NATIONAL GEOGRAPHIC: BEHIND AMERICA'S LENS ON THE WORLD

NATIONAL GEOGRAPHIC: BEHIND AMERICA'S LENS ON THE WORLD

HOWARD S. ABRAMSON

CROWN PUBLISHERS, INC., NEW YORK

Published by Crown Publishers, Inc., 225 Park Avenue South, New York, New York 10003 and represented in Canada by the Canadian Manda Group

CROWN is a trademark of Crown Publishers, Inc.
Manufactured in the United States of America
Design by Lesley Blakeney
Library of Congress Cataloging-in-Publication Data

Abramson, Howard S.
National geographic.
Bibliography: p.
Includes index.
1. National Geographic Society (U.S.) I. Title.
G3.N37A27 1986   910'.6'073   86-11596
ISBN 0-517-56109-3
10 9 8 7 6 5 4 3 2 1
First Edition

To Martha, my dear

CONTENTS

PART ONE

1. AN INTRODUCTION

> *The National Geographic Society is*
> *frequently considered equally as*
> *unassailable as motherhood and the flag.*
> Publishers Weekly *magazine*

The toastmaster was clearly a man much more accustomed to being introduced to audiences full of rich and powerful persons than to making introductions for others. But it was actually an easy task, explained the chief justice of the U.S. Supreme Court, since the main speaker who was to follow was so well known. And just to prove it, Warren Burger's introduction of that speaker consisted exclusively of stating the man's name: Ronald Reagan.

In the audience that June day in 1984 were America's attorney general, assorted cabinet members, the Senate majority leader, the White House's chief of staff, and even Anatoly Dobrynin, the Soviet Union's longtime ambassador to the United States. This was the kind of audience only Washington, D.C., can provide, and then only at the most important functions.

The President took the podium in the main auditorium of the new pink-marble-and-glass office building, one that even before its official opening was being compared to a Mayan temple, a more than $35 million expansion of a corporate giant's main headquarters. No stranger to such gatherings, Reagan looked around at his celebrity-filled audience and, seeing so much government brass, asked aloud, with his always-perfect delivery: "Who's watching the store?"

Then he told the assembled crowd about the first time he had met the current president of the publishing, broadcasting, and marketing empire that had built the structure that was being dedicated and marveled at that day:

"I informed him he was responsible for one of the biggest problems that Nancy and I were having in the transition [from private life to lofty elective office]. He looked at me wide-eyed and I told him, being in the middle of a big move from the West to the East, I said, 'Gil, I have hundreds of *National Geographics* at the ranch, and I don't know how the heck I'm going to haul them all to the White House.'"

Loud laughter greeted the speaker, the fortieth President of the United States of America. Then, after looking around at the building and some of its 500,000 square feet of floor space, Ronald Reagan said to its proud owners, "I guess you have trouble storing your old *National Geographics*, too."

There are few companies in the world that could have attracted that day's star-studded audience, and fewer still that could have gotten the President of the United States and leader of the free world to dedicate its headquarters building. But then, there's only one National Geographic Society.

*   *   *

The National Geographic Society defies accurate, or adequate, description. It runs the gamut from eleemosynary benefactor of science and of historical and geographic exploration to hard-sell mail-order house and hard-nosed diversified media conglomerate.

To many of its nearly eleven million members, the National Geographic Society is just a ma-and-pa magazine publisher that grew up. The editors are often known by their initials. The articles seem to be written by nice, albeit dull, second cousins who manage to travel a lot and send an unending stream of pretty, envy-producing postcards, with nary a mention of unpleasant happenings, such as lost reservations, washed-out bridges, or coups d'état. Rather, it is always perceived as a nice homespun organization that publishes that distinctive yellow-bordered magazine that adorns doctors' offices everywhere and features those trademark harmless photographs of all those memorable brown breasts.

And the price, $18 a year for twelve thick issues of a beautifully crafted picture magazine, seems reasonable enough—cheaper, by far, than most periodicals offered by the other big publishing chains, and for a magazine second to none for quality in the mass-circulation field.

Thus, even though the National Geographic Society makes no secret of its large circulation (one of the few things about its corporate and commercial self that it doesn't try to keep quiet), most people are still astonished when they learn of the organization's myriad undertakings and its vast wealth, or learn of its occasional questionable forays into world politics or its unabashed attempts to alter history to suit its commercial needs.

For instance:

- It is the largest scientific educational organization in the world.

- It is one of the largest and most profitable diversified publishing companies in the world, with annual receipts well in excess of $325 million.

- Its *National Geographic Magazine* has the third-largest circulation of any magazine in the United States, trailing only *TV Guide* and the *Reader's Digest,* and it is estimated that approximately fifty million people read each issue. The *National Geographic Magazine* has the highest magazine renewal rate of any commercial publication in the world, averaging around 90 percent a year.

- It is one of the country's largest mail-order houses. To support these operations, the Society, using reduced postal rates reserved for qualified educational and charitable organizations, sends out several hundred million pieces of solicitation material a year.

- It is the largest purveyor of globes and maps in the world.

It was the fifty-fifth-ranking media company in America in 1983, according to *Advertising Age*, with more media sales revenue than *Reader's Digest*, *Playboy*, and Penthouse International Ltd. Media sales account for only about 65 percent of its gross receipts, compared to 94 percent of Penthouse's. When ranked by estimated magazine revenues by *Advertising Age*, the National Geograpic Society jumps to twelfth, ahead of the New York Times Company and behind Capital Cities Communications, which is ranked eleventh.

- Its book division is unequaled, nearly always selling out its large press runs, thanks to its unparalleled market research into the Society's membership and the well over eleven million wallets that its membership represents. The eighteen major books it produced in its first eighteen years sold more than five million copies, an industry-leading average of 275,000 each.

In short, and at first glance, the National Geographic Society is just a well-run, successful publishing company, like its rivals Time Inc. and the Times Mirror Company.

It is not that simple. The National Geographic Society's publications, and the many advertising mailings it sends out to members, stress the "we" side of the organization, putting great emphasis on the fact that the Society is "owned" by its members. The first inkling that things aren't quite what they are advertised to be can be felt in the reaction of the uniformed guards to any of the Society member-owners who might attempt to visit "their" staff at the headquarters complex. Aside from a public lobby and self-congratulatory little museum on the ground floor of one of the buildings—which also features a large store at which all of the Society's goods are offered for sale—the Society is off limits to nonemployees. And attempts to visit GMG or his many aides are deflected, politely but firmly.

In its earlier days—following in the path established by its original guiding lights, Gardiner Greene Hubbard and Alexander Graham Bell—the National Geographic Society diverted substantial portions of its income to discovery and research at a time in the world's history when governments generally didn't believe that charting history should be paid for with public money. The Society funded, or helped fund, expeditions that uncovered or rediscovered many of the world's historical treasures; it pioneered the evolution of photography, especially color photography, and its use in periodicals; it was America's first window on the world, as the nation came into its own as a world power; and it gently nudged the nation into preserving some of its natural resources, including the giant redwoods of California.

The National Geographic Society is able to enlist the aid of high-minded civil servants who would never attempt to boost the corporate fortunes of private commercial enterprises, such as the President or U.S. Supreme Court justices, because it is also a "nonprofit," tax-exempt "membership" organization, ostensibly run by and for its members as a charitable institution of public geographic education. And when the Society was founded in 1888, that's just what its original members had in mind.

But as it has grown up, the Society has evolved into an organization that is quite far removed from its original stated goals, as a smaller and smaller percentage of its revenue has gone to research and exploration, and more of its booming treasury has been spent to feed its seemingly insatiable desire to grow ever larger and more profitable. More of its money is being used to raise even more money, even though its annual "profits" (what the Society calls, in the jargon of the tax business, "excess of receipts over expenses and disbursements"), $30,076,831 in 1983, already would make most corporate treasurers proud.

And even with such financial results, the National Geographic Society retains its nontaxable status, because being a nonprofit organization, according to the rules established by the U.S. Congress and the Internal Revenue Service, doesn't mean that the organization doesn't earn profits, it simply means that such profits are not distributed to shareholders. Thus, since the Society doesn't issue dividends, the government's assumption is that the "profits" go into the stated educational purpose of the organization: "the increase and diffusion of geographic knowledge."

In fact, the National Geographic Society's "surpluses"—as it politely refers to its profits when talking to the outside world— instead go to pay for employees to solicit more subscribers for its periodicals, buyers for its books, atlases, globes, films, and records; for buildings to house those employees; and for many corporate luxuries to reward the top echelons of its workforce. Finally, the balance goes into what the Society calls a "deferred capital fund." Even after paying out some of the more than $35 million in cash for the new headquarters that it opened in 1984, and embarking on a $10 million general sprucing up of the other buildings in its head-quarters complex at the same time, the Society told the Internal Revenue Service that its capital fund balance at the end of 1983 held a total of $96,908,211.72 in stocks and securities, as part of its net worth of $182,283,235. A year later, its net worth exceeded $198 million. And that figure is quite low, since the Society's valu-ation of its real estate holdings is based on the original cost of the properties, and not on the astronomical sums they would bring in downtown Washington, and other places, today.

And while over the years the National Geographic Society has funded many historical, geographic, and archaeological journeys, it today hardly fits the pattern of most nonprofit organizations or what was envisioned when the special tax treatments were created for such organizations—such as hospitals with long rows of fluores-cent fixtures lighting shiny vinyl floors and bright-white-painted walls, with ledger books open to all and with a hand always out for a donation or a grant or, if all else fails, a loan.

Rather, as we shall see, the National Geographic Society is a family dynasty, which has been in the control of one group of related people since its creation in 1888; and it has provided em-ployment, and topflight status, for much of its ruling family.

Despite their inability to disburse "profits" in the form of divi-dends, the Society's directors have lavished the best of worldly goods on themselves and their upper-echelon employees. They work in flawlessly appointed suites perched atop marble, granite, and glass towers from which they can look down on some of Wash-ington's most expensive downtown real estate, over at the for-tresslike Russian embassy, the Washington Hilton, and the *Washington Post* building. Its middle- and upper-level employees have chauffeur-driven limousines at their disposal. And not only is expense never spared on its publications or its top employees, but it is actually encouraged, partly because of the Internal Revenue Service's informal guidelines that set minimum income-to-production-cost ratios for nonprofit publications.

And while its rivals have to pay taxes and postage and to face the normal scrutiny of the world's media, the National Geographic Society is viewed as a sacrosanct deity, almost as a nonsectarian religious institution. For instance, it "is frequently considered equally as unassailable as motherhood and the flag," according to a writer for one national magazine in 1973.[1] "If the Society should ever be the target of an unfriendly investigation, which is unthinkable," said a writer for another national magazine in 1963, "a life membership [in it] and a map case [from it] should silence its harshest critic."[2]

That the National Geographic Society has been directly involved in several important historical discoveries in the world, and has at times been an invaluable source of funding for historical research and expeditions, has always been well publicized in the world's media, thanks partly to the National Geographic Society's public relations department and its always self-publicizing news service, which it provides free to any newspaper that will run it.

The "good cause" that the Society represents, coupled with its endless self-promotion and its tremendously positive media relations, has led the Society to enjoy a public image that is unmatched in American commerce today. With few exceptions, this has allowed the Society to lead a very sheltered existence, one free from scrutiny or criticism. Thus, since 1888, the National Geographic Society has quietly gone about its business, solidly, stolidly unaffected by most of the fleeting currents that sweep by it. Seemingly recession-proof, inflation-proof, politics-proof, and almost change-proof, it has grown ever larger and ever wealthier, selling the world beautiful pictures and a totally unrealistic point of view that reports only the good and, with only occasional recent exceptions, refuses even to consider the bad.

Here, for the first time, we will take an in-depth independent look inside the National Geographic Society.

2. ALEXANDER GRAHAM BELL

*The inventor was practically unknown in
electrical circles, and his invention was
looked upon, if indeed any notice at all
was taken of it, as utterly valueless.*
          Anonymous journalist, 1883

It had been a charmed life for Gardiner Greene Hubbard, the
founder of the National Geographic Society. Born the grandson
and namesake of Gardiner Greene, who was reputed to have been
the richest man in Boston at the time, Hubbard had found that
things had only gotten better as he grew up. As an adult, he became a prominent lawyer, a serious-looking man with a long beard
who was a devoted husband and the father of four lovely daughters,
who were his pride.

Many times during his life, Hubbard's imagination and interest
in new schemes had led him to make enormous new piles of
money, which he proceeded to lose in the course of implementing
his next brilliant scheme. But he always retained enough cash to
remain one of the richest men in New England as he pursued his
eclectic interests.

In 1863, Hubbard's five-year-old daughter Mabel, called May,
fell ill with scarlet fever. She recovered, but at first it was thought
that in addition to losing her hearing, she had suffered brain damage. She was bedridden for months, and silent. She responded to

nothing around her and made no actions to indicate that she even recognized her surroundings. Finally, Mrs. Gertrude Hubbard recalled how enthralled May had been when, just before her illness, she had been taken to P. T. Barnum's extremely popular exhibition of Tom Thumb and his little bride. Mrs. Hubbard had purchased her daughter a photograph of the famous pair, and, prior to her illness, May would often kiss it and say, "Little lady, little lady."

Now, Mrs. Hubbard held the photograph before her daughter's eyes in a last desperate test. "Little lady, May," her mother said. A smile came tentatively to the little girl's face, the first smile to grace that face for months. Her hand reached out for the picture. "Little lady," May said. And then she kissed the picture.[1]

After this breakthrough, May's doctors determined that she had not in fact suffered any brain damage. But when Hubbard began to search for ways to help May adapt to her new, silent world, he was astounded by the attitudes of educators toward the deaf. Over and over again, New England's leading professionals told him the same thing: May should be sent to a special school so she could learn sign language and have as happy a life as possible, under the circumstances.

Her illness had plunged Hubbard, a man used to having all important things his own way, into despair, but he continued to search for ways to treat her illness. When one of the leading educators of the deaf in America told him that "when your little girl is old enough to be taught, I predict she'll be very happy with the beautiful language of signs," an angry Hubbard abruptly picked up his hat and coat and replied sharply, ". . . I'm afraid I don't think much of your 'beautiful language' of signs! Speech is good enough for me."[2]

And Hubbard was not a man to give up easily. In addition to being a distinguished lawyer, Hubbard was a high-class huckster, a man whose active imagination had led him down many paths, and whose interests brought him great success as a promoter, from which he had learned the value of unshakable determination. He was instrumental in creating the first street railway to be seen outside of New York—which operated in Cambridge and Boston—and was the president of the company that ran the railway. He was also president of the Cambridge Gas Light Company.

Despite the early advice to accept May's infirmity, Hubbard continued his quest. Finally, he found a new hope: lipreading. Hubbard was advised to make May talk, to never let her get by with gestures or signs. To aid in this task, Hubbard enlisted her sisters and, later, a young governess named Mary True, the well-educated daughter of the minister of Bethel, Maine, a small town where the Hubbards had spent some of their summers.

Mary True, despite her lack of teaching experience, took over the education of all the Hubbard girls, although May, now eight, was certainly her most important charge. With kindness and perseverance and love, she directed the girls' schooling. Four years later, when May was twelve and ready to go off to finishing school with her sisters, Mary took a job with the Horace Mann School in Boston.

Hubbard's dogged pursuit of help for May led him eventually to a seat—which he held for ten years—on the State Board of Education as a champion of the deaf, and to the formation of enlightened schools for the hearing-impaired in Massachusetts.

One early summer day about three years after she had stopped teaching May, Mary True stormed into the Hubbard house and almost forcibly carried May from Cambridge down Beacon Hill toward dingy Boston University, where she wanted her to meet a new teacher of the deaf. May, reluctant to alter her daily routine, went along only because Mary was so insistent. "May, all the world—the world that stammers or is deaf—is talking about this man!" May later recalled in her diary. "He's a Scot who came to Boston . . . a year or two ago. . . . Oh don't look skeptical. I was, but he convinced me. And I have seen the two little deaf boys whom he taught to speak. And he has the marvelous faculty of making even children comprehend what he wants of them! [3]

Miss True led May into a nondescript dark-green room at Boston University that looked out over a small cemetery that included among its graves those of Benjamin Franklin's parents. And there, in the shadows of that room, she caught her first glimpse of Alexander Graham Bell, tall, painfully thin, and, she would later tell him, looking forty years old to her eyes. Bell was actually twenty-six; his haggard expression and ill-fitting, unfashionable clothes made him seem older.

At fifteen, May was sleek and beautiful, with long dark hair, and was always perfectly dressed and groomed, thanks to her father's lofty station in life. Despite her displeasure at her surroundings—May was not used to attending classes in a dank basement such as the room in which Bell taught—and at his physical being, she found herself drawn into the class Bell was giving. "I was forced to listen to him," she later wrote in her diary. "Himself I did not like! He dresses carelessly in a horrible, shiny broadcloth, which makes his jet black hair look shiny, too. Altogether, I do not think him exactly a gentleman. I make a distinction between teachers and gentlemen of means, lawyers, merchants etc. . . ." And then she added, with no further explanation, "I could never marry such a man!"[4]

*   *   *

Alexander Graham Bell had been born into a family of speech therapists in Scotland. His grandfather, also named Alexander Bell, had taught diction and elocution and had achieved distinction in his homeland for treating speech impediments and giving public readings of Shakespeare. His father, Alexander Melville Bell, taught at the University of Edinburgh and developed his "visible speech" method—really a form of anatomical shorthand using symbols to show the positions of the throat, tongue, and lips when making desired sounds. While he had developed the method to teach proper pronunciation of all foreign languages to English-speaking students, it soon became clear that it could also "show" the deaf how to make the proper sounds for speech. This system, with adaptations, is still in limited use today.

Young Bell, by all accounts, was a bright and interested boy. When he was almost eleven, he adopted the middle name Graham from a Bell family friend he admired, Alexander Graham. From his mother, Eliza Grace Symonds Bell, young Bell inherited musical talent and a keen musical ear. He took piano lessons at an early age and for some time actually intended to become a professional musician.

It was at this age that some of the traits that would lead to his later success began to show. He was so obsessive about his projects that he often jeopardized his health. For instance, he worked so hard at his music lessons that he often got a raging headache. And while he was never a particularly good student, his obsessiveness and desire to succeed often left him on the verge of physical breakdown. He was far from a happy student, especially in the curriculum of the day, which stressed Latin and Greek. Indeed, he continued to extol the teaching of scientific training and rail against the classical teaching methods as an adult. As a result of his poor school performance, most of Bell's early education came from private tutoring.

Bell had a great interest in sounds and acoustics even as a child. Once, his brothers discovered him on the floor next to the family dog, forcing it to open its mouth. The boys asked him if the dog was sick. No, he wasn't sick, Aleck explained, he was just teaching it how to talk. Indeed, he told his brothers, when he pressed the dog's jaws together, the animal said "ga-ga-ga." Soon they were all experimenting with the hapless dog. Before long, according to one history, the three boys had the dog saying something that sounded like "How are oo, grandma?" The pooch's fame is reputed to have become widespread.[5]

Ironically, when Bell was about twelve—a tall, dark, somewhat frail-looking boy—his mother began to lose her hearing. Later accounts tell of Bell playing the piano for her while she sat with her ear pressed against the instrument's sounding board. When he was thirteen, Bell spent a year in London with his grandfather, a time which he later said turned his life toward serious study. That year also took him away from music and influenced him to follow in his father's, and grandfather's, professional footsteps.

When he stated his decision to his father, Bell later explained, ". . . I was urged by my father to study everything relating to these subjects [acoustics and speech], as they would have an important bearing upon what was to be my professional work. He also encouraged me to experiment, and offered a prize to his sons for the successful construction of a speaking machine. I made a machine of this kind, as a boy, and was able to make it articulate a few words. . . ."6

At the age of sixteen, Bell, always an individualist, left home to break his boyhood bonds and to teach at a boys' private school. He returned to Edinburgh for a year of study at the university and then went back to Weston House Academy to teach elocution and music for another year. By 1867, at age twenty, he was filling in for his father in London, while Melville Bell was giving lectures on his visual-speech method in America.

About this time, Graham's older and younger brothers both died of tuberculosis. His father, wanting to save his last son and namesake, who was also sickly, moved the family across the Atlantic Ocean to Ontario in 1870 to escape the damp Scottish climate, which he blamed for killing his other boys. The small family resettled in North America for what was to be a two-year recuperative stay, and young Bell quickly regained his health in the sunny new land.

During his convalescence at his new home, Bell became interested in the dialect being spoken by a nearby tribe of Mohawk Indians, and he transcribed many of their words into visible-speech symbols. He was later rewarded for his efforts by being made an honorary chief by the tribe.

A year after moving to America, Bell agreed to substitute for his father on a lecture tour in America, at his father's urging. These lectures, which began in April 1871, were so successful that they led to a succession of engagements for him and to the rapid establishment of Bell as a Boston-based leader in teaching the deaf to speak. By 1873, he was a professor of vocal physiology at Boston University, which is where his path crossed that of May Hubbard.

Young Bell had developed his own method of teaching visible speech and employed it quite successfully. According to a 1946 publication prepared by the American Telephone and Telegraph Company, "he became so expert . . . that Clarke School authorities [in Northampton, Massachusetts] reported that in a few weeks he taught the children 400 English syllables, some of which they had failed to learn in two or three years under other methods of teaching. Graham's method was to teach the pupil to relate the symbol to the vocal process it described by touch or demonstration. For instance, the consonant 'P' calls for placing the tongue against the teeth, closing the lips and then opening them to ejaculate a puff of air. After writing the symbols for these processes on a black-board, Graham would open his mouth to show the tongue posi-tion—then hold the pupil's hand in position to feel the ejaculated puff of air. And so on." [7]

One acquaintance of his at this time in his life described Bell as a genial and kindly man, "so courteous and gracious in manner that you could not feel yourself an intruder though you chanced to drop into his room when some private class was under special train-ing. At the same time, though his affability sets you at ease, you could not fail to observe that he is one of the busiest of men . . . so [busy that] he has no leisure for visitors who are not interested in his work. . . ." [8]

*   *   *

By the time Mabel Hubbard was brought to him, Bell had a grow-ing reputation as a master teacher of the deaf. His visible-speech classes were encouraging the now-growing school of educationists that championed lipreading over what had been the traditional course, the teaching of sign language. The adherents of the new technique felt that signing only isolated the deaf even more, since they could do it only with themselves; lipreading, they argued, put the deaf back into the mainstream of society. The primary draw-back to lipreading was, and still is, that it is difficult for many deaf students to master.

While May was quite taken with her lessons from Bell, one day, without notice or explanation, he stopped teaching her, informing Mrs. Hubbard simply that he was turning May's instruction over to his assistant, Miss Abbie Locke. Other than his assurances that May was progressing quite well—she had been taking classes for about six months—he offered no explanation for his move.

In fact, Bell was falling in love with his young student. He was torn between his growing feelings for her and his accurate grasp of the situation: May was young, too young, too beautiful, too rich, and too outgoing. He was still shy and retiring, except when giving lessons or playing music, and poor and haggard-looking. While the Bells were a respected family in Scotland, in America he was a teacher who was barely scraping by on a small salary.

But like May's father, Bell, as he proved often later in life, was not a man who gave up a dream easily. The first step, he decided, was to separate himself from May's lessons, because he wanted her to think of him not as her teacher but as her lover.

Bell and Hubbard met several times to discuss matters involving the Clarke School, and the young teacher was invited to tea at the Hubbard home on a few occasions, at which times he impressed Hubbard with his quick mind. Soon he became a regular guest at the Hubbard's traditional Sunday dinner of roast beef and floating island pudding. Bell would play the piano for Mrs. Hubbard and what seemed to be a never-ending flow of guests to the Cambridge mansion.

Hubbard's large home was on Brattle Street, formerly called Tory Row, and then considered the best street in town. The house sat on more than five acres of prime land, surrounded by expansive lawns and shrubs, hothouses and greenhouses. And inside, the house was full of marquetry floors, velvet walls, cut-glass chandeliers, and "inherited mahogany, [which] saved the Hubbard household from the black walnut and horsehair horrors of the era," according to Catherine MacKenzie's 1928 biography of Bell.[9]

May's two younger sisters delighted in teasing Bell, and he was an easy target, with his baggy, unfashionable clothing and self-deprecating manner. When they learned that Bell had never tasted that American delicacy known as waffles, they decided to teach him how to get the most enjoyment out of them. "Pour plenty of oil and vinegar on them, Mr. Bell," advised one of them. "Oh, you certainly must try them that way! They are absolutely perfect." Only Mrs. Hubbard's timely arrival prevented Bell from a most peculiar culinary experience.[10]

But Bell had a good sense of humor all of his life, one that could be appreciated, said one biographer, by the ease with which he was able to "take in stride the teasing of May's sisters over his tail coats and whiskers" during his courtship of her, and his ability to take "the scientific criticism that often followed publication of his ideas."[11]

Meanwhile, May's older sister, Gertrude, eight years May's senior and thus very nearly Bell's own age, "was a young lady of such bewildering beauty and fascination that for a long time the susceptible Bell did not know with which sister he was in love," according to his 1928 biographer.[12] But during these regular Sunday visits to the Hubbard mansion, Bell and May spent increasing amounts of time together talking, of politics, of his history, and of teaching the deaf. One day, he offered her a confession.

When he first arrived in America, he said, he was a little suspicious of the claims made by the guiding lights behind the Clarke School, where he was teaching. That group was championing the virtues of lipreading. While he knew that physiologically, every deaf child could be taught how to speak, Bell explained to May, "I thought it was humbug about the oral school. I thought their claims regarding lipreading were too big. . . . I believed in teaching speech, but I didn't believe in speech-reading. But," he continued as he looked at her, "I am converted. You did it."[13] This was a shift in belief that was to have a major impact on the deaf world up to this day.

Following up on his father's earlier efforts to get his sons to make a machine to "speak," Bell, in addition to teaching, was now trying to construct a "harmonic telegraph," one on which many transmissions could be made simultaneously over the same telegraph wire by using differing frequencies of electrical current.

While Bell's work had begun with the desire to help the deaf, it was not only altruism that prodded him. Up until just a few years earlier, only one message at a time could be sent over a single telegraph wire—that era's primary method of fast long-distance communication. For the device that doubled that capacity, Bell was told, Western Union had paid $750,000. The invention he was working on would send six or eight messages, instead of two. If he could sell such an invention to Western Union, he was told over and over again, he would be "made for life." And he secretly knew he would then have enough money to marry even Mabel Hubbard.

Bell's growing local fame brought him several private students, in addition to May, which in turn brought him some financial backing. Thomas Sanders agreed to bankroll Bell's work on the harmonic telegraph, at least partially because he was so taken with him, and partially to keep him in Boston and teaching his five-year-old son George. A successful self-made leather merchant, Sanders wasn't rich, but was willing to gamble some money on Bell's abilities to produce the new machine. Hubbard, himself understanding the limitations of the telegraphy system, was also willing to fund Bell's research.

Bell certainly could use the money in 1873, but was embarrassed at suddenly having two such offers. In the end, he brought the men together, and they agreed to share the expenses. Bell, to assuage his conscience, insisted that a formal business relationship be establishd to spell out the arrangement, which led to the creation, although only orally at first, of what later became known as the Bell Patent Association.

On the social front, Bell had decided that his best chance of success with May lay in slowly bringing her around, to be her friend and companion until she was old enough to marry. He had thus far told no one of his secret love, contenting himself merely with being around her. But early in the summer of 1875, he got distressing news: May was to spend an unspecified period of time with her spinster cousin in Nantucket, Massachusetts. Distressed at her leaving and fearing it might mean she would never return to her parents' Cambridge home, Bell immediately took a streetcar to Cambridge, where he was now prepared to reveal his love of May to her father. But when he arrived, he found that Hubbard was out of town, and he couldn't bring himself to tell Mrs. Hubbard his news, so he beat a hasty retreat. Later, after regaining some of his courage, he wrote Mrs. Hubbard a letter.

Mrs. Hubbard was certainly surprised. She was fond of Bell, and had thought something might develop between Aleck and Gertrude, but May? May was a child, and a deaf one at that. And while she and her husband had hoped that one day May would lead a normal family life, they were less than sure it would happen. And since she was so young, they hadn't really begun to think about marriage and a family for May. Mrs. Hubbard summoned Bell to her house the next day. "We have known you intimately for well over a year," she told him, "and I have never seen nor heard anything to alter my opinion that you are a truly fine man. I do think, however, that Mabel is not ready, not old enough, to hear your confession. And I feel sure that her father will be of the same opinion."[14] Rather, she advised him, wait until she was older, when she would know her own mind better. Wait one year, she said, and if he was unswayed, then he should ask for her hand.

When Gardiner Greene Hubbard got the news, he was less than pleased. "I consider Mabel such a child that if Mrs. Hubbard hadn't said one year, I would have said two," he told a dejected Bell.[15] After agreeing to the one-year probation, Bell promptly fell into a depression when May left for Nantucket. Finally, he told Mrs. Hubbard he couldn't bear to wait and implored her to accompany him to Nantucket, where he would tell May the entire story. She refused to go, after simply repeating what she had said before. And, she added, he looked terrible; she suggested that he visit his family in Canada and take a rest. Instead, he trekked up to Nantucket and again unburdened his soul in a letter, this time directly to May. But the next day, when he went to the cottage to see her, May's cousin wouldn't let him in. Heartbroken, he returned to Boston.

Late in August, however, May returned to Cambridge. As he arrived on a cloud of hope for the next Sunday's dinner, May took him aside. She told him, "I like you. I don't love you, but I do like you. Is that enough—now?"[16]

Convinced he would win May's heart, Bell heeded Mrs. Hubbard's advice and went to his parents' home in Canada to recuperate from his latest in a series of stress-induced illnesses and to continue working on his harmonic telegraph and a new invention in which he had gotten interested. In the course of working on the harmonic telegraph, Bell became convinced he could move actual sound waves over wires, not merely the dots and dashes of the telegraph. He and Thomas Watson, an assistant he had hired with the money from Sanders and Hubbard, spent increasing amounts of time and attention on the new machine, at the expense of work on the harmonic telegraph. This diversion eventually angered Hubbard and led to a confrontation.

Soon after May's declaration of interest, Bell received a sharp letter from her father, demanding that Bell refocus his attentions on the telegraph and forget his dream machine, which had never worked. Further, Hubbard said, it was time for Bell to abandon his visible-speech classes as well, and to focus any time not spent on the harmonic telegraph on serious scientific research, not on futuristic technological frills, which would have little economic value even if finally perfected.

While Bell was certainly ready to give up his classes, and longed to be free to spend nearly all of his time in the laboratory, he was driven to be a commercial success so that he could begin life with May. By Thanksgiving, only three months after returning from Nantucket, May told Bell that she did indeed love him. They agreed to marry, but Bell—who was now called Alec by his friends, having lost the "k" somewhere along the line—insisted they wait until one of his inventions bore fruit, so that he would have enough money to take care of her in a style at least somewhere close to that provided by her wealthy father.

Finally, Bell found the breakthrough he had been searching for on his dream machine, which he had steadfastly refused to abandon. His discovery was accidental. Several other people were already working on the transmission of speech over their own conceptions of telephones, but no one else was experimenting with undulating electric current. With what he thought to be the key in his hand, and with the goal of a life with May in the offing, his single-minded determination to succeed led him to a feverish work pace as he tried to perfect his telephone before any of his competitors could complete theirs. The pace proved too much for the still-frail Bell, however, and he again became ill. But first came success, and his famous words: "Mr. Watson, come here, I want you."[17]

For the second time in just a few months, Bell saw how doggedness and determination, when added to his ingenuity, would pay

21

great rewards. Bell returned to his father's Ontario home to recuperate once more, and as he rested from the rigors of the laboratory, he began to write out his ideas for the required patent application on the telephone.

The first patent for Bell's telephone was granted on March 7, 1876, but little in the world changed when it was registered. "The issuance of Bell's patent," wrote one journalist in 1883, ". . . attracted little or no attention in the telegraphic world. The inventor was practically unknown in electrical circles, and his invention was looked upon, if indeed any notice at all was taken of it, as utterly valueless."[18]

Bell, broke and having already taken a year's advance on his salary at Boston University, continued refining the telephone patent, but was depressed over the lack of interest, financial or scientific, that others had shown in his work. However, after having "telephone conversations" at public exhibitions with his assistant, Watson, first 16 miles apart and then 143 miles apart, he realized there was enough general curiosity about the telephone to hold regular public demonstrations, and that people were actually willing to pay to attend them.

Bell's first public lecture on the telephone brought him $85. Bell—the romantic, even if still churchmouse-poor—spent the money to have a silver model of the telephone made, which he presented to Mabel.

* * *

Hubbard began to ponder the telephone's potential applications and realized that he had been wrong about its commercial prospects. So now he threw his considerable talents as a promoter and an entrepreneur behind Bell and his invention. While Sanders established the New England Telephone Company for their little Bell Patent Association, Hubbard quickly moved to export the idea to the rest of the industrialized world.

As soon as the patent began to show signs of having serious economic significance, a welter of litigation commenced, mostly from men who claimed that they had already invented the telephone, and that Bell had stolen their ideas. But only Bell, the courts later definitively ruled, had been working with undulating current to carry the sounds over wires, the vital element that made the Bell telephone work.

After being awarded a second patent for his telephone design in January 1877, Bell went on tour to give more lectures and demonstrations and turned the business side of the telephone over completely to Hubbard and Sanders. Sanders alone risked $110,000, and bankruptcy, as his part of the effort to put the Bell Telephone Company on its feet.

Believing himself freed from the need to make a living, and with his future father-in-law running the Bell Telephone Company, Bell married Mabel Hubbard at the Brattle Street mansion in July 1877. Bell gave May the telephone patent rights and all of his shares in the company, save one which he kept, as a wedding gift (along with a strand of pearls)—and off they went, on their way to England both to honeymoon and to discuss his invention with investors there.

But first, a visit to his family was in order. As Bell and his aristocratic bride walked up the path leading to the Bell house, a small woman darted out from the house and without explanation broke an oat cake over May's head. As May stood there flabbergasted, Bell introduced his mother and explained that it was an old Scottish custom to break a cake over a bride's head as a precaution against her ever being hungry for as long as she lived in her husband's house.

Bell's farsightedness is well illustrated in an 1878 letter to some potential investors in England, in which he wrote that one day it was actually conceivable that "cables of telephonic wires" would connect homes and factories and shops, "establishing direct communication between any two places in the City. . . . I believe that in the future, wires will unite the head offices of Telephone Companies in different cities and a man in one part of the Country may communicate by word of mouth with another in a distant place."[19]

One company that did not have to be sold on the potential economic and technological impact of the telephone was one of America's giant industrial firms and probably its most powerful at the time: Western Union. The firm's analysts quickly understood just what Bell's machine could do to Western Union's nationwide communications monopoly. The telephone, they could see, would quickly make their telegraph network obsolete.

Even while Bell had been going around giving exhibitions of his invention, Western Union had quietly put together a three-inventor team—including Thomas A. Edison—with orders to produce a similar device, without infringing on Bell's patents. But the men were unable to do so. Despite this failure, Western Union teamed with two of the inventors (Edison took no part) and created the American Speaking Telephone Company in December 1878.

While the Bells were again visiting London, where May gave birth to their first child, Elsie May, in May 1878, the new Western Union subsidiary firm advertised in several American newspapers that it would soon be producing "superior telephones by the original inventors."

The experienced Hubbard understood the tactic immediately. By taking the initiative, Western Union had put the fledgling Bell Telephone Company in the position of having to initiate lengthy and expensive copyright-infringement litigation against the giant established firm and its batteries of lawyers. And by teaming with inventor Elisha Gray, who had indeed been working on a telephone for some time and could at least make claim to being its inventor, or perhaps one of its inventors, Western Union had strengthened its case.

When Bell received a cable from his father-in-law explaining the new turn of events and imploring him to return to the United States immediately to prepare for the trial, he was completely deflated and defeated. All of his hard work, he could see, was going down the drain. Well, he was no fool, he explained to his wife. He had made up his mind: He would leave London, all right, but only to take his wife and daughter to Canada, where he would find a teaching position, such as his father's and his father's father's, and live a quiet and respectable life, he told Mabel.

He sent Hubbard a terse telegraphic reply to his cable. "I am not coming to Boston. Will go to Quebec." And at this most disheartening time of his life, he told his wife, as she later revealed, "I have lost the telephone."[20] But when their ship docked, Watson was there to meet them. He implored Bell to come back to Boston in order to help their fledgling company win the suit that had been filed against Western Union. Finally, after appealing to Bell at least to save the financial investments of his father-in-law and Sanders, Bell agreed to go to Boston after depositing his daughter and wife at his parents' home in Canada.

The trial over ownership of the telephone invention rights dragged on for a year. Bell's deposition was so long and detailed that it was later published as a book. Finally, Western Union's counsel advised his client to seek a settlement, apparently convinced that the firm could not win the case in court. Eventually an agreement was made whereby Western Union received one-fifth of the patent rights, and Bell retained the balance. While not a complete victory, the deal clearly established Bell as the inventor of the telephone, or at least four-fifths of it.

Overnight, the Bell Telephone Company's stock jumped to $995 a share. And in time, Bell won all the other suits; in each case, he was found to have been the first to "conceive and apply the crucial idea of the undulatory current, in contrast to the older art of interrupted current, which all of the other inventors who had been working on the telephone had been employing."[21]

*   *   *

Later, after the lawsuits were won, the Bells moved to Washington, D.C., to spend more time with May's family; Gardiner Greene Hubbard's business—and especially his increasing workload involving the telephone business—required him to be in the nation's capital more often. Hubbard had for many years maintained a large home in Washington and found the winter climate there more to his liking than New England's. Bell returned to the lab to let his fertile mind roam across the landscape of his interests, spending much of his time in trying to better the plight of the deaf and pursuing his belief that mankind's next frontier was the air.

Despite his many accomplishments during his long life in varied fields, Bell, when asked, always described himself simply as "a teacher of the deaf." And around the Bell home, May's deafness was not a major impediment, in large part thanks to her attitude, and Bell's, toward her handicap. After their two daughters were old enough to fight with each other, May would control them by warning, "Children, if you don't behave, I'll close my eyes and then I won't hear a thing."[22]

Over the years, Bell had also fallen in love with his adoptive home. In Washington, in 1882, he became an American citizen. He often spoke of his great pride in being an American. Years later, when he died, the epitaph over his grave, which is carved out of solid rock on top of a mountain, reads: "Born in Edinburgh . . . Died a citizen of the U.S.A."

At the same time that Bell was leading his dream life as a successful inventor and a happy father, many of his father-in-law's spare hours were spent at the Cosmos Club, a gentleman's social club in downtown Washington, and in activities involving the Smithsonian Institution, America's fledgling national museum. And by 1887, Hubbard and five friends were dreaming of a new learned society for Washington, one that would champion the new breed of world explorers, who would—in their own way—make the earth smaller, just as Bell had done with his wires and modulating-current transmitting equipment.

3. THE GEOGRAPHIC FRONTIER

> *Dear Sir: You are invited to be present at a meeting to be held in the Assembly Hall of the Cosmos Club, Friday evening, January 13 [1888], at 8 o'clock, for the purpose of considering the advisability of organizing a society for the increase and diffusion of geographic knowledge. . . .*
>
> *Invitation letter*

In the 1880s, Washington, D.C., was still a dusty backwater town, even judged by nineteenth-century American standards. Although its population had climbed to nearly 180,000, the capital was really just America's newest tourist attraction for the rich and powerful. Washington offered itself as the cradle of a federal government that was growing rapidly in size and in importance as it assumed and consolidated the powers formerly exercised by the states. Industrialization was changing the face of America, and the founder's planned confederation of independent nation-states no longer suited the country.

The North's victory in the Civil War sealed the demise of that confederation and marked the start of an era of swift federalization. "What transpired in Richmond, Columbia, or Baton Rouge, indeed in Albany, Topeka, or Sacramento, now mattered far less than what politicians decided on Capitol Hill; Americans must go to Washington to be in the swim," wrote historian Constance Green.[1] Thus, Washington's winter social season quickly became the most important one in the nation, one that was not to be missed. And society and government soon became the city's only primary products, for while commerce and industry thrived in New York, Philadelphia, and Baltimore, it faltered in Washington. This may have been due in part to the fact that Washington was abandoned at the start of each summer by anyone who mattered, leaving the town to the local blacks who were too poor to flee Washington's oppressive hot weather.

In addition to its failure to industrialize, the city proved incapable even of managing its own treasury. After its territorial government went bankrupt in 1874, following several years of teetering on the brink of insolvency, the federal government took over Washington's affairs. Being run by the United States promised the residents a solvent government, but it also stripped Washingtonians of all their self-governing powers. But becoming a federal city helped inspire the only real economic boom the town was to have: real estate. Now that the federal government was in control, the wealthy could rest assured that taxes would remain low and that municipal services would always be provided.

Thus stabilized, Washington began to grow into a real city. "While the vulgarity of a new plutocracy had permeated much of official society during most of the post–[Civil] War decade, after the panic of 1873 [as the city headed for bankruptcy], the social carpetbaggers had gradually ceased to exercise much influence. Old residents imbued with a strong sense of tradition, newcomers ready to share in community responsibilities, and a number of cultivated, highly trained men willing to risk the precariousness of government employment had succeeded in restoring dignity to social intercourse," according to Green.[2]

Although the government was attracting more businesses and tourists, which provided employment for the locals, Washington was far from being a classy outpost of civilization in the American wilds. While new hotels were springing up, the proprietors of the capital's restaurants were still learning their craft and the city's serious clothiers were few and far between. A few local clothing stores were opened, using as models such leading retailers as Wanamaker's of Philadelphia and Marshall Field's of Chicago, but despite advertisements offering shoppers the latest fashions Paris had to offer, Washington, as one young woman put it, was not "a brag shopping place." [3] Even Washington's own political clout was minimal; local attempts to stage a world's fair in the late 1880s to commemorate Columbus's discovery of America failed, and Chicago instead landed the official celebration.

* * *

As the twentieth century approached, America and its place in the world were undergoing an extreme and historically important change. Some thirty years after the Civil War, the industrial revolution was well under way, practical science was entering a golden age, and Americans were beginning to look around them, beyond their own borders to the rest of the world. This new interest in the world fostered an era of global exploration. Americans were beginning to believe that there was nothing they couldn't accomplish, no obstacle that couldn't be overcome or world they couldn't explore. Also, there were rumblings of an impending war in Europe, as the British Empire continued to unravel and Germany demanded a major role in a realigned Europe. And Americans weren't sure what effect such a war half a world away would have on their young nation.

Despite these new worries, the United States was booming. The spreading trackage of its railroads was opening new territories and creating new markets. The telegraph provided almost instantaneous communication between cities and towns. America was a nation of readers: Already approximately a hundred periodicals were being published, led by the popular trio *Harper's Weekly*, *Leslie's*, and the *Independent*, which offered a mix of fiction and hair-raising true tales of adventure. Samuel Langhorne Clemens, as Mark Twain, was the nation's best-read author. And the newspaper industry, thanks to technology, was going through a wave of wild expansion. The telegraph, which came into commercial use in 1844, had boosted newspaper publishing and led in 1892 to the establishment of the Associated Press, through which newspapers could share their dispatches. The invention of a practical linotype machine in 1885 generated a newspaper boom unmatched in the industry by speeding up typesetting and reducing the manpower needed to produce a newspaper. From 971 daily newspapers in 1880, twenty years later Americans had their choice of 2,226 daily papers, nearly all of which offered their readers lurid tales under screaming headlines about events throughout the world.

In spite of all this commercial expansion in many of America's cities, and the threat of the looming war, Washington was still a calm place. Wrote one late-nineteenth-century visitor from England: "Compared with New York or Chicago, Washington, although it is full of commotion and energy, is a city of rest and peace. The inhabitants do not rush onward as though they were late for the train or the post, or as though the dinner hour being past they were anxious to appease an irritable wife." Wrote another, "It looks a sort of place where nobody has to work for his living, or, at any rate, not hard."[4]

Washington seemed mostly populated with bankers, generals, scientists, and scholars in those days—in addition, of course, to politicians. In order to provide themselves with local entertainment, the usually part-time Washingtonians founded social clubs, and helped sponsor artistic, literary, and scientific activities, primarily through various formal associations they created. The men of money and of war were mostly drawn to the Metropolitan Club, while the second rung of aristocracy—primarily government scientists and faculty members from local colleges—spent their time at the Cosmos Club. The Cosmos Club was a blue-bloods' gathering spot in downtown Washington that was housed in the building where Dolley Madison had spent her last years; in the club congregated some of America's brightest, if not her wealthiest, men.

Washington now attracted more and more scientists, and they played an ever larger role in the growing government and, ultimately, in the city of Washington itself. Joseph Henry, secretary of the Smithsonian Institution, in 1871 remarked that no other city in America had "in proportion to the number of its inhabitants, so many men actively engaged in pursuits connected with science as in Washington."[5]

And these learned and wealthy men needed more entertainment than a mere prestigious drinking club could offer. While Washingtonians were proud of the four universities that had already been established in the city, and of the Library of Congress and the fledgling Smithsonian Institution, they needed more. The town was practically devoid of any serious music or theater. "In music," according to historian Green, "Washington lagged behind other big American cities. A week, or at most a fortnight, of opera presented by companies on tour was her quota for the season. Occasionally a well-known instrumental soloist gave a concert, but professional performances were few," owing in large part to the town's lack of a large concert hall.[6] And even when one of the city's local musicians became a big success, the city didn't benefit. By the time John Philip Sousa, who headed the U.S. Marine Band, became world-famous for his "Washington Post March," he had already left the Marine Corps and the town in order to start his own band in New York City. In fact, by the time Sousa's march became famous, he had sold the score to a Philadelphia publisher for $35.

So, in order to make up for this lack of local entertainment, a number of "scientific associations" were founded by Washington's leading citizens. And while they for the most part met at the same men's clubs their members used for general socializing, these clubs had purpose. Not only were the new groups designed to emulate the British penchant for clubs and associations, but they were designed to help explain the rapidly changing world to its members, and to provide a convenient place for government officials, educators, and the leaders of the commercial and industrial sectors to meet and discuss serious matters of mutual interest.

America's period of territorial expansion and consolidation was mostly concluded. Factories were luring young people off the farm into the nation's cities. America's time as a provider of raw material for Britain's factories was over; America was herself an industrial power. Fresh inventions were continually changing the face of manufacturing. It was a new world for America, and its leading citizens wanted to know more about it.

The most prestigious of the scientific associations formed in Washington at this time was the Philosophical Society. Begun in 1871, it attracted the most learned of the town's intellectuals. The Philosophical Society aimed its efforts "at investigation of the positive facts and laws of the physical and moral universe." [7] As Washington's population expanded over the next twenty years, six similar societies were formed, although none ever rivaled the Philosophical Society in importance, because while the Philosophical Society spent its energies looking into some of life's great mysteries, most of the newer groups concerned themselves primarily with the popularization of the sciences. However, many eminent members of the Philosophical Society also joined with other educated men in these newer groups, despite their making, in Constance Green's phrase, "no pretense of nurturing erudition." [8]

In 1888, these scientific organizations moved to join forces for publishing and for securing public speakers. They formed a loose federation under the leadership of Gardiner Greene Hubbard, who that same year began his own scientific organization. All seven of the societies that were functioning in the latter part of the 1880s met at the Cosmos Club. That club was the logical choice for the meetings, since its primary requirement for admission was simply high achievement. And it had been created in large part because New York friends of prominent Washingtonians had constantly twitted them for having no respectable gathering place equal to New York's Century Club.

Maj. John Wesley Powell, who three years later would become the second director of the U.S. Geological Survey, was the driving force behind the Cosmos Club's founding in 1878. He convinced the members of the Philosophical Society to join with him in establishing the new club, both to fill the acknowledged need for such a place and to prevent a rivalry from eventually developing between the society and the new club.

*   *   *

One of the seven scientific organizations was formed in early 1888 when six wealthy and noted Washingtonians, led by Gardiner Greene Hubbard, sent out invitations to their fellow patricians to join them in the formation of a society to specialize in their favorite pastime, which they were later to describe as "the increase and diffusion of geographic knowledge." The new organization was to have a dual purpose: It was to be a sort of explorer's club for the armchair-bound that could offer "good works" and provide entertainment, and to provide professional geographers a place to meet their colleagues and mingle with prospective employers.

Hubbard joined with five celebrated geographers and explorers, including Henry Gannett, chief geographer of the U.S. Geological Survey and noted mapmaker of the Rocky Mountains; A. W. Greely, who had led the Lady Franklin Bay Polar Expedition in 1882 and held the American record for travel to the farthest-north point on the globe; Henry Mitchell of the U.S. Geological Survey; A. H. Thompson of the U.S. Coast and Geodetic Survey; and Commodore J. R. Bartlett of the U.S. Hydrographic Office.

Hubbard's Boston law practice had long caused him to divide his time between Boston and Washington; in the capital, he was often arguing cases before the Supreme Court and presenting the causes of his clients to various governmental agencies. This had led him to take an active role in the capital's social evolution. Indeed, Hubbard was an influential figure in both Washington and Massachusetts. Although not a scientist himself, Hubbard was a regent of the fledgling Smithsonian Institution, which had been founded in 1836 in Washington, through a bequest by an English chemist, as America's national museum.

Thirty-three men responded to the invitation from the six noted gentlemen and met at the Cosmos Club, which is today still a bastion of old-line exclusivity in downtown Washington. At that first general session—held in the Cosmos Club's Assembly Hall, a handsome masculine room full of oversized black leather armchairs and large gaslight chandeliers—they agreed that it was indeed "both advisable and practicable to organize at the present time a geographic society in Washington."9

Influenced by both the lack of large numbers of professional geographers and explorers in Washington, and owing to Hubbard's central influence in its formation, the group agreed from the outset that it would be a far more accessible organization than the nation's then-leading geographic group, the New York–based American Geographical Society. The resolution adopted at that first meeting stated that "this society should be organized on as broad and liberal a basis in regard to qualifications for membership as is consistent with its own well-being and the dignity of the science it represents."[10] In other words, it was to be restrictive and exclusive, but moneyed amateurs would not be excluded.

Every civilized nation in the world at the time had a geographical society, but most of them were government-affiliated or at least government-recognized. Membership was limited to the aristocracy and the educational establishment. But in America, even geography was to be democratized. The exploratory group that met in Washington decided to open its rolls to all learned and interested citizens. In effect, of course, it meant that membership was open to all interested members of the ruling class. The American Geographical Society, on the other hand, was an organization of and for professionals.

Founded in 1851 as the American Geographical and Statistical Society—it changed its name twenty years later to the American Geographical Society of New York—the organization centered its efforts on building an enormous research library and on producing a few unprecedented maps, including "The Millionth Map of Hispanic America," so called because of its 1,000,000:1 scale. The map, actually a collection of 107 maps, is so detailed that it has "not only been used in the settlement of international boundary disputes, but has had many other critical peacetime and wartime uses, as well as contributing toward the promotion of better Inter-American relations," according to a circular published by the organization. It has been called "the greatest single mapping project in history."[11]

The American Geographical Association well met the outside world's image of an organization of people concerned with boundary lines and global features: It was technically oriented, populated with bookish people, and never very far out of debt. As the twentieth century neared, it had only a few thousand members; the primary service it provided, in addition to the library for New York–based professionals, was its noted journal, the *Geographical Review*.

Such a select, private organization was clearly not on Gardiner Greene Hubbard's mind when his budding group met in Washington one week after sending out its invitation letters. At that meeting, the new group adopted bylaws proposed by a committee of its founding members and formally agreed to incorporate in the District of Columbia. Another week later, on January 27, 1888, the National Geographic Society held its first official meeting, also at the Cosmos Club.

This conclave of formally dressed, bearded, stern-looking educated men must have presented quite a sight. "The moment [of founding] has since been immortalized in a painting . . . " noted one writer. "It looks like a cross between old photographs of Driving the Golden Spike at Council Bluffs, Utah [upon completion of the transcontinental railroad in America], and Aristotle Contemplating the Bust of Homer." [12] After hanging for many years in the foyer outside the conference room where the Society's board of directors met, this picture now hangs in the Bell Room, in Hubbard Memorial Hall, which has been restored to its original condition.

"I am not a scientific man," Gardiner Greene Hubbard told the 165 leading citizens of Washington who attended the group's first meeting, "nor can I lay claim to any special knowledge that would entitle me to be called a 'geographer.' I owe the honor of my election [as president of the Society] simply to the fact that I am one of those who desire to further the prosecution of geographic research. I possess only the same general interest in the subject of geography that should be felt by every educated man." [13]

Hubbard said that by his very election, the founders had shown that the Society was not going to be confined to professional geographers, "but will include that large number of people educated in other professions, who, like myself, desire to promote special geographic research and exploration by others, and to diffuse that knowledge."

He continued, "In union there is strength, and through the medium of national organization we may hope to promote geographic research in a manner that could not be accomplished by scattered individuals or by local societies. . . ." These were high-sounding words for a little club, even with its pretentious name. And the world hardly stopped and took notice of its birth. Although many local luminaries were involved in its creation, the Society's formation was not big news, even in Washington's society-struck newspapers, where a party at the White House was sure to get prominent coverage, complete with a list of all the invited guests.

In fact, the formation of rich men's scientific associations had become ordinary news. About the only thing that seemed to set this club apart from the others was that it planned to specialize in geography. There was no reason to think it would ever be anything special. Even the National Geographic Society's main reason for existence—still quoted today prominently in every issue of its magazine, "Organized 'for the increase and diffusion of geographic knowledge'"—was lifted from the will of James Smithson, the founding benefactor of what was to become America's national museum. The will, as quoted in the 1836 act of Congress that formally recognized the museum, included a bequest "for the purpose of founding, at Washington, under the name of the Smithsonian Institution, an establishment for the increase and diffusion of knowledge among men. . . ."

Hubbard, who was a regent of the Smithsonian, apparently decided to adapt the Smithsonian's credo as the National Geographic Society's own. Hubbard must have been quite taken with Smithson's deed, since he seems to have borrowed freely from it in formulating his own vision of the National Geographic Society. Hubbard moved to shape his fledgling society into the kind of altruistic organization Smithson had in mind—only Hubbard wasn't going to do it posthumously, surely wasn't going to hand the reins over to strangers, and wasn't going to contribute the sums of money Smithson had provided.

The *Washington Evening Star* gave the founding of the Society one paragraph on page one of its four pages, listing its incorporation and its officers, and noting its stated objectives. The January 28 edition of the *Washington Post* failed to note the National Geographic Society's founding, spending most of its space recounting crimes and mishaps from around the world, including the year's worst blizzard in the Midwest and the strange disappearance from a local cemetery of a recently buried woman, whose body was later found on the dissecting table of a medical school in town.

4. HUMBLE BEGINNINGS

*The first issues [of the Society's magazine]
were dreadfully scientific, suitable for
diffusing geographic knowledge among
those who already had it, and scaring off
the rest. . . .*
Magazine writer Anne Chamberlin, 1963

Conditions in Washington at the turn of the century were good for
the formation of an organization like the National Geographic
Society. The federal government was sponsoring a comprehensive
exploration and survey of the western United States, which drew
to the nation's capital each winter an increasingly large number of
specialists in the sciences related to geography. Many of these same
men carried on expeditions during the rest of the year and met
their peers and employers only in Washington during the winter.

Almost all geographic work at the time was government-spon-
sored. The young nation, having recently ended its Civil War and
having dispatched its native Indians to reservations, was still taking stock of itself. Boundaries were being drawn; homestead acts
divided the range; mineral deposits were being found; interconti-
nental railroads crisscrossed the land; America was on the move.
And big business was on the scene to grab the lion's share of commerce. The large railroads, oil companies, meatpackers, and steel
companies created giant monopolistic trusts to lock up and protect
their businesses.

Since their primary employer was based in Washington, most

geographers established residence there too. During the winter, when the government was in full swing as the executive and legislative branches rushed to finish their business before Washington's legendary summers took root, the scientists and geographers would be there in search of funding for their projects. Thus the National Geographic Society, its founders believed, would serve as both an off-season headquarters for wintering geographers and a central clearing house when the professional geographers were out in the field. The amateurs, Gardiner Greene Hubbard among them, could amuse themselves all year long.

The National Geographic Society's founding fathers had decided to "increase and diffuse" geographic knowledge mostly by holding meetings at which members could present papers and give lectures, and to publish those papers and other works in a journal to be called the *National Geographic Magazine,* which would be sent to all members. Volume I, Number 1 of its publication, covered in terra-cotta-colored cardboard, made it to market in October 1888, and everyone who has ever written about it agrees that it was slim, dull, and technical. The cover price was 50 cents, and the magazine included a detailed analysis of the blizzard of '88 and a lead article titled "Geographic Methods in Geologic Investigation" and another titled "Classification of Geographic Forms by Genesis." The issues that followed, on its irregular publication schedule, were hardly more exciting than the premier issue, featuring dry dissertations by the Society's professional members.

"The first issues," summed up one writer, ". . . were dreadfully scientific, suitable for diffusing geographic knowledge among those who already had it, and scaring off the rest. . . ."[1] And besides being uninteresting, the magazine had no set publication schedule; it was seemingly printed whenever its volunteer staff could manage to get enough material to the printer to fill an issue.

Hubbard was not a man of letters, and responsibility for production of the magazine fell on several of the members who claimed an understanding of magazine publication but were in fact academicians. As a result, the magazine featured dull, ponderous articles on technical subjects by professionals, many of whom were government employees reporting on their continuing research projects. The magazine's advisers were also politicians, in the way of professional educators everywhere, and many of the articles made their way into the *National Geographic* more on the credentials of the writers than because of the merits of, or widespread interest in, the articles. In fact, Washington was still a small enough town, and the United States a young enough nation, for all of the powerful elite to know one another. The governors and the governed lived elbow to elbow, as one big and somewhat friendly family.

Dues were set at $5 a year, with all members receiving the magazine as a premium of membership. Dues were kept low in order to attract many members. Life memberships were also available for $50. But by May 31, 1895, seven and a half years after the Society's founding, the total membership was only 1,178, small compared to the enrollments of other societies in Washington.

In the Society's first ten years, its sole contribution to the "increase" of geographic knowledge was the sponsoring of an expedition to Mount St. Elias in Alaska in 1900. The expedition discovered Mount Logan; at 19,850 feet, it was North America's second-highest peak. But the Society had no money with which to sponsor such expeditions, and all of the funds for this project were provided by Gardiner Greene Hubbard.

Even this successful expedition failed to generate much outside interest in the National Geographic Society. While the founders had insisted that the National Geographic Society be an organization for interested and educated laymen, most of those it had attracted were high-ranking government workers and geographers who looked to the government for funding. The venerable American Geographical Society already existed in New York and was publishing its own well-respected journal, with all its activities aimed exclusively at professional geographers, who didn't urgently need another geographical society, even one situated in their home base.

So, in 1898, with membership rolls still hovering around a thousand, the Society's directors decided to take a chance on an all-out effort to make a success of their club. Under Hubbard's guidance, the Society set out to build up its little magazine's subscription base by publishing it monthly and offering it for sale on newsstands to the public.

The idea behind the project was to generate interest and memberships in the Society through the spread of the magazine, as well as to gain needed income through the street sales of a publication that the Society was already committed to producing for its existing membership. Hubbard, who had accomplished so much in his full life, was disturbed by his inability to build up the organization. And so he adopted the strategy that had been so successful for him in the past: a full-scale charge.

But it was a dismal failure; apparently America was not ready for a big geographical society. Not only did the newsstand drive not make money, but the Society ended up spending all of the cash it had obtained from selling "lifetime" memberships—which guaranteed a member a lifetime of magazines and privileges—while the Society still had the obligation to provide the services.

And at the Society's darkest hour, with its treasury empty and its ledgers showing $2,000 in debts, Gardiner Greene Hubbard died.

* * *

Up to this time, Alexander Graham Bell, despite his continuing closeness to his father-in-law and their joint involvement in the Bell Telephone Company, had expressed little interest in geography or the National Geographic Society and had not taken an active part in the organization, except to pay his dues. Rather, Bell was spending his time on the pursuits that most interested him—anything to do with flight or with sound and the deaf.

He developed the method of recording sound on wax disks and cylinders for phonograph records, replacing Thomas Edison's metal-foil process and creating the record industry as we know it. Bell gave his share of the patent rights to the Volta Bureau to fund its research into the causes of and cures for deafness. Bell was a leading advocate of the fledgling aviation industry and helped fund, with Mabel's active assistance (since she had controlled all their money since the day Bell gave her the telephone company stock as a wedding present), a circle of aviation buffs that led to the development of the aileron—a movable wing extension that increases lift on takeoff—which is still fundamental to modern airplane construction.

In 1891, he contributed $5,000 toward aviation experiments being conducted by S. P. Langley. Five years later, Bell was one of the witnesses of the successful flight over the Potomac River near Washington of Langley's sixteen-foot pilotless model, which was steam-powered. "The sight of Langley's steam aerodrome circling in the sky convinced me that the age of the flying machine was at hand," he later said. [2]

Bell was elected a regent of the Smithsonian, and his enthusiasm for Langley's work helped the aviator obtain a $50,000 contract from the War Department. But Langley's full-scale model, which carried a pilot, crashed into the Potomac during its trial, and the project dissolved in ridicule, setting back the entire cause of aviation until the Wright brothers' later successes at Kitty Hawk, North Carolina.

Hubbard's death could easily have meant the end of the National Geographic Society. With its treasury empty, its most active member and guiding light dead, and its other members' interest flagging, the little organization certainly seemed doomed. But some of Hubbard's closest associates had another idea: Alexander Graham Bell.

Bell was the logical successor to Hubbard and the only candidate for savior of the Society that these men could find. But when these gentlemen first approached Bell with the suggestion that he step in and fulfill his father-in-law's dream of making a success of the National Geographic Society, they were rebuffed. Bell told them that he was not the right man for the job, since he wasn't a geographer. And Bell knew that despite its expansive name, the Society was little more than a local club, and a moribund one at that.

But the success of the National Geographic Society had been a grand dream of Hubbard's, one of the few he had had that he had been unable to fulfill. Bell, obviously more from family loyalty than anything else, finally agreed to accept the appointment. He also no doubt enjoyed the prospect of tackling a seemingly impossible situation and coming up with the solution, such as teaching the deaf to speak, or man to fly, or sheep to breed only twins.

After surveying the situation, Bell agreed with the Society's board that the *National Geographic Magazine* was the key to any future success, but in a completely different way than they had envisioned. Bell had come to the conclusion that people would read about geography only if it was presented in a light, entertaining way. "To sugarcoat the pill" was a phrase heard around the halls of the Society for many years. He further decided that the best way for the Society to proceed was to stop trying to boost its membership rolls by selling subscriptions to the magazine. Instead, he wanted to reverse the process and offer the magazine strictly as a bonus for membership in the Society. At the same time, he wanted to appeal to prospective members' other emotions—the altruistic and the not so unselfish—by offering them membership in a select geographic society.

Bell believed that most people want to learn, and that many people—not just the very rich—would like to support scientific exploration and research, if they could only do so on a reasonable financial scale. He also realized that a select society would appeal to snobbishness, to the strong desire of some members of the middle classes to copy the rich and to join clubs and organizations. Bell well understood the vicarious thrill readers might get out of "traveling" to strange and exotic lands through the magazine.

Fortunately for the Society, as Bell matured and became more confident in himself and secure in his place, he became quite an effective salesman for his causes. "He was fearlessly honest and scornful of shams, but he had the showman's innate appreciation of an effect," biographer Catherine MacKenzie wrote. "The world was a stage, and his was a genius for entrances and exits. . . . His long white hair and flaring white beard, his homespun knickerbockers and his old black tam-o'-shanter, his animation, and ample gestures, were the expression of a perfectly valid histrionic sense after a fashion that mere flamboyant affectations never are."[3]

It was this flair for showmanship that led him to make a fundamental decision: to put "pictures in the *National Geographic Magazine* when that periodical's life crept feebly from one annual deficit to another. The magazine was little more than a Society bulletin, distributed to less than 1,000 members—using occasional pictures and maps, it is true, but often with no relation to the text," wrote MacKenzie in her 1928 biography.[4] Such a redesigned magazine, Bell said, should not rely upon subscriptions or newsstand sales. Rather the Society should seek members who were eager to learn, interested in increasing knowledge, and willing to help support exploration and research through modest annual dues.

The first roadblock to Bell's vision was not even the public, but the Society's own board of trustees. The board was composed mostly of staid professionals, to whom geography was more a religion than an avocation. But Bell persisted. The first step, he decided, was to hire a person full-time to supervise the magazine and solicit new members; up until now, the only paid Society employee had been a clerk. The magazine was run completely by volunteers, and thus rarely met deadlines or had a distinctive style. Bell quieted most of the opposition to this part of his plan when he volunteered to pay the salary of the new employee himself.

At that time, the NGS had two classes of membership: "active" members, those who lived in the Washington, D.C., area, received the magazine, were invited to the Society's lectures, and paid $5 a year; and nonresidents, who paid $2 and got only the magazine. At the time there were eight hundred local and two hundred nonresident members. "Dr. Bell advised that the distinction . . . be abolished, arguing that people disliked to be classed as nonresident, or corresponding, members, because of a prevalent feeling that nonresident members had few privileges," according to one Society history.[5]

As the trustees continued to haggle over these changes, Bell turned to the task of finding the new employee to take over the daily operation of the Society and the magazine. Bell, a man of vision, not only had a person in mind, but apparently realized he could resolve another pressing personal matter at the same time.

In the summer of 1897, Bell's wife, the mother of several marriageable daughters, had read a story in *Harper's Weekly* about the latest class of Amherst College graduates. The article discussed with great interest the twin brothers Gilbert Hovey and Edwin Prescott Grosvenor, whose father, Edwin Augustus Grosvenor, a clergyman who chose teaching over the pulpit, was a friend of Mr. Bell's. The senior Grosvenor was at the time a professor of European history at Amherst. The twins made up the college's tennis doubles team, had won many scholastic honors, were members of Phi Beta Kappa, and dressed alike to confuse their classmates. The *Harper's Weekly* article said, "Interest in the commencement at Amherst seems to have been divided between President Gates and the Grosvenor twins . . . both of whom were graduated this year and both with distinction. . . . At the alumni dinner the graduates had fun with the twins, and did their best to have as much seemly fun at commencement as possible."[6]

After reading the article, Mrs. Bell invited the twins to a house party at the Bell summer house in Nova Scotia. Her daughter Elsie, a radiant nineteen-year-old, brown-eyed and slim-waisted, was very much taken with Gilbert. At the end of the summer, Gilbert took a job with a boys' school in Englewood, New Jersey, teaching languages, algebra, and chemistry, but Elsie and Gilbert Grosvenor continued to write to each other.

About a year later, Elsie decided that Englewood, New Jersey, was too great a distance from Washington, D.C., for her ever to have a serious relationship with Gilbert, and she sought her father's advice on the problem. Bell, ever the opportunist, wrote Professor Grosvenor that he was looking for a capable young man to brighten up his magazine and asked, feigning indifference and impartiality, whether either of the twins would be interested in the job.

While that's not exactly the official version offered in the archives of the Society—which shows young Grosvenor in the traditional male-aggressor role in pursuit of his blushing prize—Gilbert Hovey Grosvenor found himself being interviewed for the job by Bell in Washington in the spring of 1899.

"Dr. Bell showed me copies of the popular magazines of the day—*Harper's, Century, McClure's, Munsey* and others. Could we develop a geographic magazine that would be as popular as these? I thought we could, but emphasized that we should proceed slowly and feel our way for a time," Grosvenor later wrote of this meeting.[7] Several years before, Bell told Grosvenor, he and Gardiner Greene Hubbard had spent $87,000 in a vain attempt to establish a magazine called *Science*. "After two unprofitable years, they were glad to sell the name for $25, even though they had paid $5,000 for that name," Grosvenor recalled.[8]

And if Grosvenor agreed to take over the *National Geographic Magazine*, Bell promised him, he was willing to invest a similar amount of money in the attempt to revive it. "This statement, however, alarmed me," Grosvenor said. "Sheer weight of money, I felt, would not ensure success. The answer lay elsewhere. I replied that I would take the job only if he limited his gift to $100 a month for my salary—considerably less than I was getting at Englewood. Dr. Bell's surprise was evident, but it was also apparent that Mrs. Bell was pleased; she did not want him to lose another large sum in magazine experiments."[9]

In a later reminiscence, Grosvenor wrote that Bell was "reluctant" to agree not to underwrite the Society with any more than the $100 a month, but that "Mrs. Bell gave me strong support. 'Bert,' she said, 'all our money is in my name. Mr. Bell gave his share of the telephone patent to me as a wedding present. I feel that I hold in trust for him all that I own. You are right to insist that he limit his donation. Money is not the answer. You have a difficult job, and as you said, you must proceed slowly.'"[10]

The job appealed to Grosvenor for several reasons. First, it would give him a chance to woo Elsie, and he was already quite infatuated with her. It would also bring him to Washington and give him a close working relationship with Bell, already a leading citizen of the nation. And the job would give Grosvenor the opportunity to indulge his interest in exotic foreign lands. Grosvenor had been born in Constantinople and had spent all of his early years abroad, before his father brought the family back to the United States.

After his meeting with Bell, Grosvenor returned to New Jersey and asked the headmaster of the boys' school for permission to leave immediately, well before the school year ended, because of this extraordinary opportunity in Washington. The headmaster agreed, but not before offering up a humbling final thought to Grosvenor, who was not yet a year into postcollege life. Grosvenor later wrote, "His final words to me were, 'Remember, Grosvenor, Mr. Bell wants you mainly because you are your father's son.'"[11] Perhaps it would have been more accurate to say that Bell wanted him because he was Elsie's beau.

5. GROSVENOR I

> *. . . The organization was not so poor as it seemed. Dr. Bell's idea of membership in a society, not merely subscription to a magazine, was sound and a great initial asset.*
>
> Gilbert H. Grosvenor

When Gilbert H. Grosvenor arrived in Washington on April 1, 1899, Bell took him to the National Geographic Society's headquarters for a sobering inspection tour. The Society's "offices" consisted of half of one small rented room on the fifth floor of a building across from the U.S. Department of the Treasury in downtown Washington; the other half of the room belonged to the American Forestry Association.

The Society's part of the small room was littered with old magazines and newspapers, a few shabby pieces of furniture, and a few books of records, which seemed to be the only visible property of the Society. Mixed in among the two rickety chairs and small table were six enormous boxes full of magazines that had been returned by newsstands following Hubbard's abortive attempt to boost circulation. There was not even a desk for the young editor. "No desk! I'll send you mine," Bell told Grosvenor; that very afternoon a beautiful Circassian walnut rolltop was delivered. [1]

Despite its lowly financial condition—the Society had already spent the $2,000 raised through the sale of life memberships—the organization had some valuable assets, especially Bell's interest and

attention. And Bell had already devised a plan to save the floun-
dering Society. Grosvenor—time perhaps having taken the uncer-
tainty out of his and Bell's hopes—wrote thirty-seven years later,
". . . The organization was not so poor as it seemed. . . . Why not
popularize the science of geography and take it into the homes of
the people? Why not transform the Society's magazine from one of
cold geographic fact, expressed in hieroglyphic terms which the
layman could not understand, into a vehicle for carrying the living, breathing, human-interest truth about this great world of ours?
Would not that be the greatest agency of all for the diffusion of
geographic knowledge?"[2]

Gilbert Hovey Grosvenor, then twenty-three, was hired to be
the Society's only paid employee on a three-month trial basis. He
was replacing both a volunteer editor of the magazine, a statisti-
cian at the Department of Agriculture, and the Society's only paid
worker, who held the title of assistant secretary.

Grosvenor began by studying "geographic" books that had been
successful in the ultimate testing ground, the marketplace. He read
Darwin's *Voyage of the Beagle,* Dana's *Two Years Before the Mast,* and
Joshua Slocum's *Sailing Alone Around the World.* "What was there
in Herodotus' travels, written 2,000 years earlier," he wondered,
"that gave the book such life that it had survived 20 centuries and
was still going strong? . . . Finally I was convinced I had the answer: Each was an accurate, eyewitness, first-hand account. Each
contained simple, straightforward writing—writing that sought to
make picures in the reader's mind."[3]

But while Bell was a man of action who wanted quick response
once a path was chosen, young Grosvenor was more concerned
with the continuing battles that were raging within the board of
trustees over the Society's future. The board was still sharply divided between members who supported Bell and his policies of
growth through the popularization of geography, and traditionalists
who were reluctant to appeal to the masses for support for their
club. Some of the trustees were not convinced geography could—
or should—be put into nontechnical, populist terms.

Adding fuel to the already crackling fires of dissension on the
board was one of the publishing industry's most successful men,

who had his own designs on the *National Geographic*. Soon after taking over the Society, Bell went for publishing advice to S. S. McClure, head of the publishing firm and the very successful 370,000-circulation magazine that bore his name. McClure told Bell emphatically that all of Bell's ideas were wrong. His advice: "(1) Publish the *National Geographic* in New York, since it is impossible to establish a popular magazine in Washington; (2) change the magazine's name to something simpler; (3) abandon the plan to build circulation by membership in a geographic society; (4) depend upon newsstand sales and advertising to increase the circulation; (5) never mention the name National Geographic Society in the magazine, since people abhor geography."[4]

Bell and Grosvenor were aghast. They reminded the board how precarious newsstand sales could be, as they had found out. A magazine issue that was dated January would be published and distributed in December, but the news dealers wouldn't pay for the copies until July. And since there was no way of knowing how many copies of an issue were unsold until payment was received, there was no way to gauge future printing runs without six-month delays.

"Yet many siren songs were sung to us by the news dealers," according to Grosvenor. "They proposed that we sell subscriptions to them in bulk, which would permit them to resell the magazine at a cheaper price than the membership fee in the Society. . . ." And, Grosvenor later said, during the meetings he and Bell had with the Society's directors over the organization's course, "I caught several men exchanging winks when Dr. Bell enlarged on his idea that geography could be made interesting."[5]

While these battles raged within the board, and while Bell and Grosvenor postulated formulas for success, there was real work to be done. As the Society's only employee, Grosvenor wrote, "I was even obliged to address the magazine envelopes myself. The names of the members were then printed on long slips, and it was the practice to cut these slips up with a pair of scissors and then paste them on the envelopes. After addressing one edition of 900 copies in this way, my first investment in office furniture was the purchase of an addressing machine for $20."[6]

At the same time, Grosvenor's romance with Elsie Bell was having troubles of its own. Her mother, Mabel Bell, apparently was having second thoughts about Grosvenor's suitability for her daughter. While it is impossible now to determine why Mrs. Bell's feelings had changed about Grosvenor and his quest for Elsie's hand, since just about the only accounts of this period in the lives of all the participants were written by Grosvenor, Mrs. Bell clearly tried to separate the two.

After Bell introduced Grosvenor to the board members and the volunteers of the Society, he left for his laboratory at Cape Breton, Nova Scotia, where he normally summered. ". . . His family soon followed—but not until Mrs. Bell obtained a promise from Elsie and me that we would not correspond with one another during the summer." Mrs. Bell, Grosvenor wrote, did, however, ask her mother, Hubbard's widow, who was still living in Washington, to look out for him.

"When Dr. Bell learned of his wife's action," Grosvenor later wrote, "he slyly made Elsie his secretary when writing to me, and all the many letters I received from him that summer were in her familiar handwriting. That helped both of us, but Elsie never inserted a personal note. She kept her word to her mother, and so did I."[7]

Meanwhile, Grosvenor got off to such a good start at the Society that less than a month into his three-month trial period, Bell wrote to inform him that the members of the "editorial committee have been so much pleased with you, and appreciate so highly the benefits already derived from your assistance, that they consider it unnecessary to wait," and hired him permanently at the agreed-upon $100 per month.[8]

Grosvenor immersed himself in his work, realizing he had two jobs to do. First, he had to find new members quickly; the Society needed the money and the morale boost an expanded membership would bring. And at the same time he had to make the *National Geographic* into a professional-quality magazine; no more could deadlines slide or unreadably technical articles occupy its pages because he had nothing else with which to fill them.

Luckily for the National Geographic Society, in an age when

many viewed "promotion" as the huckstering of unprincipled traveling salesmen, and to be avoided at all cost, Grosvenor's father had a quite different view, which had rubbed off on his son. The elder Grosvenor, during his tenure as a professor of European history at Amherst College, had written a book about Constantinople based on his many years living there while he was teaching, and had done a good deal of self-promotion to ensure its success.

"Dignified promotion had proved its worth" in his father's pursuits, Grosvenor later wrote, "and I have never forgotten the lesson it taught me. To some people, the word 'promoter' is an unattractive designation, but I have been one all my life. Promotion in good taste and for a good cause is a creative enterprise, esssential in the publishing field."[9]

This belief meshed nicely with Bell's own sense of promotion, and would prove to be a vital key to the Society's future fortunes. In line with his "promoter" instincts, in order to help boost the rolls of the NGS, Grosvenor initiated what would become another trademark National Geographic Society marketing technique, that of the unsolicited "nomination" of prospective members. The technique involves sending letters to potential members informing them that they had been recommended by their friends, and inviting them to send in their dues. ". . . I began by asking prominent men to nominate their friends for membership. Initially that meant seeking nominations from my father and Dr. Bell," Grosvenor wrote. ". . . As fast as the names came in—all distinguished men and women—the Admissions Committee would approve them, and letters would be sent inviting the nominees to join. . . ."[10]

But just as he was implementing the new sales program, the first solicitation letter quickly ran afoul of the sensibilities of the traditionalists on the Society board, who were obviously still in the majority. While Grosvenor had gotten Bell's approval for the letter before the scientist left for Cape Breton with his family for the summer, the board "condemned [it] . . . in a most emphatic way; in fact," he later wrote Bell, "the different men tore it so to pieces, the idea, language, begging character, and undignified method of procedure as they put it, that nothing was left when they finished. . . ." The board named a committee to write a letter to Bell explaining their objections, but to add insult to injury, Grosvenor continued, "as each wished the other to write it . . . I had to do it myself."[11]

Eventually, a solicitation letter satisfactory to the board members was written and sent to the many nominees whose names Grosvenor was able to garner; he was helped in all these efforts by a volunteer assistant, Elsie Bell.

Before sailing for an extended vacation in Europe with his family on June 30, 1900, Bell again met with the Society's trustees to discuss the organization's future. The primary bit of business had been a formal vote by the board, at Bell's urging, to overrule the five-member executive committee, where much of the opposition to Bell's plans was centered. The committee had wanted to follow New York publisher McClure's earlier advice and move the magazine to New York and separate it from the Society, but Bell's motion to override it was carried.

Believing he had finally settled matters, he departed, sure the board was willing to give his plan a trial period, even though many of them were not happy about his plans. However, only days after Bell began his journey by boat, a revolt broke out anew, the plotters no doubt taking advantage of the slowness of that era's means of transportation. Several dissenting members of the board of directors reopened negotiations with McClure to take over publishing and distributing the *National Geographic Magazine* from New York City. At the same time, the board's executive committee refused to accept any of the 1,100 prospective membership "nominees" Grosvenor had harvested from his father and two of the trustees for the next wave of membership solicitation letters.

Next, to complete the coup d'état, the executive committee moved to fire Grosvenor. Just how much of the board's intransigence was based on opposition to Bell's plans and how much, if any, was caused by antipathy to Grosvenor is lost to time. According to Grosvenor, "The dispute [over his employment] concerned the spelling of such words as Peking and Porto Rico. Two members of the committee took violent sides on this question and would not speak to each other."[12] And, he said, he found himself in the middle of the dispute. However, upon reflection, that explanation seems frivolous.

Things were so bad during that hot summer of 1900, Grosvenor recalled, that "occasionally I clambered onto the fire escape outside my window for a breath of air, and one day I heard beneath me the strident tones of a hurdy-gurdy playing Sousa marches. On the curb, an organ grinder cranked tinny tunes while a monkey capered, grimaced, and bowed. It was absurd, ridiculous—and delightful. Listening every day to the hurdy-gurdy became my sole diversion from care, and today, 63 years later, it seems I can still hear Sousa's stirring music. During those days," he continued, "my father counseled, 'Just be patient, be patient.' His advice brought to mind a line from Longfellow's 'A Psalm of Life': 'Learn to labor and to wait.'"[13]

On top of all these troubles, Grosvenor was still fighting the battle for Elsie Bell's hand. Grosvenor's announcement to the Bells of his desire to marry Elsie had actually led to this latest Bell family voyage to Europe. While Grosvenor later wrote that the Bells had taken the news of his intentions to marry Elsie "with affectionate approval," Mabel Bell had placed another hurdle for the young sweethearts to climb. Mrs. Bell, with her husband's approval, suggested that there be a few months' separation, so that the two could be sure of their hearts, and the Bells took Elsie to Europe for an extended cooling-off period.

After receiving Grosvenor's panicked word about the shocking turn of events at the Society, Bell returned to Washington in August and quickly quelled the insurrection. He reconvened the board of managers, as the directors were then formally called, and its members unanimously reaffirmed Grosvenor's status as permanent editor of the magazine and even increased his salary by two-thirds, to $2,000 a year, with the additional $800 to come from the Society's treasury, not from Bell's pocket. Then Bell returned to his family in Europe.

Despite the troubled situation, Grosvenor later wrote, a new development "soon drove all but happy thoughts from my mind."[14] The executive committee's opposition to Grosvenor, as no doubt related in detail by her father, had angered Elsie and made him the deserving underdog in her eyes, fighting for her father's, and grandfather's, vision of the future against his short-sighted enemies. Difficulties have a way of bringing young couples closer together, Grosvenor later wrote. On August 30, 1900, his father's birthday, Elsie agreed to marry Grosvenor, and they made plans for a wedding abroad.

Elsie, a large and handsome woman, had seemingly inherited her father's wide-ranging interests and sense of adventure and both her parents' wanderlust and doggedness. As a seven-year-old, Elsie had accompanied her family on what was to be a tour of the Newfoundland coast as the Bells searched for a place to build a summer home. One foggy morning, the ship they were on, the S. S. *Hanoverian,* hit some rocks and began to sink. Bell assisted his wife and daughters into lifeboats, and they all made it safely ashore. Later asked about her frightening experience, Elsie replied, "It was the best part of the trip."[15]

Despite her family's wealth, in the Victorian tradition, Elsie had not gone to college; but by the time she met Grosvenor, she was extremely well traveled, had attended schools in France and Italy, and took a great interest in the world and the National Geographic Society. She had been at least indirectly involved in the Society since childhood, and as a girl of ten had accompanied her grandfather, Gardiner Greene Hubbard, to the Society's first public lecture.

London was chosen as the site of the Grosvenor-Bell wedding. Elsie, now twenty-two, had been born there while her father was in England to demonstrate his invention to Queen Victoria. Gilbert Hovey Grosvenor and Elsie May Bell were married at King's Weigh House Chapel on October 23, 1900, the wedding anniversary of Grosvenor's parents. "Even King's Weigh Church . . . proved symbolic," according to Grosvenor, since "it stands a block from Gilbert Street, just off Grosvenor Square."[16]

After the wedding, the newlyweds began a memorable honeymoon, being "royally entertained" by geographic societies in Paris and Berlin, Grosvenor recalled—another reward for membership in the armchair-explorer-club circuit, as visiting members of foreign geographic clubs were always well taken care of by the local organization—as part of a planned whirlwind tour of all Europe. But as they were enjoying the start of their new life, sampling the treasures the Old World could offer to young, upper-class tourists, matters in Washington were again taking ominous turns.

While the young couple was in Vienna, Grosvenor received belated word of what was going on at home: Despite their belief that the battle with the trustees had been settled once and for all, Grosvenor was told that the executive committee had actually signed a contract with one of S. S. McClure's firms, McClure, Phillips & Co., to print the *National Geographic Magazine* in New York.

The Grosvenors and the Bells, who had also remained in Europe after the wedding in England, all returned to Washington. Bell, firmly backing his new son-in-law and his own vision of the National Geographic Society, set about undoing the misdeeds committed in his absence, while Grosvenor went to New York to join the fray directly with McClure.

The first two issues of 1901 were printed at McClure's plant before Grosvenor could undo the executive committee's action. "But the reversal was won," he wrote. "I brought the magazine back to Washington, where I had it printed at half the cost of New York publication." Apparently, the executive committee, in addition to underestimating Bell's tenacity and resolve, hadn't fully appreciated all that was involved in having McClure print the magazine, and especially hadn't understood what the big-city printing bills would total. "The executive committee was happy to escape from the New York printer . . . and we shook hands," Grosvenor said.[17]

This battle, and the executive committee's total capitulation after its brief affair with McClure, marked a turning point in the evolution of the magazine, the Society, and the role Grosvenor was to play in both of them. The in-house opposition was forever stilled, and Bell was free to shape the Society in his own image.

And soon thereafter, Grosvenor—now clearly Bell's surrogate-director—was made editor of the magazine and director of the Society, with full control over both. With his new strength and independence, Grosvenor was able to scuttle the publications committee and the obstructionist role it had been playing in overseeing his operation and stifling his attempts to expand the viewpoint of the *National Geographic*. The example he always cited to illustrate the committee's operations concerned an article submitted in late 1899 by C. C. Georgeson, who worked for the U.S. Department of Agriculture, on what he saw as the possibility of developing successful commercial farms in parts of Alaska.

At that time, Georgeson's position seemed radical, especially to the committee. While Grosvenor said later that he found the author's point of view a sound one, others on the committee ridiculed it, particularly one member whose view of Alaska was colored by the fact that when he had climbed glaciers there years before, he had suffered from the cold. The article was rejected at the time by the committee, but as if to underscore his newly acquired authority, Grosvenor ran it in the March 1902 issue.

After their shortened honeymoon, Grosvenor and his wife redoubled their efforts to garner new members for the Society, primarily by hounding their families for the names and addresses of potential enlistees. They also took full advantage of Bell's prominence and of the fact that William Howard Taft, who was then serving as the first U.S. civil governor of the Philippines and would later serve the nation as secretary of war, President of the United States, and chief justice of the U.S. Supreme Court, was Grosvenor's second cousin.

Grosvenor later explained how "while the battle raged" with the recalcitrant board members, he and Elsie "drew up a list of prominent friends we felt sure would welcome the chance to support the Society and its journal. To each, we mailed a dignified brochure soliciting National Geographic membership. Even we were surprised by the response: Nearly every reply brought an enthusiastic acceptance and—to our delight—a check for dues. . . ." But, in Grosvenor's words, "the membership campaign was a foundation on which to build, but the real challenge lay in the magazine. No promotion, however inspired, would sell a journal that could not sell itself. . . ."[18]

Even though he still had no budget with which to buy manuscripts, he set about the task of transforming the magazine from a collection of professional treatises to a popular, money-making periodical. Grosvenor was helped along in his efforts by the increased stirrings of American interest in the rest of the world, as the nation began to move to the forefront of the industrialized world. And for the first time in its short history, the United States was becoming a colonial power. After beginning a buildup of its armed forces, late in the nineteenth century the United States began a move to forge a confederation of North America and South America in an organization called the Pan-American Union, and to enforce the Monroe Doctrine declaring American primary in the affairs of its hemisphere.

In 1895, a group of Cuban revolutionaries, encouraged and financed by exiles living in the United States, began threatening Spanish control of their homeland. By burning Cuba's important sugar and tobacco crops, the rebels were able to paralyze the nation, and Spain responded by sending 200,000 troops to Cuba. Anti-Spanish feelings were whipped into a frenzy in the United States by an orchestrated campaign, highlighted by the publication in a New York newspaper in February 1898 of a private letter written by Spain's Washington minister that criticized President William McKinley. Less than a week later, the American battleship *Maine* was destroyed at anchor in Havana harbor; war became inevitable.

The Spanish-American War of 1898 won the United States possessions—the Philippines, Cuba, and Puerto Rico—and suddenly Latin American countries and customs were of interest and concern to Americans. Moreover, Americans, bound more closely together by crisscrossing railroad lines and the wires that connected Alexander Graham Bell's growing network of telephones, wanted to know more about one another.

Grosvenor, with the general blueprint already laid out for him by Bell, went about putting the populist stamp on the National Geographic Society that founding father Hubbard had talked of, but that had never before been realized. The magazine's personality changed: Articles were less academic, of broader interest; thought was applied to layout and graphics to make the stories more appealing to the eye. And membership grew.

6. THE KEY

As Alexander Graham Bell became convinced of his son-in-law's ability to carry out his blueprint for making a success of the National Geographic Society, he began to move out of the picture, and Gilbert H. Grosvenor took an ever-larger share of the responsibilities for running the organization.

Grosvenor, a thin and serious-looking young man with a prominent mustache and sharply parted straight hair, relished his authority. With Bell's proxy firmly in his pocket, he moved to continue implementing Bell's populist theories and putting his own stamp on the Society and its magazine. This decision was made despite lingering resistance from the trustees. They were still divided over the direction the Society should take, with the traditionalists continuing their fight to appeal to a select, professional audience, and Bell's supporters pushing for his plan for a general, mass appeal.

As close a relationship as Grosvenor and his father-in-law had developed, they were quite dissimilar people. Bell was an effusive and by now huge man, witty and theatrical, quick-tongued, a lover of food and smoke, a man of immense and wide-ranging interests.

While he ended up known primarily as the inventor of the telephone, he could just as easily, and probably just as happily, have been an aviator or sheep raiser or piano player.

Grosvenor was equally full of dedication and energy, but, after 1899 at least, it seemed that his efforts were all directed at the furtherance of the National Geographic Society and its magazine. He was a man of steady and moderate habits. He didn't drink or smoke or tolerate abusive language from anyone around him.

An obsession of the Chief's—as Grosvenor became known to all on his staff—that quickly became a hallmark of *National Geographic Magazine* prose was his insistence on short paragraphs. One illustrative story involves William Howard Taft, Grosvenor's cousin, who was often quite helpful to the Society during his career, which led eventually to the White House. It seems that Grosvenor's gratitude toward his second cousin "did not blind him to the fact that his kinsman, as a writer, was given to sensational violations of this [short paragraph] principle." He instructed a staff member to break one of William Howard Taft's manuscripts into short paragraphs. "Grosvenor's subordinate called the Chief's attention to the fact that an editor had already broken up the manuscript into one-sentence paragraphs, but that the ex-President's sentences were rather long. 'Well, break up the sentences,' said Grosvenor. 'The Bible does it. That's why people read the Bible. And that's why they read the *National Geographic.*'"[1]

* * *

When Grosvenor took control at the *National Geographic,* photography was in its infancy, and graphic arts, at least as applied to periodicals, was nonexistent. The *Geographic* featured a single column of basically uninterrupted type, broken only occasionally by a large capital letter and a small headline.

Most reproductions at this time were still being duplicated for publication using the slow and costly steel-engraving method of the nineteenth century. While this gave superior quality to the prints, the expense involved severely limited the use of photographs and other reproductions in periodicals. While the *National*

Geographic had carried its first photograph in 1896, and had run a few since then, the illustrations had been used only to record facts and had generally been small and of mediocre quality.

After taking over, Grosvenor slowly began to change the magazine's look. In addition to insisting on short paragraphs, he increased the page size and switched to two columns of type on each page. But the biggest breakthrough would grow out of a book written by Grosvenor's father four years earlier on the history of Constantinople, now called Istanbul.

The senior Grosvenor's manuscript had already been accepted by his publisher when he discovered that a man in Philadelphia, Max Levy, had invented photoengraving, a method of reproducing pictures that didn't require the laborious and expensive craftsmanship of the older processes.

Grosvenor's father immediately rushed to Boston with three hundred photographs that he had brought from Constantinople, and persuaded the publisher to reproduce 230 of them, according to young Grosvenor. The book that resulted, in October 1895, was said to be the first scholarly work to be profusely illustrated by photoengravings.

In addition to the expense of reproduction, another roadblock to getting photographs into the magazine was that photographs were scarce, especially those of geographic interest. So, Grosvenor began to hunt for them in every place he could think of. Then he bought himself a camera, and eventually became one of his own best photographic sources. Early issues of the magazine contained many more charts and drawings than photographs, and most of the photographs that were used were printed small; because of their size and the technology of the day, they nearly all looked as if they were taken on cloudy days.

But Grosvenor soon found a large, reliable, and inexpensive source of photographs: the federal government. "It was like striking gold in my own backyard," he said, when he discovered that various government agencies would lend him engravings of photos they had already used in their own publications. "These photoengravings were available to other publications, but none were

interested," Grosvenor said. At the time, all the successful commercial magazines were still showing "an amazing indifference to
the winds of pictorial change. An official of *Century Magazine* actually told me that they—and the public—considered our half-
tones [the common name for the new photoengravings] vulgar and
preferred steel engravings costing $100 a plate. Our halftone plates
cost us $7 or $8 each. . . . ."

Even the *National Geographic*'s own ruling editorial board—
"frowned on photographs unless they were 'scientific,'" Grosvenor
reported. As Grosvenor moved to expand the use of photographs
in the magazine, one top officer of the Society's board, in a thinly
veiled warning to him, had assured the readers of the National
Geographic that "'the excessive use of pictures and anecdotes is
discouraged. . . . Superficial description and pictorial illustration
shall be subordinate to the exposition of relations and
principles.'"[2]

This dispute over photographs represented the last major stand
of the board members who wanted the Society and the magazine to
have its primary appeal to professionals. But Grosvenor was already
successfully working photographs slowly into the *National Geographic* on a regular basis when the magazine's most significant
turning point came in December 1904, and came, as is so often the
case, out of necessity.

Grosvenor was "deeply discouraged," he explained to one writer
almost sixty years later, because he faced an eleven-page hole in
the January 1905 issue that he was laying out and had no suitable
material to occupy the space. "There is no tyranny so absolute as a
printer's deadline, but I simply did not have a good manuscript
available," he recalled.[3]

While still contemplating his dilemma, he opened a recently
delivered package that was still sitting on his desk. The package
included a packet of fifty unsolicited photographs from a Russian
explorer who had visited Lhasa, Tibet—the seldom-visited, inaccessible mountain capital known as the "forbidden city." The explorer offered the photographs for publication in the *National
Geographic Magazine* at no charge, in return for a credit in the

magazine. "The photographs were the first of Tibet's capital and were so extraordinary that I decided to use them to fill the pages," Grosvenor said.

So, despite the amount of money that even relatively inexpensive photoengravings would cost—especially considering the lack of money in the company coffers—Grosvenor decided to use all eleven blank pages in the issue to display the photographs. "When I went home," he wrote, with no doubt more than a little historical embellishment, although opposition was sure to come from the minority traditionalist faction on the board, "I told my wife that I expected to be fired for publishing eleven solid pages of scenic pictures—particularly since the plates had been paid for from our own slender resources."[4]

But when the January 1905 issue was published, "my anxiety was soon dispelled when members of the Society stopped me on the street to tell me how much they had enjoyed the first photographs of romantic Lhasa. A few days later . . . I was unanimously elected to the Board of Managers and appointed a member of the executive and finance committees. . . ."[5]

Emboldened by his success, Grosvenor tried it again. "Soon," he wrote, "another pictorial windfall came my way." The next month, William Howard Taft, who had been govenor-general of the Philippines before becoming secretary of war, and later President, informed Grosvenor that the War Department would be publishing the first census report on the Philippines in April, and that it would be filled with illustrations. ". . . Mr. Taft had distinctly said 'photographs,' and that word had become as musical to my ear as the jingle of a cash register to a businessman. The appeal of the Lhasa pictures, and others in the magazine, had clearly vindicated my faith in photoengravings."[6]

Grosvenor selected thirty-two full-page plates—a total of 138 pictures—for the April 1905 magazine. It would have cost the Society several thousand dollars to obtain such photographs and hundreds more to make that many plates at a commercial shop—money the Society did not have, Grosvenor said. The Philippines issue brought such a flood of new members that he had to put it back on the press to meet the demand.

The National Geographic Society had started 1905 with 3,400 members. By December its rolls had soared to 11,000, a gain of more than 200 percent. Grosvenor had discovered a vital key to making a success of the Hubbard dream.

As Grosvenor moved to impose his view of the world upon the *National Geographic,* one of the first things to disappear from the magazine's vocabulary was all mention of things deemed distasteful. "Too often in my long lifetime have I seen unfair and erroneous statements made about other nations in the name of 'objective reporting' or 'constructive criticism,'" Grosvenor later wrote. "The *Geographic* has always dealt in facts, not bias, rumor or prejudice."[7]

As he modified the magazine, he evolved a set of what have become known as the "Seven Principles," still the guiding hand of the National Geographic Society. In an article in the magazine in 1915, he detailed his beliefs for his readers, the credo by which the magazine would run:

• The first principle is absolute accuracy. Nothing must be printed which is not strictly according to fact. The magazine can point to many years in which not a single article has appeared which was not absolutely accurate.

• Abundance of beautiful, instructive and artistic illustrations.

• Everything printed . . . must have permanent value, and be so planned that each magazine will be as valuable and pertinent one year or five or ten years after publication as it is on the day of publication. . . .

• All personalities and notes of a trivial character are avoided.

• Nothing of a partisan or controversial nature is printed.

• Only what is of a kindly nature is printed about any country or people, everything unpleasant or unduly critical being avoided.

• The content of each number is planned with a view of being timely. Whenever any part of the world becomes prominent in public interest, by reason of war, earthquake, volcanic eruption, etc., the members of the National Geographic Society have come to know that in the next issue of their magazine they will obtain the latest geographic, historical and economic information about that region, presented in an interesting and absolutely nonpartisan manner, and accompanied by photographs which in number and excellence can be equalled by no other publication.

Grosvenor, in reviewing the imposition of his "Seven Principles" on the *National Geographic,* told an interviewer, "I was brought up on the Golden Rule and was always taught not to criticize other people. . . . That same rule pays off when you are dealing with countries. . . . Some people have to criticize—there is a need for it and someone has to do it. But I didn't want to; the world is so big and there is so much to say. . . ."[8]

* * *

As Grosvenor was taking firm control of the Society, the Bell and Hubbard families moved to ensure that the Society would live on. In 1903, despite the fact that the Society had only some three thousand dues-paying members, the families built the organization's first home of its own, on Washington's fashionable 16th Street. Named Hubbard Memorial Hall, it was designed to prove the Society's permanence and to aid in its claim of being a national organization.

". . . When I first moved into it," in the fall of 1903, Grosvenor later wrote, the new building ". . . bulked as large as a palace in my mind, and I resolved that we would prove worthy of so splendid a headquarters. . . ."

Now that the Society had a permanent home, Grosvenor decided that it needed to have a recognizable symbol of its own, a flag. He turned the project over to his own Betsy Ross, his wife Elsie, with the admonishment, "Most organization banners I had seen were marvels of confusion and cryptic symbols. Clearly, what the Society needed was a simple and dignified standard, both at-tractive and instantly recognizable." What resulted, and endures, was an almost childlike pennant of three horizontal bars of color: green for the sea, brown for the earth, and blue for the sky. "At my suggestion," Grosvenor wrote, "Mrs. Grosvenor added the So-ciety's name in white block letters."[9]

Another crucial turning point in the National Geographic So-ciety's history came when Hubbard Memorial Hall was opened. At that time, Bell asked to be relieved of the presidency so he could pursue his other interests without distraction. While he surely wanted more time to himself, his departure, he knew, would mark the real beginning of his son-in-law's regime.

Bell had been elected to fill the vacancy on the Smithsonian Institution's board of regents caused in 1898 by his father-in-law's death; it was a post he filled with relish, and to which he wanted to devote more time. The eclectic nature of the Smithsonian's in-creasing purview better fit Bell's interests than did the relatively restricted concerns of the Society.

The Smithsonian had been established in Washington in 1846, after years of congressional haggling, putting to work a $500,000 legacy from a French-born English citizen and chemist, James Smithson, a man who had never even visited America.

The bequest was so unusual, and came with such a general in-struction—"to the United States of America, to found at Wash-ington, under the name of the Smithsonian Institution, an establishment for the increase & diffusion of knowledge among men," the words which Hubbard later put to his own purpose when he founded the National Geographic Society—that a fight raged through Congress as to whether the money should even be ac-cepted, since some viewed it as snide charity.

Finally in 1846, and by the barest of margins, the House passed a bill creating a national museum with the bequest. The Senate fol-lowed suit.

In 1900, after joining the board, Bell, among others, began lob-bying to have Smithson's body moved to the United States for reburial as a sign of gratitude for his bequest. A quarrying operation in Genoa, Italy, was going to require that Smithson's body be exhumed anyway, but Bell had failed at three successive annual board meetings to gain approval, apparently owing to the fact that Smithson had been born the illegitimate child of Hugh Smithson, the Duke of Northumberland.

In 1903, Bell asked Grosvenor to write an article to help build public support for the relocation of Smithson's remains to the United States; he free-lanced the story to the New York Herald Syndicate, and indeed contributed to such a public call. At the next regents' meeting, in December of that year, Bell was authorized by the Smithsonian board to go to Genoa and escort Smithson's body to Washington.

But aboard the ship that was taking him back to New York, Bell began to worry about the reception he and Smithson's body were going to receive. He cabled Grosvenor and asked him to arrange for a suitable ceremony upon the ship's arrival in America. The young editor, not at all sure of protocol, wrote President Theodore Roosevelt. "It would seem appropriate that a government vessel, a ship of war, a revenue cutter, or even a tug be detailed to meet the *Princess Irene* when she enters the harbor of New York and receive Smithson's remains," Grosvenor wrote.[10]

Roosevelt came through with flying colors, sending a warship to greet the ship and arranging for the body to be received later at the Washington Navy Yard by a large military escort. Bell was very pleased; the President's attitude also stifled any simmering public dissent over honoring Smithson, whose body was reinterred next to the main building of the institution bearing his name. Grosvenor's warm relations with Roosevelt were later to have important benefits for the National Geographic Society. Roosevelt came to symbolize American aggressiveness and assertiveness throughout the world, and the Society's connections to him boosted its claims to representing America's interests. Many times Roosevelt used the power of his office to come to the Society's aid.

Bell's next task for the Smithsonian was to serve on a committee to decide whether the art collection of Charles Freer—which he had bequeathed to the Smithsonian, on the condition that the organization provide a suitable place to display it—was worth having. "Bell was naturally responsive to beauty," said Catherine

MacKenzie in her 1928 biography, "but he made no pretense of critical appreciation of the arts. He had no interest in literature as such. When he read a novel, he wanted a good plot and plenty of action."[11]

Bell and three colleagues from the Smithsonian board journeyed to Chicago to view the collection. Unfortunately, Bell's colleagues shared his narrow art sensibilities. "Politely and gloomily," reported MacKenzie, "the four surveyed the 950 pieces of pottery from the Far East and Central Asia, the priceless group of ancient Chinese and Japanese bronzes, and the ceramics so rare that they were still unidentified. Not even the 100 framed paintings of James McNeill Whistler and the entire decorations of the Peacock Room could move them to any enthusiasm for this dingy array, valued at more than a half-million dollars [in 1910]. They looked to Bell like 'a lot of old pots,' and his distinguished confreres thought so, too."

But, luckily for the nation, Bell had taken one of his daughters, Marian, along with him, for she had more sophisticated tastes and could appreciate the importance of the collection, which is now housed in its own building as part of the Smithsonian's collection in downtown Washington. "And it was Marian Bell's insistence, Bell always said—with delighted chuckles—that saved the Freer collection" for the people of the United States. [12]

Bell's more informal Smithsonian connections are perhaps best illustrated by the time Bell and S. P. Langley, then head of the Smithsonian, along with astronomer Simon Newcomb, spent an entire afernoon at the Bell family's Beinn Bhreagh estate in Nova Scotia trying to determine why it is that cats always land on their feet when they jump. "Two of the investigators, on hands and knees, watched carefully while the third dropped the cat from a verandah onto a cushion on the ground. The findings of the investigation have never been made public—nor has the cat's opinion of the proceedings."[13]

The last official tie between Bell and the Society was cut in January 1905, the month the historic issue of the *National Geographic* was published, filled with photographs of Tibet, when the board passed a resolution thanking Bell for his generous support and stating that the organization was now making enough money to pay all of Grosvenor's salary. Bell continued to write occasional articles for the *National Geographic,* including one on turtles and lizards in the June 1907 issue. That article was printed under the pseudonym H. A. Largelamb, a name that utilized the letters of Bell's name and that he had contrived in his youth. Bell told Grosvenor he chose to use the pseudonym because he was not a naturalist and didn't want to seem to be posing as one. Grosvenor said he was later able to show his appreciation of Bell's efforts by devoting thirteen pages in the same issue to printing the full text of Bell's arguments for the adoption of the metric system in the United States.

As Grosvenor shaped the *National Geographic Magazine* into his own image, he also decided that the publication would avoid all mention of things that he found distasteful not only in the editorial matter but in its advertising pages as well. Thus, the Society to this day still accepts no advertising for tobacco products, alcohol, or patent medicines. Staff members were used to seeing their abstemious and reserved Chief in the hallways of the Society's headquarters, always wearing his tie and jacket. However, Edwin Grosvenor, the Chief's twin, who had gone on to a successful career as a lawyer in Washington and New York, would occasionally come to the Society headquarters to visit his brother. During their college days at Amherst, they would often dress alike and purposely confuse people about their identities. Edwin, however, liked to smoke and had an active sense of humor. So, as told in the understated tones of *The New Yorker,* "he sometimes caused a certain amount of confusion by strolling through the Geographic offices puffing a large cigar and greeting editors in a proprietary way. . . ."[14]

PART TWO

7. THE BIG NAIL

Reached the North Pole April 21, 1909.
Discovered land far north.
September 1, 1909, telegram from Dr.
Frederick A. Cook

I have the old Pole, Roosevelt safe.
September 5, 1909, message from Robert
E. Peary

The world grew a lot smaller in the first week of September 1909, when a prize that had tempted men for centuries and that had tantalized the imaginations of many more was finally captured. In fact, much to the world's amazement and, later, its chagrin, two people made their claims to having done it during that one week.

On September 1, the strikingly handsome Dr. Frederick A. Cook, a dapper and mustached physician from New York who doubled as a part-time explorer, sent a telegram after a Danish ship delivered him to Lerwick in the Shetland Islands group, north of Scotland. Cook told the world simply, "Reached the North Pole April 21, 1909. Discovered land far north."

But no sooner had the accolades and awards begun to pour in than the world heard from another quarter. The ship *Roosevelt* steamed into Indian Harbor in Labrador bearing civil engineer and explorer Robert E. Peary. On September 5, and he told the world, "I have the old Pole, Roosevelt safe." The reference to President Theodore Roosevelt, his longtime supporter—for whom Peary's ship was named—concerned a bet the President had made on who among the world's explorers would get to the North Pole first.

Roosevelt's enthusiastic backing of Peary added a new expression into the nation's lexicon: "Bully for Peary." Peary, a single-minded, dedicated explorer who had spent a major portion of his life in trying to reach the North Pole and who viewed the frozen north as his private exploration domain, informed the world that he had reached the North Pole on April 6, 1909.

The race to reach the North Pole had long captured the world's imagination and stirred intense nationalistic feelings; explorers sought the prize for the pride of their homelands. After Cook's claim was received, one newspaper published a table listing 743 men who were known to have died in pursuit of the North Pole, going back to Sir Hugh Willoughby, an English Arctic explorer, and his crew of sixty-one, who perished near Lapland in 1553, during the reign of Queen Mary I.

For years, newspapers had daily followed the progress and failures of the major assaults on the pole. Now headlines from coast to coast and country to country told of the latest developments, as men combated nature to reach an imaginary point that marked the top of the world—which the Eskimos called the Big Nail—for little more gain than to be able to say they were first. Following Cook's and Peary's claims, the world's press at first seemed prepared to award the men equal praise for their work and laugh about the coincidence of the timing of their discoveries. No one thought to question the claims or to demand proof; both men were known to the press, although Peary was clearly the more famous.

But just a few days later, on September 7, Peary sent a second telegram that was to forever change history: "Don't bother about Cook," he telegraphed. "He has simply handed the public a gold brick." Peary's words ignited a public battle that was to fascinate all the world, and especially Americans, for many months to come. For, as America entered the twentieth century finally established as a commercial and political world power, no longer was exploration of interest only to the wealthy Explorers' Club patricians. Now geography and exploration had meaning and interest for all Americans, from Africa to Tibet, and especially the North Pole. There was a magic about Arctic exploration that captured the public's fascination and curiosity. Now that controversy had arisen as a

Alexander Graham Bell, as he looked around the time he was awarded his first telephone patent in 1876. *(Library of Congress)*

Bell at the official opening of the long-distance telephone line between New York City and Chicago in 1892. (*Library of Congress*)

Mabel Hubbard Bell with some of her grandchildren (from *left*, Gertrude Grosvenor, Melville Bell Grosvenor, and Mabel Grosvenor), in 1906. (*Library of Congress*)

Picture of the Gilbert H. Grosvenor family taken in 1907. (*Library of Congress*)

Bell spent many of his later years working on kites and hydrofoils. Here he seems to be pondering a nagging question as he sits on a hydrofoil in Nova Scotia in 1908. *(Library of Congress)*

Photo of these Philippine women began what has become perhaps the best-known *National Geographic Magazine* trademark. In his own history of the Society, Grosvenor wrote, " . . . In rejecting prudery he [Grosvenor] had the full support of President Bell. Since that time many pictures in the magazine have shown women of the world in true native dress." *(Library of Congress)*

U.S. President Theodore Roosevelt and William Howard Taft during a snowstorm in early 1909. Both often came to the aid of the National Geographic Society, and to Grosvenor, who was Taft's cousin. Roosevelt was instrumental in Taft's nomination and election. *(Library of Congress)*

Dr. Frederick A. Cook was the first man to claim having reached the North Pole. On September 1, 1909, after being lost in the Arctic for a year, he told the world that he had accomplished the long-sought deed on April 21, 1908. (*Library of Congress*)

Robert E. Peary aboard his ship, the *Roosevelt*. On September 5, 1909, Peary told the world that he had reached the North Pole. Later the National Geographic Society would play a key role in getting the world to accept Peary's claim and to reject Cook's. (*Library of Congress*)

Hiram Bingham discovered and charted the long-lost Inca city of Machu Picchu in Peru, with the financial backing of the National Geographic Society and Yale University. Bingham later found the remains of a road that linked the mountaintop city with Cuzco and its ancient Inca ruins, such as the fort pictured here. (*Library of Congress*)

Bingham was later elected to the United States Senate and was an avid flyer. Here, as president of the National Aeronautical Association, he is pictured *second from right*, with Elinor Smith, *left*, then holder of the world's women's sole endurance record for aviators, and Amelia Earhart, the first woman to fly across the Atlantic Ocean. (*Library of Congress*)

result of this discovery, the world wanted to know who had really conquered the North Pole. In the forefront of support for Peary and his claim was the National Geographic Society.

Dr. Frederick A. Cook was forty-four years old, and quite a Renaissance man; he already had a reputation as a good doctor and explorer, although he was considered a maverick, long before his fateful journey to the north. A founder of the Explorers Club in New York and its second president (Peary was its third), Cook had joined the 1891 expedition to northern Greenland led by Peary, who was then a civil engineer attached to the U.S. Navy. That Peary expedition was part of Peary's complicated strategy to reach the North Pole.

Cook led other expeditions to the north in 1893 and 1894, and was credited with having saved the expedition's ship, the *Miranda,* after it struck an iceberg during the 1894 journey. After the *Miranda* hit the iceberg off of southern Greenland, Cook traveled ninety miles through rough seas in a small open boat and returned with a rescue ship. Next, Cook joined the Belgian Antarctic Expedition of 1898–99, of which Roald Amundsen was second in command. Amundsen, who in December 1911 became the first man to reach the South Pole, later gave Cook much credit for the success of the 1898–99 mission. As a result of his efforts, Cook was knighted by the king of Belgium.

One of the costs of dedicating oneself to exploration in an age when railroads and steamships were the primary means of travel, and especially to Arctic exploration, where it was dog sleds and foot power, was the all but complete loss of a normal social and family life. Explorers were away from home for years at a time. This may, in fact, have enhanced exploration's appeal for Cook. The year before his first expedition with Peary, his wife, Libby, gave birth to a child who survived only a few hours. A week later, Cook's wife was also dead.

Meanwhile, Peary had begun his fourth northern expedition in 1899, after getting a five-year leave from the navy. His route to Arctic exploration had also been a circuitous one. After graduating from Bowdoin College in 1877, Peary spent two years as a land surveyor in Maine, and another two years as a draftsman for the

U.S. Coast and Geodetic Survey in Washington. He joined the navy as a civil engineer with the rank of lieutenant in 1881; three years later he was sent to Nicaragua to help scout out possible locations for a proposed ship canal to connect the Atlantic and Pacific oceans.

Peary said that his interest in the Arctic was inspired by his reading in 1885 of an account by Nils Adolf Erik Nordenskjöld, a Swedish geologist and explorer, of an expedition to the interior of Greenland. Peary obtained a six-month leave from the navy in 1886 and made his first journey north. Now, in 1901, two years into his latest trek, no word had been received from Peary, so a relief expedition was organized under the leadership of a group called the Peary Arctic Club. Cook was asked to serve in an advisory position and as the unpaid surgeon for the expedition, even though Cook and Peary had had a falling-out over Cook's publication of an article on Greenland's Eskimos. Cook had also bridled under Peary's order that none of the men who journeyed with him could write anything having to do with the expeditions: Peary wanted to be sure that his writings after he finally reached the pole would have no competition. Cook had written a book about the medical findings he had made among the natives encountered during his expedition with Peary, and Peary had objected to its publication.

After returning home from the Peary rescue mission, Cook married a widow, Mary F. Hunt of Brooklyn, who had a daughter, Ruth, from her previous marriage. Cook had few hobbies or pastimes other than a passion for automobiling and a growing preoccupation with the North Pole. In 1903, he organized a party to scale Mount McKinley, the highest peak in North America, and one that had never been climbed. Cook's attempt, from the southwest, failed. Three years later, he tried again. Finally, he found a route to the top along the northeast ride of the mountain, and so tamed Mount McKinley, placing himself in the top rank of American explorers.

While most of Peary's later expeditions were well-financed, highly organized operations, Cook was much more a seat-of-the-pants explorer; he had none of the politically and financially powerful backers who filled the Peary camp. Thus, when John R.

Bradley, a big-game hunter and millionaire, offered in 1907 to finance a Cook expedition to Greenland, he accepted. Bradley's
primary motivation was not to further man's knowledge; rather,
the Arctic represented one of the few places in the world in which
he hadn't yet shot a hunting trophy. Cook set sail in July 1907.

While the world well knew of Peary's publicized plans for another assault on the North Pole, Cook and Bradley told no one of
their trip. They had agreed to treat the journey as a hunting expedition to the north, and if conditions seemed right, Bradley would
return, while Cook would stay over a winter and prepare to make a
dash to the North Pole the following year. "He [Cook] was to photograph Eskimos and I was to shoot walrus and polar bear," Bradley
later explained. With money provided by Bradley, Cook bought a
schooner and outfitted it for the trip.

> When all these preparations were complete, Dr. Cook and I
> were lunching one day [in New York] . . . and he said to me,
> "Why not go for the Pole?" I replied: "Not I. Would you like to
> try for it?"
> He said: "There is nothing that I would rather do. It's the
> ambition of my life."
> He thought it would cost only about $8,000 or $10,000 more
> to furnish equipment for this purpose. Finally I said: "We'll fit
> this expedition for the Pole and say nothing to anyone about it."
> . . . We figured it this way: In case we got up to Etah and
> found the natives were not well or the dogs scarce or any other
> conditions unfavorable, we could call it a hunting trip and re-
> turn quietly home again. [1]

On July 3, the ship, which Cook named the *John R. Bradley*, left
Gloucester, Massachusetts, bound for Sydney, a port on Cape
Breton Island in Canada, and the first leg of the journey. He and
Bradley were accompanied by Mrs. Cook and their daughters Ruth
and Helen, who were to disembark at Cape Breton and await the
return of the *Bradley* in the fall; if Cook didn't make a run for the
North Pole, when the ship returned, the rest of Cook's family
would join him and they would return together to Brooklyn. Thus,
in less than four months, Cook had planned the journey, pur-

chased and provisioned the ship, and departed for the North Pole.

By contrast, Peary had for years been preparing and raising funds for his eighth Arctic exploration, and what was billed as his last. He had already resigned himself to another year of fund-raising when one of his principal supporters, Herbert L. Bridgman, learned of a letter from Cook dated August 26, 1907, a month and a half after the party had left from Gloucester. Cook was by then in Etah, on Greenland's western coast, and the letter was carried by Bradley, who mailed it from Sydney, Cape Breton Island, on October 1, following his return. Cook, finding things quite to his liking in Greenland, had decided to stay over the winter in preparation for an assault on the pole in the spring.

Cook's letter, addressed to the Explorers Club and later released to the press, said, "I have hit upon a new route to the North Pole and will stay to try it. By way of Buchanan Bay and Ellesmere Land [in Arctic Canada] and northward through Nansen Strait over the Polar Sea seems to me to be a very good route. There will be game to the 82nd degree, and here are natives and dogs for the task. So here is for the Pole. Mr. Bradley will tell you the rest. Kind regards to all."

The Peary camp was aghast. They redoubled their efforts to ready their ship and raise money, and Peary's expedition set sail on July 6, 1908. Peary was crestfallen; he had made it clear to all that he felt his entire life's work hung on his reaching the North Pole first. And he seemed to view Cook's threat to that award seriously.

That was the way things stood until the first week of September 1909.

* * *

After his return to civilization, Cook told a waiting world that he had set up his base camp in northern Greenland, some seven hundred geographical miles from the Pole. After Bradley had left him, he waited out the Arctic night at his camp until February 1908, meanwhile arranging for support teams of Eskimos and their dogs to accompany him. When he departed for the pole, his intention was to follow his new route over the frozen waterways between

Ellesmere Island and Grant Land. On March 20, Cook said, he left his last support party and struck out with two Eskimos, two sledges carrying eight hundred pounds of supplies each, and twenty-six dogs on the most perilous leg of the journey, the final dash to the North Pole itself.

Compared with the unheralded nature of Cook's venture, Peary had everything, including a brass band, which greeted President Roosevelt when he boarded Peary's ship on Long Island for a tour the day after the ship's formal launching from New York's East River. While the world had read about several of Peary's seven earlier missions, the coverage had been irregular and mostly dependent on scarce news at the time of his missions. Now, however, with many rich and powerful men behind him, Peary's latest mission became downright businesslike. Rights to his story of this eighth attempt on the pole had already been sold to the Hearst newspapers and the *New York Times*. Peary's friend Herbert Bridgman, the business manager of the *Brooklyn Standard Union* and viewed by many as Peary's press agent, had whipped up interest from newspapers around the nation.

Bridgman had organized the Peary Arctic Club in 1900 to muster financial support for the explorer's North Pole quests. He had served as historian for the relief expedition that rescued Peary, and, according to one account, he "did more than any other to help and encourage Peary in his efforts to reach the Pole."[2] In return, Peary later named Cape Bridgman in Greenland in his honor.

Among the many powerful friends Peary had developed were the men who ruled an emerging lay scientific exploration and publishing company, the National Geographic Society.

* * *

The very first issue of the *National Geographic Magazine,* in October 1888, had contained among its prosaic offerings "Across Nicaragua with Transit and Machete," the tale of a young, unknown civil engineer named Robert E. Peary, recounting his travels as he scouted out a route for the proposed ship canal.

Peary's relationship with the Society was renewed in May 1895, when Peary's wife, as sweet and friendly as he was acerbic and gruff, scoured the country for contributions for an expedition to retrieve her husband from the Arctic before another long winter set in. Peary had no way of getting a message back, short of sending a member of the party to a city that had a telegraph station. When no word had been received, it was presumed that he had failed once again to reach his primary objective, the North Pole, and that he was in need of help. At this time, Gardiner Greene Hubbard, completely charmed by Mrs. Peary and impressed with her dedication to her husband and his dream, took up the cause and became a staunch supporter of Peary's.

Josephine Peary was a charming and likable woman, seemingly possessed of as strong and adventuresome a spirit as her husband. When her husband obtained an eighteen-month leave from the navy in order to probe the Arctic regions, Mrs. Peary joined his 1891 expedition to Greenland and became the "first white woman" to winter with an Arctic expedition. Two years later, she joined him on another expedition to Greenland, where she gave birth to their daughter, Marie Ahnighito—who had the distinction of being the most northerly born "white girl" in the world.

But rather than make an outright financial contribution to Peary's rescue, according to the Society's records, Hubbard got the National Geographic Society's board of managers, "as a slight recognition of interest in and approval of the plan, [to] vote . . . to appropriate a sum sufficient to pay the expenses of a lecture by Mrs. Peary and to give her the gross receipts" derived from the lecture admissions. This allowed the Society, "at comparatively small expense, to add $400 to the fund—a result especially gratifying by reason of the fact that Lieutenant Peary is one of our own good members."[3]

"This incident furnished in itself a good example of the practical effectiveness of our organization in aiding actual geographic research as well as increasing and diffusing geographic knowledge," according to a statement in the magazine. Another person involved in the fund-raising, Fitzhugh Green, Peary's biographer, reported that the evening Mrs. Peary spent at the Society "netted

$2,000," and that a second lecture a few days later brought in the final $1,000 she needed to bring her husband home.

The event marked an important milestone in the Society's evolution. Now, for the first time, it was participating in a geographic event, and not merely recording its occurrence.

The next major breakthrough, both for the Society and for Peary, came in 1906 when editor Grosvenor—ready to follow through on Hubbard's interest in Peary, now that Hubbard was dead, and apparently aware of the potential advantage the Society could reap—advised the board that the organization's net receipts were now great enough to permit it "to begin annual grants for research, and I recommended that the Society subscribe $1,000 towards the cost of Peary's [latest] assault on the Pole." This was to be the Society's first grant of its own money for the express purpose of exploration. From this time on, Peary and the Society were inseparable, at least from the Society's point of view.

But the most important part of the Society's involvement in Peary's quest was that Grosvenor had clearly decided that it could be the turning point in the organization's evolution. While the Society was surely on firmer footing than when he had taken over, its future success was still far from assured.

At first tentatively, and then wholeheartedly, Peary's quest became the Society's own. Grosvenor had seen, correctly, that the discovery would spark an unprecedented interest throughout the world in other geographical topics and that if the Society was perceived in the public's eyes to be directly involved in it, Peary's work would inspire a boom in membership, and Grosvenor wasn't about to let this once-in-a-lifetime opportunity elude him.

Ironically, on December 15, 1906, the Society, at its annual dinner, honored both Peary and Cook, who would soon be combatants, in what was believed to have been their last joint appearance. Cook was introduced by Bell:

"I have been asked to say a few words about a man who must be known by name, at least, to all of us—Dr. Frederick A. Cook, president of the Explorers Club of New York. We have had with us, and are glad to welcome, Commander Peary of the arctic regions, but in Dr. Cook we have one of the few Americans, if not the only American, who has explored both extremes of the world, the Arctic and Antarctic regions. And now he has been to the top of the American continent, and therefore to the top of the world, and tonight I hope Dr. Cook will tell us something about Mount McKinley."

President Roosevelt followed Cook on the program, and presented Peary with the first Gardiner Greene Hubbard Gold Medal for having attained a point closer to the North Pole during his most recent expedition than anyone else had ever come. "You did a great deed," said Roosevelt, "a deed which reflected credit upon you and upon your country." Peary replied, "To me, the final and complete solution of the polar mystery . . . is the thing which is intended that I should do, and the thing that I must do. . . ."4

8. KANGAROO COURT

If Peary says he reached the Pole,
I believe him.

              Dr. Frederick A. Cook

After reading . . . [Cook's first-person
story on his discovery in the New York
Herald], *there can be no question of Dr.*
Cook's success or the accuracy of his
findings. It is stamped with the
genuineness of his work. . . ."
National Geographic Society President
                Willis L. Moore

In September 1909, as soon as Cook claimed success in reaching the North Pole, the world's accolades began to pour in, much to Cook's amazement. As he sailed to Copenhagen, he spoke to several fellow passengers and was astonished at their enthusiasm. "The anxiety of the newspaper correspondents on board gave me an idea that my story might have considerable financial value," Cook later wrote, revealing that he had $40 in his pocket when he landed in Denmark. Upon arriving in Copenhagen, he was overnight the toast of Europe: the king of Belgium greeted him, the Royal Danish Geographic Society awarded him a gold medal, and the University of Copenhagen honored him. When told in Copenhagen of Peary's "gold brick" charge by a journalist, Cook is said to have replied simply: "If Peary says he reached the Pole, I believe him."[1]

From here, the saga took on astounding, Machiavellian overtones. Peary, it seems safe to believe, didn't even claim to have attained the North Pole until he was informed that Cook had claimed to have done so. He quickly fired off his "gold brick" charge against Cook. Peary stated that he had not only reached the North Pole, but that no other "white man" had ever set foot there. The Eskimos who accompanied Arctic explorers were of no consequence to him.

Friends of Peary's, many of whom were connected to the National Geographic Society, and the Society itself, under Grosvenor's direction, immediately initiated a campaign both to prevent other governments and geographic organizations from honoring Cook and to get the sponsoring organizations to withdraw these honors already conferred upon Cook. One of the few men who went to Nova Scotia to await the *Roosevelt's* arrival with Peary was Gilbert H. Grosvenor.

A clear holding strategy had been devised by Peary's backers: They would deny Cook the laurels while they built their campaign to ensure Peary's recognition as the first white man to set foot on the top of the world. As soon as Cook's message about reaching the pole had been received, the Explorers Club of New York, now headed by Peary's friend Bridgman, had invited Cook to be its guest of honor at an upcoming dinner. After Peary's message was received, some members suggested that he also be invited. But Bridgman would have none of that: Unless Cook's invitation was withdrawn, he declared, he would resign. Cook solved the club's dilemma by asking the organization's members to withdraw his invitation.

Before Peary made his claim, the National Geographic Society had also intended to honor Cook. The Society's new president, Willis L. Moore, had said of Cook the day before word was received from Peary, "After reading [Cook's first-person story of his discovery in the *New York Herald*], there can be no question of Dr. Cook's success or the accuracy of his findings. It is stamped with the genuineness of his work. . . ."[2]

On the day Peary made his claim, Moore said that he too would probably be honored by the Society. Moore, a former newspaper printer, had been named to head the nation's weather bureau by President Grover Cleveland in 1895, after working his way up from an appointment to the meteorological section of what was then the Signal Corps. He became president of the Society in 1905.

But the day after Peary's claim, Moore said, following a meeting of the Society's board of managers, "It is customary to await proofs by explorers before action is taken. . . . Before we can award medals to either Peary or Cook we must first have positive proof that one or the other has been to the Pole. . . ." That same day, however, Moore sent Peary a telegram that said, "In answer to your telegraphic report to this Society that you reached the North Pole, the National Geographic Society, through the action of its Board of Managers, today extends to you its heartiest congratulations on your great achievement."[3]

In public, the Society moved quickly to install itself as the world's "impartial" arbitrator of the dispute. Of course, few members of the public or the press were aware of the Society's long-standing relationship with Peary, and fewer still knew that the Society had actually quietly pledged $25,000 toward the cost of Peary's latest run for the Pole.

The Society, as part of the Peary group's strategy, "invited" Cook and Peary to send their records to Washington for examination, promising to award a gold medal to the one who was found to have the valid claim. This alone showed an interesting bias. Cook seemed fully prepared to accept that Peary had also reached the North Pole and was willing to share the glory; only Peary and his most ardent supporters, and especially Grosvenor and the National Geographic Society, refused to acknowledge that Cook could have made it and insisted that only one claim could be valid.

The Society fired off telegrams to most of the world's geographic societies asking them to hold off judgment until the Society, claiming to be the rightful judge of a claim by American explorers, issued a verdict—even though the Society, unlike most of its counterparts around the world, had no official government standing. Messages were also sent to the Royal Danish Geographic Society and the University of Copenhagen asking them to withdraw the honors they had bestowed on Cook.

At the same time, while Grosvenor and the Society were still ballyhooing themselves as the only impartial arbiters of the dispute, a telegram was sent to Peary by the Society: "Board of National Geographic Society wishes to act on your expedition at regular meeting next Wednesday [October 20]. Can you not immediately forward us sufficient records to justify action then?"[4]

The Society's board, at Grosvenor's urging, appointed a three-man subcommittee to judge the claims. The members, however, hardly composed a neutral jury. Henry Gannett, a Society board member and a close friend of Peary's, was already, according to the *New York Times* (itself a supporter of Peary's claims), "considered a skeptic on the question of the discovery of the Pole by Cook." Interestingly, one writer later found that while the Society, in public relations material sent out to publicize the committee, described Gannett as "chief geographer of the U.S. Geological Survey," the government agency reported that he had only been one of their part-time geographers.[5] O. H. Tittman, one of Gardiner Greene Hubbard's cofounders of the Society, was the superintendent of the U.S. Coast and Geodetic Survey, to which Peary had been technically assigned while he was on his expedition. Colby M. Chester, a retired rear admiral, was a longtime critic of Cook.

At the committee's request, Peary sent them some data through Charles J. Nichols, a lawyer from Portland, Maine. While never revealing just what the data were, the committee let it be known that the material covered Peary's trek only up to the point where his companion, Robert A. Bartlett, turned back, well short of the North Pole. The committee then asked Peary to appear himself and to bring his records and his equipment. He took the train to Washington and met with the Society's representatives on November 1. Two days later, the committee ruled that "Commander Peary has submitted to this subcommittee his original journal and record of observations, together with all his instruments and apparatus and certain of the most important of the scientific results of his expedition. These have been carefully examined by your subcommittee, and they are unanimously of the opinion that Commander Peary reached the North Pole, April 6, 1909."[6]

As to the question of whether or not anyone reached the pole prior to 1909, the committee recommended that the board create another subcommittee to study the matter.

The Society then embarked on a clandestine attempt to get the U.S. State Department to intervene with the Danes and secure

Cook's records, which had been supplied by the explorer to the University of Copenhagen. When the State Department refused to become enmeshed in the controversy, the Society wrote the University of Copenhagen directly, asking that the Society's representative be included in the school's investigation of Cook's records and offering to present some of what it termed, "the unwritten history of the case."

According to a report by a Copenhagen correspondent of the strongly pro-Peary *New York Times,* Danish scientists "would have welcomed the inclusion of an American scientist of established reputation as a member of the commission [investigating Cook's claims], but resented strongly the suggestion of the National Geographic Society [that it] should be represented at the inquiry, on the ground that the society had no scientific standing whatsoever. When the American Society's request was proffered, the Copenhagen University authorities, so the story goes, had inquiries made by the Danish representative in Washington, from whom it received a reply that led the Danes to look upon the offer as a little less than an insult."[7]

At this point, according to an inquiry conducted by Russell W. Gibbons, then a college student who became interested in the topic and published a paper in 1954 on it, "through intrigue of the National Geographic Society and its government contacts, the way was paved for final acceptance by Congress" of Peary's claims. "Gilbert H. Grosvenor . . . as chief mogul of the Society, became Peary's chief lobbyist," wrote Gibbons. "The plan was to line up foreign geographic societies in honoring Peary so that the 'verdict' by the Society's 'investigating committee' would be accepted by the public and Congress without question. The [U.S.] Diplomatic Service was lined up and Grosvenor's medal solicitors preceded Peary on his 1910 trip to Europe. There the commander took the medals, and to the world it appeared as a scientific acknowledgment of his success.

"It was an instance, however," Gibbons continued, "of how a geographic society can prostitute its name and how 'science' can succumb to politics. . . ."[8] Years later, Gibbons, after publishing several articles on the subject, became president of the Frederick

A. Cook Society, a small group dedicated to restoring Cook's claims.

Despite the number of prominent explorers and polar researchers who supported Cook's claim, it soon became clear, Gibbons wrote, "that the armchair explorers and the kitchen geographers such as were found in the National Geographic Society were to be the deciding factors" in awarding Peary history's laurels for reaching the North Pole.

The instrument they were going to use to destroy Cook and his claims was the press. The method they were going to employ was to assassinate Cook's character.

Neither Cook nor Peary could back up his claims with the scientific evidence of plottings and solar observations necessary to verify having reached the North Pole. Peary had failed to make accurate solar observations; Cook claimed he had left his detailed observations with Harry Whitney, a rich sportsman, like Cook's Bradley, who had accompanied Peary to Greenland. Whitney had remained behind in Etah when Peary left on his expedition. In fact, Peary had installed Whitney in Cook's cabin. Whitney was the first white man Cook encountered after returning to the village from his adventure. Whitney had no particular allegiance to Peary, and when Cook departed, Whitney had agreed to take Cook's detailed records of the journey and his personal belongings back to the United States. But when Peary returned to Etah and was preparing for the journey home, angry over Cook's claims, he refused to let Whitney bring Cook's trunks back to the United States. Thus, Cook had few records of his expedition.

In September 1909, Cook returned to the United States from Europe to great acclaim. Despite Peary's charges and the campaign being waged against Cook under the leadership of Grosvenor and the Society, Cook was honored by his native Brooklyn upon arrival in New York Harbor; later that month the Arctic Club of America gave a banquet in his honor. But on the very day he was being given the keys to the City of New York, October 15, the city's press prominently carried a fascinating story: The man who had accompanied Cook on his ascent of Mount McKinley in 1906, Edward Barrill, suddenly declared that the ascent was a hoax, that he and Cook had invented the entire episode. Barrill, a former blacksmith, was then living with his wife and five children in Darby, Montana, where he said he was now engaged in the real estate business. The affidavit that he signed was released to the press by the Peary Arctic Club.

Cook knew that some of Peary's supporters were expending great efforts to look into his earlier expedition to Mount McKinley. The *New York Times* had earlier revealed that Gen. James A. Ashton, a lawyer with the largest practice in Tacoma, Washington, had been hired by a "New York law firm to obtain all information possible regarding the disputed ascent of Mount McKinley by Dr. Cook."[9] When Cook learned that the unnamed New York law firm was one run by one of Peary's largest sponsors, he immediately wired Barrill in Montana asking him to come to New York to hold a joint press conference with Cook at which they would describe their ascent of the mountain.

Instead, the next installment in the affair was the publication of Barrill's affidavit. The clear, and no doubt intended, implication of the entire affair was that if Cook would lie about climbing to the top of Mount McKinley, surely he would lie about having reached the North Pole.

The *New York Herald,* the only local newspaper that showed sympathy to Cook—it was running his story of the North Pole discovery at the time—sent a reporter, Roscoe C. Mitchell, to Missoula, Montana, to talk with Barrill. Barrill admitted to the reporter that he had been offered $5,000 to sign an affidavit declaring Cook's climb a fraud, and the reporter found that a Tacoma bank had indeed given Barrill $1,500 around the time he filed the document. Barrill told the reporter he didn't know the man who had offered him the money, nor did he know the stranger's motives. Meanwhile, another man who had accompanied Cook to Mount McKinley offered to support Cook publicly, if the doctor would provide him an expenses-paid trip to New York.

"Though he [Barrill] had boasted of reaching the apex of the North American continent with the doctor [Cook] after the expedition," Gibbons wrote, "and had maintained it for three years, suddenly he was put forth by the pro-Peary press as an unimpeachable witness, in spite of the fact that he had completely changed his testimony. Such fabrications and forgery were easily seen by the unprejudiced eye and would not bear honest investigation. Yet it came to be believed by the large American public that Cook had lied. . . ."[10]

Barrill's hoax claim, coupled with the outcome of the North Pole controversy, cost Cook the credit for having been the first man to have climbed Mount McKinley, even though the argument still rages among aficionados of Arctic history.

At the end of 1909, the University of Copenhagen reported the findings of the committee it had asked to investigate Cook's claims. One of the investigating panel's members reported to the press: "As there were certain questions of a special astronomical nature with which I myself was not sufficiently acquainted, I called in our greatest astronomical scientist . . . who put an exhaustive series of mathematical, technical and natural scientific questions to Dr. Cook. . . . Dr. Cook answered all to our full satisfaction. He showed no nervousness or excitement at any time. I dare say, therefore, that there is no justification for anybody to throw the slightest doubt on his claim to have reached the pole and the means by which he did it. . . . [And I am] entirely satisfied with the evidence."[11]

After receiving the report, the university eventually concluded that the evidence was convincing, but also circumstantial; since there were no contemporaneous solar observations (that close to the North Pole, compasses were of little value), there was no absolute proof that Cook had reached the North Pole.

Back in the United States, the only part of the university's report that the press seemed to hear was that there was no proof to support Cook's claim. Peary's claim, of course, had been authenticated—by his own statements, and by his supporters at the National Geographic Society. It is interesting to note that at a congressional hearing a year later in the United States, Peary's supporters had to admit that he, too, lacked the absolute proof that the University of Copenhagen had sought in Cook's papers. But this was not deemed very newsworthy by the press. Many of Peary's backers were themselves publishers, which no doubt contributed to his media successes. But the reporters of the day seemed swept into the event; Peary, with his long experience and naval rank and powerful backers, seemed to them to be the man who should have discovered the pole, while Cook was an unconnected free-lance stranger.

The later congressional hearings that challenged Peary's claims were held because Peary wanted to be made an admiral in the navy before he retired and to receive an admiral's pension in return for his many services to the United States. But despite the best orchestrations that his supporters could arrange, the hearings turned into quite a trial. The House Naval Affairs Committee bottled up the bill to promote and pension Peary, and appointed a subcommittee to investigate Peary's claims further. This was in part due to the strong objections of Naval Secretary George von Lengerke, who told the committee it was "inappropriate to confer upon him [Peary] a title for which his previous education, training and service have not fitted him."[12] Calling the National Geographic Society's investigation of Peary's records "perfunctory and hasty," the committee asked on March 4, 1910, that Peary submit his original records for its review. Peary adamantly refused.

Three days later, a congressman from New York reported Peary's explanation: "Commander Peary and his friends say that contracts signed months ago with his publishers render it impossible to make his records and scientific data public now. . . ." But Representative Henry T. Helgesen of North Dakota speculated, with more than a little justification, that the delay was to give Peary the chance to "prepare some 'original records' and bring about a climate friendlier to the passage of the bill."[13] Whatever the case, it was ten months before the records were submitted.

The day after Peary's claim to having reached the North Pole was "authenticated" by the National Geographic Society in November 1909, Peary signed a contract for a ten-part series of articles to be published in *Hampton's Magazine,* and a contract for a book to be published by the Frederick A. Stokes Company, for which he received the large fee of $75,000. After Peary's version of events had appeared in *Hampton's,* his book, *The North Pole,* was readied for publication in September 1910. When it appeared, it boasted an introduction by Theodore Roosevelt and a foreword by Gilbert Grosvenor—in which he called Peary "the peer of Hudson, Magellan, and Columbus"—and a map supplied by Grosvenor and the National Geographic Society.

Peary biographer William Herbert Hobbs, in his *Peary*, would later claim, "While in retirement . . . Peary had completed his serial narrative of the successful expedition."[14] But according to the editor who handled the series at *Hampton's*, Peary had "little or nothing" in the way of a manuscript when the magazine contract was signed; a free-lance writer, Elsa Barker, had written it, based mostly on his answers to questions she posed to him during meetings in New York. Peary, according to Hobbs, said that his book "has been planned and written in hotels, on trains and streetcars and taxicabs, even on steamers, and everywhere and anywhere I might find a few spare hours or minutes during the last year."[15]

Added the biographer, "Despite the handicaps of the writing of *The North Pole*, its literary quality is of high order. Peary . . . if he had not chosen a career of an explorer, might have achieved a reputation as a writer." But according to writer Andrew A. Freeman, A. E. Thomas, a free-lancer, claimed, "It is perfectly true that I wrote the bulk of Peary's *North Pole*. I should think 80 percent would be about right." And, he added, "It was a dull book, because Peary was a dull man, and it was impossible to get much lively human material out of him. . . ."[16] Neither ghostwriter was ever acknowledged by Peary.

Cook, clearly depressed over the furor being raised and weary of the attacks on his character and his claims, retreated from the public eye and went to Europe. Turning aside many more financially lucrative offers for his story—one newspaper had offered his brother $1,000 just for Cook's address in London—Cook eventually signed a contract with *Hampton's Magazine* so that he could address the same audience to which Peary had told his ten-part version of events in the Arctic.

After agreeing on a general outline for the articles during meetings in London with an editor from *Hampton's*, Cook quietly returned to the United States. At a meeting in Troy, New York, while waiting for the magazine's publisher to arrive, a subordinate editor proposed a scheme. In Cook's words: "As he outlined it, I was to go secretly to New York, submit myself to several employed alienists who would pronounce me insane, whereupon I was to write several articles in which I should admit having arrived at the conclusion that I reached the Pole while mentally unbalanced! . . . This plan, I was told, would 'put me right' and make a great sensational story!"[17]

Cook said he was staggered by the idea. But Hampton himself soon arrived and agreed to Cook's earlier outline for the articles. Cook retired to a hotel in Newburgh, New York, wrote the articles and, after approving and initialing the galley proofs, returned to London to conclude some personal matters before his public return to the United States, which was going to be timed to coincide with the publication of the articles in *Hampton's.*

In his articles, Cook had explained that given the instruments of the day, it was virtually impossible for him or Peary to have been sure that they were standing at the exact mathematical North Pole. But what came out in the January 1911 issue of *Hampton's,* after being loudly trumpeted in the daily press in advance of publication—all just as Congress was about to resume deliberations on Peary's requested promotion and pension—was "Cook's confession" that he hadn't actually reached the North Pole and an admission that he had been affected by the "mirage-effects" of the polar region. Newspaper headlines everywhere featured the "confession" and the plea of "insanity." In bold italic type, Cook's "confession" sliced across the cover of *Hampton's:* "Dr. Cook's confession. Did I get to the North Pole? I confess that I do not know absolutely. Fully, freely and frankly I shall tell you everything.'"[18]

The article is actually far from what it was billed to be by the prepublication hype or by the magazine's cover. The general impression gained by reading it is that Cook was prepared to state what should have been obvious, at least to all the professionals familiar wih the affair: that it was impossible for him to state unequivocally that he had touched the magic spot, the North Pole. A soul-baring Cook tried to explain patiently and calmly that he believed he had reached the pole, but that even if he hadn't spied the Big Nail, he had gotten very close after an unprecedented two-

and-a-half-year journey during which he had suffered unimaginable hardships, including being lost and having to winter with his two Eskimos in a hole in the ground, chewing leather for nourishment until the spring thaw.

"I have been called the greatest liar in the world, the most monumental impostor in history," Cook began in the January issue of *Hampton's,* the first of four installments. "My claim to the discovery of the North Pole has been adjudged a willful, premeditated, and brazen fraud, and I a cheat who hoaxed an entire world for gain. I believe that, in a very undesirable way, I stand unique, the object of such suspicion and vituperation as have assailed few men. Returning from a life savage in its drain on body and mind, I was tossed to the zenith of worldly honor on a wave of enthusiasm, a world-madness which startled me. In the ebb of that wave I was plunged into the depths of suspicion and discredit, a victim of my own folly and the sufferer from a storm of adverse circumstances."[19]

Chief among his "follies," according to Cook—and rightly so, in retrospect—was his silence, his refusal to answer the character-asassination campaign of Peary's supporters, and especially Peary's friends at the Peary Arctic Club and the National Geographic Society. But in the article, Cook committed another folly: He was too honest and open in a medium better suited to short, flip answers.

"Did I get to the North Pole?" Cook asked in extra-dark type, the only time the editors of *Hampton's* used boldface in the article. "Perhaps I made a mistake in thinking that I did; perhaps I did not make a mistake. After mature thought, I confess that I do not know absolutely whether I reached the Pole or not. This may come as an amazing statement; but I am willing to startle the world if, by doing so, I can get an opportunity to present my case. By my case I mean not my case as a geographical discoverer, but my case as a man. Much as the attainment of the North Pole once meant to me, the sympathy and confidence of my fellow-men mean more."[20]

This paragraph is basically the extent of Cook's "confession," although later in the article he discusses the mind-altering effects of the journey caused by lack of food, overexertion, snow blindness, and loneliness. And not only were Cook's words taken out of context in the publicity material sent around by *Hampton's,* but they were altered by the magazine.

At a later congressional inquiry, one of the editorial copyreaders of *Hampton's,* Lillian Eleanor Kiel, testified: "We cut through the galley proofs and inserted what has been known to the world as Dr. Cook's confession of mental unbalancement. The 'confession' was dictated to me by a sub-editor. Dr. Cook was on the ocean to Europe to get his wife and children. I then thoroughly believed the confession was authorized by Dr. Cook. I was horrified later to find that he knew absolutely nothing about it."[21]

One writer later called this incident the "most dastardly deed in the history of journalism. . . . It was deliberate misrepresentation and chicanery. . . ."[22]

Cook, later trying to reconstruct what had happened, said he had agreed to try to explain to the readers of *Hampton's* that locating the exact spot of the North Pole would be impossible. "I had made the admission that I was uncertain as to having reached the exact mathematical Pole, the same admission Mr. Peary would have to make if he had been pinned down. . . ." Cook later wrote. "By picking up garbled extracts from my articles about the impossibility of a pinpoint determination of the Pole and the crazy-mirage effects of the Arctic world, these news stories were construed to the effect that I had admitted that I did not know whether I had been at the North Pole, and also that I admitted to a plea of insanity."[23]

9. FRUITS OF HISTORY

> *I have given more time and thought to this alleged discovery [of Peary's] than I have to any other public question that I remember to have undertaken to investigate in my whole life, and the more I have investigated and studied the story, the more thoroughly convinced have I become that it is a fake, pure and simple. . . .*
>
> Congressman R. B. Macon

As Congress prepared to resume action on the Peary promotion and pension bill in early 1911, Cook's "confession" in *Hampton's Magazine* had left as the only real issue for the legislators the validity of Peary's claim to have reached the North Pole. The magazine articles had eroded nearly all remaining public support for Cook's claims, leaving Peary as the only contender for the nation's accolades.

Now, with Cook's claim demolished and with a firm battle plan in hand, Peary and his supporters began to work even harder to pave the way for the passage of the bill that would promote Peary to admiral and secure him a healthy government pension.

Members of Congress received a message from President William Howard Taft, citing Peary's "unparalleled accomplishment" of reaching the North Pole that, he said, was "approved by the most expert scientists. . . . I recommend fitting recognition by Congress of the great achievement of Robert Edwin Peary."[1] This was the same Taft who had on several occasions helped Grosvenor—his second cousin—obtain photographs from the U.S. government for use in the *National Geographic Magazine,* and who had himself written articles for the magazine. Lest the members of Congress not fully understand his own position, Peary published and distributed a pamphlet, *How Peary Reached the North Pole*, subtitled "An Expedition over the Ice That Went to Its Mark with the Precision of a Military Campaign and Reached the Goal Sought for Centuries."

Peary finally appeared before the House Naval Affairs Subcommittee on January 7, 1911, where he faced forceful questioning from at least two of the members, Ernest W. Roberts, Republican of Massachusetts, and Robert B. Macon, Democrat of Arkansas. Roberts, who served nine terms in the House, was most interested in the National Geographic Society's role in the affair, maintaining that since the Society undertook to determine the "real" discoverer of the North Pole and the veracity of Peary's claims, the organization itself must bear public scrutiny. Roberts zeroed in on the Society's claim that it had thoroughly examined Peary's original records and his instruments and based its verification on those elements. Under questioning from Roberts, Peary was evasive and forgetful, refusing to trust his memory and deflecting questions to others, and especially to the National Geographic Society.

After Peary was finally prodded to say that the meeting with the National Geographic Society's subcommittee was held at one of the member's homes, he couldn't remember how long it had lasted or at what time of day it had been held. Next, Roberts asked about the explorer's instruments. A combative, petulant Peary eventually revealed that he had not brought the trunkful of instruments that he had used to take his sightings during his journey to the house, but rather that the committee had gone to the Pennsylvania Railroad Station to examine them. They went to the station after dark.

Roberts: When you got to the station, what did you or the committee do with regard to the instruments? How did the instruments come down [with Peary from Maine]?

Peary: They came in a trunk.

R: After you reached the station and found the trunk, what did you and the committee do with regard to the instruments?

P: I should say that we opened the trunk there in the station.

R: That is, in the baggage room of the station?

P: Yes.

R: Were the instruments all taken out?

P: That I could not say. Members of the [Society's] committee will probably remember better than I.

R: Well, you do not have any recollection of whether they took them out and examined them?

P: Some were taken out, I should say; whether all were taken out, I could not say.

R: Was any test of those instruments made by any members of the committee to ascertain whether or not the instruments were accurate?

P: That I could not say. I should imagine that it would not be possible to make tests there.

R: Were those instruments ever in the possession of the committee other than the inspection at the station?

P: Not to my knowledge.

Roberts, in his later minority report on the day's proceedings, called Peary's testimony "delightfully vague and uncertain." He went on, "The occasion [the meeting with the National Geographic Society subcommittee] was a most momentous one in his career, for the report of this committee was to settle in the public mind the mooted question of having attained the Pole, and the fact that the incidents of that day made no sharper impression on his mind than is shown by his testimony, is very conclusive evidence that the examination of his records was anything but minute, careful or rigorous."[2]

Roberts, in the manner of a prosecutor building a case for the jury, also questioned Peary about the photographs that had appeared in his book. Peary claimed that they showed him and his party at the North Pole, but the shadows failed to match the times of day Peary said they were taken. Under Roberts's questioning, Peary contradicted what he had written in his book about when the pictures were taken.

When the subcommittee studied Peary's diary, Roberts noted that it "shows no finger marks or rough usage; a very cleanly kept book." He said, "It is a well-known fact that on a long Arctic journey ablutions even of the face and hands are too luxurious for the travelers. Pemmican [a condensed mixture of beef, fat, and dried fruits] is the staple article of food. Its great value lies in its greasy quality. How was it possible for Peary to handle this greasy food and without washing his hands write in his diary daily and at the end of two months have that same diary show 'no finger marks or rough usage' . . . ?"

Roberts also questioned the authenticity of a certificate Peary's traveling companion, Robert A. Bartlett, gave to Peary as he left him on the last leg of the quest, only 133 miles from the North Pole. The one-paragraph note said he was leaving Peary at latitude 87° 47'.

Roberts: When were those figures [the latitude] inserted?
Peary: Immediately after the observation.

R: Why did he [Bartlett] use two pencils on that record?

P: That I cannot say.

R: I should judge that evidently that was a different pencil; that looks like an indelible pencil, and this looks like an ordinary lead pencil. Do you know whether or not Bartlett signed that after making his observation, after putting down the figures?

P: Yes, sir; I think he did.

R: It looks like a different pencil entirely.

P: Yes sir; that was signed at the time, and of course it was done after the observation was made.

R: It seems rather strange that he had such an assortment of pencils there—three pencils. Those entries were all contemporaneous—made the same day?

P: Yes, sir.

Roberts also questioned Peary about whom he had informed of his discovery and when.

R: Captain Peary, when you returned from your dash, the first people you saw were those at the ship?

P: Yes, sir.

R: You of course told them of the trip?

P: No, I did not. I did not go into any details in regard to the trip.

R: Did you tell them that you had reached the Pole?

P: I told Bartlett; no one else.

In other words, Peary told the committee that after returning from the realization of his life's ambition, he encountered his waiting band of support personnel and told no one of his accomplishment except for Bartlett. And no one else ever testified that he had even heard Peary make the claim that he had told Bartlett of his success until Peary testified before the committee.

This creates another interesting conflict in Peary's story. Despite his testimony to the committee, in his book, *The North Pole*, Peary revealed that he had ordered one of his crewmen, George Borup, to take two Eskimos and travel to Cape Columbia and erect a monument. The three men, at Peary's orders, built a stone mound with a pole in the middle on which were mounted signs pointing east, west, north, and south. On the north sign was written "The North Pole, April 6, 1909, 413 miles." "The strange contradiction between Peary's sworn statement before the House subcommittee and his instruction to Borup must remain an enigma, since Peary never attempted to explain this discrepancy. Borup himself sheds no light on it in his book, A *Tenderfoot with Peary*," according to Theon Wright in his 1970 book *The Big Nail: The Story of the Cook-Peary Feud*. [3]

Congressman Macon knew he faced an uphill battle. "I realize that my efforts to defeat the passage of the bill . . . are Herculean in their proportions when I consider that I have the combined influence of the administration [and] a paid lobby of the Peary Arctic Club and the National Geographic Society to contend with. . . ." [4] In a later dissenting speech to the full House of Representatives, as reported in the *Congressional Record*, he was also quite skeptical of Peary's lack of memory concerning the National Geographic Society's investigation. "Think of it, gentlemen. Do you think that if you were trying to have the crowning act of your life consummated, that you would not have some definite knowledge about anything that was done in connection with its consummation? He [Peary] said that he did not remember to have told anyone of his discovery upon his return except Bartlett, and I have heard of no one who ever heard of his having told Bartlett of it until he made the statement before this committee. Messrs. Gannett and Tittman said that there was no evidence before them of his ever having told anyone that he had discovered the Pole until he flashed his wire to New York to that effect, and that was only done after he had heard that Cook had reported a short time before that he had discovered the Pole. . . ." [5]

After Peary ordered Bartlett and the rest of the crew to return to their base camp, he and Henson, with their four Eskimos, made the dash for the pole. While the entire group was together, they had averagd 9.03 nautical miles a day; on his return, Bartlett and his group averaged 14.7. But while Peary and his group said they spent two days at the pole, and would have had to travel 300 miles to the pole and back in addition to the approximately 250 miles covered by Bartlett, Peary arrived back at the *Roosevelt* only three days behind Bartlett's group. Thus, Peary had to have averaged 26.7 nautical miles a day, a mark unequaled in the history of polar exploration. By comparison, Cook never claimed to have advanced more than 15 miles a day.

Indeed, it is here that Peary's claim seems fatally flawed. In his two-hour speech on the floor of the House, Macon reviewed every fact and claim that grew out of the controversy, and concluded that Peary had never reached the North Pole. "I insist," said the incredulous Macon of Peary's claim to have covered 91.8 statute miles without sleeping, "that such a thing cannot be done, and no one who has any knowledge of the limitations upon human endurance will for a moment contend that it can be done."[6]

Peary's biggest defender on his claimed speed before the committee was Grosvenor, who pointed to Peary's earlier expeditions, during one of which Peary had claimed a speed of 22.8 miles a day. "Grosvenor's argument, designed to counteract suspicion among Cook's supporters that Peary could not possibly have made the speeds he said he made, merely added to this suspicion," reported author Wright, who reminded his readers that no one else in the history of polar exploration had matched Peary's claimed average speed during his dash, "a period in which . . . *there were no reliable witnesses*" (Wright's emphasis).[7]

At the conclusion of the hearing, the panel's chairman, Congressman Thomas S. Butler, a supporter of Peary, told the explorer: "We have your word for it, and we have these observations to show you were at the North Pole. This is the plain way of putting it, your word and your proofs. To me, as a member of this committee, I accept your word; but your proofs I know nothing about at all."[8]

In all, said Congressman Macon, Peary's statements before the committee show "his movements after Bartlett turned back were as uncertain, unstable, and as unreliable as the wind. He took no observations except at or near the Pole, and hence his every act or movement was based upon guesses or estimates. Everything seemed to be of a negative or indefinite character from the time Bartlett turned back until his final appearance before the Geographic Society in Washington, that passed upon his proofs."[9]

Of Peary's diary, Macon said, "It is much more reasonable to believe that he prepared it in some office after his return home than it is to believe that he prepared it in an igloo under the circumstances and conditions described by him."

In conclusion, Macon said, "I have given more time and thought to this alleged discovery than I have to any other public question that I remember to have undertaken to investigate in my whole life, and the more I have investigated and studied the story, the more thoroughly convinced have I become that it is a fake, pure and simple. . . .

"I have had some men tell me that they believe Peary discovered the Pole, because they could not understand how a man in his position in life would make a claim of having discovered it unless he had really done so. That kind of a statement presupposes that men occupying responsible positions in life always tell the truth about their achievements, but we cannot afford to accept that kind of a supposition as a true guide to the acts of men, no matter how important the position or how high the standing held by them."[10]

But Peary's supporters had conducted their dual campaign to destroy Cook's claims and his reputation as a means for boosting Peary's. In the end, despite the clear objections of some, and with loud "cat-calls of 'selfish egotist,' 'braggart' and 'bogus hero'" ringing through the halls of Congress from members who were unconvinced by Peary's case as the bill came up for a vote, Peary obtained most of what he sought, including his promotion and his pension. [11] His opponents won some points, but they were mostly esoteric, and have been lost from history with the passage of time. For instance, while Peary asked to be promoted to rear admiral and retired, the bill that eventually passed called for him to be placed on the retired list of the Corps of Civil Engineers with the "rank of rear admiral" and an annual pension of $6,000. The bill failed to recognize Peary officially as the North Pole's discoverer, instead commending Peary "for his Arctic explorations resulting in reaching the North Pole."

Since 1911, there have been many books written about the North Pole controversy, and nearly all maintain that there was clearly no basis in fact for valuing Peary's claim to having reached the North Pole above Cook's. Both claims are fatally flawed by the lack of supporting documentation, but they are equally flawed. Cook maintained that his supporting evidence was left behind in Greenland because of Peary's refusal to carry Cook's trunks, which had been left in Harry Whitney's care, back to the United States; Peary seems to have purposely failed to take verifiable observations, despite his complete knowledge of what was required as proof.

In *The Big Nail*, Theon Wright theorizes that Peary, knowing he couldn't reach the North Pole, ordered Bartlett back to the ship, keeping with him only his servant Matt Henson and the Eskimos, none of whom could serve as effective witnesses.

"There actually is no justification for assuming that Peary consciously intended to lie about his journey to the Pole," wrote Wright. "He may not even have thought of it as faking. There is ample evidence from his charts that Peary had never been a careful navigator, and it is quite possible that he did not particularly care how far he went into the Polar Sea, as long as he could reasonably justify his claim of having attained the Pole. To assure that justification, he did two things: He avoided taking longitudinal observations, which might have given a verifiable position; and he avoided taking along reliable witnesses. . . .

"This may seem a preposterous conclusion to draw, yet it is the only one that fits the facts. Peary never demonstrated any real devotion to accuracy, and his attitude toward scientific precisions, or even what might be termed scientific interest, was wholly negative and almost amoral. . . ."[12] To support that statement, Wright recalls a letter Peary wrote to Dr. Henry Bryant of the Philadelphia Academy of Sciences discussing the statements of many scientists that more important than any "race" to the North Pole was the knowledge to be gained through observations at the pole.

Wrote Peary, according to his biographer, Fitzhugh Green, in his *Peary, the Man Who Refused to Fail*: "You know as well as I do that the talk of having secured all the scientific information that is desirable, and not considering the Pole alone as of any special value, is all rot. You and I are no longer chickens, and we both know that no man would give a few facts of so-called scientific information the slightest weight, if balanced against the Pole."[13]

What seems clear so many years after the events is that Peary and his supporters—led by Grosvenor, Bridgman, and the Peary Arctic Club—set out to destroy Cook's claim in the only way they could without also destroying Peary's: by assassinating Cook's character, not by attacking his claim directly. And they succeeded.

These supporters managed to put Cook and his integrity on trial in a kangaroo court, without inspiring the same accounting of their own man. In 1934, Dr. J. Gordon Hayes, a professor of geography at Cambridge University, in *The Conquest of the North Pole,* wrote, "Peary's character was of the daimonic type, and his daimon drove him mercilessly. The American newspapers called him 'a weather-beaten fanatic.' He was such an enthusiast that it was no idle boast that he never would be content until he was famous. Yet this nearly broke him down. . . . He was probably the only explorer whose troubles came near turning his brain."[14]

Not everyone was blind to the evidence. William J. Armbruster, a college professor, wrote in a St. Louis newspaper, "Mr. Peary's testimony before the congressional committee is itself sufficient to show that the committee of the National Geographic Society did not make a proper examination of the data, and in declaring Mr. Peary the discoverer of the North Pole, without having made a proper and sufficient examination of the data, they perpetrated a gross iniquity upon the people of American and the world. . . . Mr. Peary charged Dr. Cook with having handed the people a 'gold brick.' Mr. Peary handed the public something much worse."[15]

To add to the furor, Peary ordered that his papers be sealed until the year 2000, by which time he knew that all the principals in the North Pole controversy would be dead. But the die was cast for history's recognition, and over the succeeding years, atlases, history books, and encyclopedias accepted Peary's claim as the valid one, unaffected by the minor alterations that Congress had made to the claim. According to one historian, Peary's victory was assisted by a $250,000 war chest that was established by his wealthy backers. And today, Robert E. Peary—who died of anemia in 1920—is still generally recognized as the undisputed discoverer of the North Pole.

Concluded Theon Wright: "Whatever may be the verdict of historians with respect to Cook, the conclusion as to Peary's claim is unescapable. The reasons for the vague and indefinite research that has pursued this question over the years may be difficult to understand, but one thing is beyond question: The perpetuation of the myth that Peary discovered the North Pole has no possible justification in fact or tradition."[16]

The National Geographic Society served Peary even better than the rest of his supporters, for it has continued to support his status as the North Pole's discoverer in issue after issue. Grosvenor also jumped at the chance to work Peary's name and claim into articles, and the Arctic and Antarctic were favorite topics for decades to come.

This culminated in a trip Grosvenor took in 1953 in Peary's wake, which resulted in an article in the *National Geographic Magazine* entitled "We Followed Peary to the Pole," describing Grosvenor's voyage in an air force plane over Peary's supposed route to the North Pole. In the article, Grosvenor proudly stated that the *National Geographic* had already carried "some 90 articles about life at the top of the world."[17]

The National Geographic Society has never wavered from its complete support of Peary, and even today it reacts vehemently to any attempt to examine the issue. During the production of a 1983 movie, *Cook and Peary: The Race for the Pole*, which concludes that Cook was the true discoverer of the North Pole, the Society tried to influence the sponsor of the made-for-TV film to pull out and to persuade the network not to run it. After this failed, the Society took the unprecedented step of writing an editorial in the March 1984 issue of the magazine to denounce the film and its makers; in the editorial the president of the Society repeats many of the falsehoods against Cook and in favor of Peary.

The Society said the film was full of "blatant distortion of the historical record, vilifying an honest hero and exonerating a man whose life was characterized by grand frauds. . . . Peary's claim is backed by astronomical observations made by others as well as himself, soundings taken through the ice, and by the testimony of his companions, including Eskimos. . . ."[18] At best, these statements are partial truths, and they make it clear that the campaign against Cook by the National Geographic Society is not yet finished, since some people still believe that Cook, and not Peary, was the true discoverer of the North Pole.

*　　*　　*

Dr. Frederick A. Cook retired from the arena defeated but un-bowed, somehow tenaciously clinging to the belief that history would eventually right the wrongs inflicted upon him. In his 1913 book *My Attainment of the Pole,* Cook recommends that his readers also obtain Peary's *The North Pole,* and place the books side by side. Cook's story was published before Peary's, and their observations of what they saw at the pole were very similar. Cook points out that "the striking analogy apparent in the Peary pages either proves my position at the Pole or it convicts Peary of using my data to fill out and impart verisimilitude to his own story. . . ."

Cook's words for the National Geographic Society's role in the affair were harsh. Under a chapter titled "How a Geographic So-ciety Prostituted Its Name," he said that the Society "very early assumed a meddlesome air in an effort to dictate the distribution of Polar honors; . . . They began a series of movements that would put a dishonorable political campaign to shame." He said the Society's role "is generally misunderstood because of its pretentious use of the word 'National.' In reality, it is neither national nor geo-graphic. It is a kind of self-admiration society, which serves the mission of a lecture bureau. It has no connection with the govern-ment and has no geographic authority save that which it assumes. As a lecture bureau it had retained Mr. Peary to fill an important position as its principal star for many years."[19]

And during the time the Society was conducting this anti-Cook campaign, he reported, "its moving spirits, Gilbert Grosvenor and Admiral [C. M.] Chester [a Society trustee], were publicly and privately saying things about me and my attainment of the Pole that no gentleman would utter. That Mr. Peary was a member of this Society; that his friends were absolute dictators of the power of appointment; that they were stock owners in Mr. Peary's enter-prise—all of this, and a good many other facts, were carefully sup-pressed. To the public, this Society declared they were 'neutral, unbiased and scientific'—no more deliberate lie than which was ever forced upon the public."

Cook said, "With shameless audacity this Society helped Mr. Peary carry along his press campaign [against Cook's honor] by dis-

seminating the cowardly slurs of Grosvenor, Chester, and others."
In all, he said, "I climbed Mount McKinley, by my own efforts,
without assistance; I reached the Pole, save for my Eskimos, alone.
I had spent no one's money, lost no lives. I claimed my victory
honestly; and as a man believing in himself and his personal rights,
at a time when I was nervously unstrung and viciously attacked, I
went away to rest, rather than deal in dirty defamation, alone. At
a time when the tables seemed turned, when the wolves of the
press were desirous of rendering me, I came back to my country—
alone.

"I have now made my fight," he said of his book. "I have been
compelled to extreme measures of truth-telling that are abhorrent
to me. . . . [But] I have confidence in my people; more than that, I
have implicit and indomitable confidence in—Truth."[20]

* * *

Fate was still not through with Dr. Cook. In the 1920s, he was an
oil promoter in Fort Worth, Texas, with a firm, the Petroleum Producers' Association, that had fallen upon hard times. This was the
era of the Harding administration's Teapot Dome scandal, in
which federal oil reserves were secretly "leased" to private oil firms,
and which led to the imprisonment of Secretary of the Interior
Albert B. Fall for bribery. Thus, in the words of one historian, "the
federal prosecutors were looking for [oil-industry-related] scape-
goats to satisfy public opinion."[21]

Cook was indicted for using the mails to defraud because a brochure that he wrote and mailed to prospective investors showed a
picture of an oil-well gusher coming in. The case received a large
amount of publicity, and Cook, who was almost sixty, was sen-
tenced to fourteen years and nine months in a federal penitentiary,
with no credit for the sixteen months he had already spent in a Fort
Worth jail awaiting trial.

". . . After a quarter of a century of ignoring the activities of oil-
stock swindlers, the federal government decided to prosecute, and
singled out the company headed by the conspicuous Dr. Frederick
Cook. . . . " wrote the *Literary Digest.* [22] While it is impossible to

verify today the motivations of those federal officials who were behind the prosecution, Cook and many of his associates felt that the oil-swindle charges were retribution pure and simple; the rich and powerful men who had backed Peary and who were still in lofty positions of power had one last reply to Cook for his criticism of them and their explorer.

Cook was convicted despite the fact that he was found to have been the largest single investor in the company and had drawn no salary or commission as its head. During the five years he spent at Leavenworth Penitentiary, one of his company's oil properties, bought at a U.S. marshals' sale by another firm, came in, and reaped the new owners millions of dollars. The find was part of the Yates Pool, the largest oil reservoir found in the continental United States during the twentieth century, and formed the basis of the Marathon Oil fortune in the United States. [23]

While in prison, Cook refused to see any visitors, including his children, except for explorer Roald Amundsen, the discoverer of the South Pole, who had originally defended Cook when the affair with Peary began, but had later allowed his name to be used by the Peary forces against Cook. After his meeting with Cook at the prison in 1926, the Associated Press ran a dispatch:

"Dr. Frederick A. Cook is a 'genius' in the estimation of Capt. Roald Amundsen, and, no matter what he may or may not have done in business, deserves the respect of the American people for his intrepid explorations. Dr. Cook may not have discovered the Pole, but Commander R. E. Peary also may not have, and the former has as good a claim as the latter." The reporter quoted Amundsen as saying, "Cook was the finest traveler I ever saw. He was practical. He never would say quit. Why, I remember once when he needed a camera in the worst way, Cook had a lens. Around that lens he built a camera, and it worked. I've never been able to duplicate some of his feats. He was a fine physician too." [24]

The report was widely circulated. When it reached the headquarters of the National Geographic Society and the ears of Grosvenor, the Society's director went wild. First, Amundsen's invitation to address the Society two months later was withdrawn. Said Grosvenor, after hearing of the dispatch, ". . . I felt compelled on behalf of the Society to withdraw an invitation to Amundsen to speak. . . . Amundsen stated that the interview was garbled, but a telegram [Amundsen sent] to the *New York Times* [with which he had a contract for his upcoming dirigible flight to the North Pole] . . . was not a retraction of his reflection upon Peary."[25]

Within four years of Peary's award from the Congress, some of his most important earlier "discoveries" were repudiated and removed from the government's official maps, including Peary Channel in northern Greenland, which was found by later explorers not to exist, and his claimed discovery of Jesup Land, which turned out to be Axel Heiberg Island in northern Canada, discovered years before by Otto Sverdrup, a Norwegian Arctic explorer.

The Navy Department also rejected the deep-sea soundings taken by Peary on his expedition to the North Pole, which Tittman had told the House committee was "the most valuable scientific result of the expedition." E. Lester Jones, superintendent of the Coast and Geodetic Survey, "later made known that the soundings were worthless because the nautical positions Peary gave for them were unreliable."[26]

In general, however, as good as Peary's recognition as the discoverer of the North Pole was for him, it was even better for the National Geographic Society. Despite some loss of credibility within the professional community, the Society had taken on a position of trust and leadership with the general public of America. From a circulation of some 10,000 in 1905, the Geographic grew to 107,000 in 1912, just months after President Taft had signed the Peary pension bill.

10. EXPANDING HORIZONS

> *Suddenly, without warning, under a huge overhanging ledge the boy showed me a cave beautifully lined with the finest cut stone. It had evidently been a royal mausoleum. . . . It seemed like an unbelievable dream. Dimly I began to realize that this wall and its adjoining semicircular temple over the cave were as fine as the finest stonework in the world.*
>
> *Explorer Hiram Bingham*

Proud of their success in getting Peary declared the discoverer of the North Pole, and overwhelmed with the new business that had resulted, Gilbert Grosvenor and his colleagues at the National Geographic Society began to understand fully the possible rewards that could result from their work. Grosvenor, now in his mid-thirties and a board member of the Society as well as editor of its magazine, was firmly in control of the organization's destiny. With the Society suddenly flush with money and members, Grosvenor began to consider ways he could live up to the Society's stated reasons for existence. While it had begun—through the magazine—to "diffuse" geographic knowledge, it had hardly been "increasing" the world's store of it.

The Society's sole geographic project in the nineteenth century had been the sponsorship of the 1890 expedition to Mount St. Elias in Alaska. That expedition, completely paid for by Gardiner Greene Hubbard, had led to the discovery of Mount Logan—at 19,850 feet, the second-highest peak in North America. Another sixteen years had passed before the Society contributed $1,000 to Peary's unsuccessful 1906 assault on the North Pole. This grant had represented the first time the Society's own funds were used for exploration; it was followed by the $25,000 grant to Peary, which helped underwrite the supposedly successful 1909 journey to the top of the earth.

With the Society's income rising quickly in the wake of its North Pole success, Grosvenor informed the directors in 1911 that the organization was now solvent enough to put away 15 percent of its dues each year to support expeditions, research, and related projects and, for the first time, to start living up to the second part of its often-stated goal.

Grosvenor's motivation was not simply altruistic: The *National Geographic Magazine* needed material to fill its expanding number of pages and to feed its growing audience. So now began, at Grosvenor's behest, the Society's policy of providing money to explorers and researchers to chart paths around the globe, on occasion to find new treasures to share with the world, and, more often, to tell easy-to-understand tales of exotic places that most of its members would never visit. Despite Grosvenor's loud protests that he was only funding the research in the holy name of science, these explorations, no matter how large or small, always yielded the fruits that were so necessary to keep the magazine interesting.

*   *   *

In 1911, a group of explorers under the directorship of a Yale University professor thirsting for adventure on his summer vacation was scouring Peru in search of the city of Vilcabamba, the legendary long-lost final capital of the Incan civilization. Hiram Bingham, a dashing and handsome thirty-six-year-old who looked like Abercrombie & Fitch's idea of the well-dressed white explorer eventually appealed to Grosvenor and the National Geographic Society to join with Yale University in sponsoring him.

Bingham had gotten interested in the Incas in 1909—the same year Peary was again hunting for the North Pole—after he had toured a number of known Incan ceremonial sites. He had come to exploration in an unusual way. His great-grandfather, for whom he was named, had been a zealous Protestant missionary who had spearheaded the drive to end tribal religions in Hawaii; he also managed to get his rivals, the Catholic missionaries, thrown off the islands. According to one writer, the character Abner Hale in James Michener's novel *Hawaii*, "the overbearing, bigoted and generally villainous preacher, is clearly modeled on Hiram Bingham, Sr."[1] Bingham's parents had also been missionaries, although far less successful ones. They spent several miserable years in the Gilbert Islands until, in poor health, they returned to Hawaii. Their primary accomplishments were to create a written language for the Gilbertese and then to translate the Bible into it.

Hiram Bingham III had deeply disappointed the family by refusing to become a missionary, choosing instead to teach. The Binghams, although venerated in Hawaii, never had much money; however, Hiram III, to the great chagrin of both families, married Alfreda Mitchell, heir to the Tiffany fortune.

The Incas ruled Peru and neighboring areas and developed an advanced society before they were routed by the Spanish conquistadors in the sixteenth century. Much of the evidence of their civilization was adulterated by the Spanish conquerors, and it had been plundered by the treasure hunters of the ages ever since. The modern world's attempts to understand the accomplishments of the Incas, and their fate, were severely hampered by the fact that the civilization had never developed a written language, and thus left no records or even hieroglyphics. The only written records of the Incas were made by the Spanish chroniclers, after the defeat of the Incas, who sent their accounts to Spain after interviewing many of the old inhabitants who knew Incan oral legends and fables.

According to the Spanish accounts, the Incas migrated from a high plateau near Lake Titicaca, on the border between modern Bolivia and Peru, to occupy the town of Cuzco. In 1438, another powerful tribe, the Chanca, invaded from the west. With the enemy just outside the city, the Inca ruler Viracocha fled with his eldest son in order to preserve the royal line, leaving the town's seemingly doomed defense to another son, Pachacuti. Against overwhelming odds, the Incas defeated the Chanca. This victory seemed so clearly miraculous to the Incas that they attributed it to divine intervention. Stones on the battlefield had risen up and been transformed into warriors who fought with the victorious Incas, according to their tales. As a result, Pachacuti was chosen as the new Inca ruler, and he soon embarked on a headlong career of conquest and social reorganization.

Under Pachacuti, the Incas became regional rulers and developed an advanced civilization. He is said to have devised both the Incas' governmental system and their religion, and under his leadership, the Incas soon ruled a large portion of South America's western coast. If the Spanish chroniclers are correct, the entire reign of the Incan empire was only about ninety years.

The Spanish, venturing south after their conquest of the Aztecs in Mexico, overwhelmed the Incas at Cuzco in 1533. The brave and disciplined Inca troops were no match for the guns and horses of the Spanish, neither of which the Incas had ever before encountered. It is believed that Manco, an Inca prince, fled with some of his followers to a retreat in the hills to the north, where he established the tiny kingdom of Vilcabamba. In 1572, the Spanish overran this last outpost of Incan civilization.

After returning from his 1909 trip to Peru, Bingham sought financial backing to search for the major lost cities of the Incan civilization. Yale agreed to fund him, and in 1911 Bingham and his crew set out to uncover the lost capital of the Incas, which many explorers had searched for, and some had claimed, incorrectly, to have found in earlier times.

Bingham and his troupe had trekked for six days after leaving Cuzco by foot, with much of their walk following an ancient footpath that was sometimes cut along the edge of sheer precipices and sometimes on brackets built into the sides of overhanging cliffs. At a small plantation, the expedition set up camp near the owner's grass-thatched hut. The owner, named Melchor Arteaga, soon came to them to inquire about their business.

"He turned out to be an Indian, rather better than the average, but overfond of 'fire-water,'" Bingham later wrote in the *National Geographic Magazine*. "His occupation consisted in selling grass and pasturage to passing travelers and in occasionally providing them with ardent spirits. He said that on top of the magnificent precipices near by there were some ruins at a place called Machu Picchu [which means "old peak"], and that there were others still more inaccessible at Huayna Picchu ["new peak"], on a peak not far distant from our camp. He offered to show me the ruins, which he had once visited, if I would pay him well for his services. His idea of proper payment was 50 cents for his day's labor. This did not seem unreasonable, although it was two and one-half times his usual day's wages."

At dawn on July 24, 1911, a miserably cold and wet day began. A number of the party found other things to do in order to avoid having to investigate their host's tale, but Bingham felt obliged to check out the farmer's story; he, Arteaga, and an armed escort supplied by the Peruvian government set off. The first obstacle they faced was a primitive bridge across the turbulent Urubamba River. "The 'bridge' was made of half a dozen very slender logs, some of which were not long enough to span the distance between the boulders but had been spliced and fashioned together with vines!" Bingham later wrote. His companions crossed by gripping the bridge planks with their toes; Bingham crawled over on all fours.

After more than half a day's hard climb brought no evidence of the claimed ruins, Bingham began to think "that my time had been wasted. . . . However, the view was magnificent [and] the water was delicious. . . . So we rested a while and then went on to the top of the ridge. . . ."[2]

The trio happened upon a hut occupied by two men who were farming in this remote area, the pair explained, in order to be far from the army, which was always looking for "volunteers," and from the tax collector. While Bingham could see that they were using terraces built by the Incas into the mountain for their plantings, he was still unconvinced he would find any important ruins, since many such Incan terraces dotted the countryside in that part of Peru. Bingham's guide and the two farmers decided to stay and chat—Arteaga because he had seen the ruins before and the farmers because they were so isolated and were hungry for news or gossip—and a young boy was provided to show Bingham the nearby ruins.

After negotiating the peak called Machu Picchu, the explorer found himself in a tropical forest. "Suddenly, without warning,"

Bingham wrote, "under a huge overhanging ledge the boy showed me a cave beautifully lined with the finest cut stone. It had evidently been a royal mausoleum." Next the boy showed him a wall and, half hidden beneath the vegetation, an Inca temple resembling the famous Temple of the Sun in Cuzco. "It seemed like an unbelievable dream. Dimly I began to realize that this wall and its adjoining semicircular temple over the cave were as fine as the finest stonework in the world."[3]

Slowly, as his eyes adjusted to the dense forest in front of him, he could make out more and more structures under the thick growth. He knew he had made a major discovery, but instantly wondered whether anyone would believe him. "Fortunately," he wrote, "in this land where accuracy of reporting what one has seen is not a prevailing characteristic of travellers, I had a good camera and the sun was shining." Bingham wrote that "the superior" stonework he found, the presence of grand edifices and the "unusually large number" of high-quality stone dwellings "led me to believe that Machu Picchu might prove to be the largest and most important ruin discovered in South America since the days of the Spanish conquest."[4]

One thing that excited Bingham the most was the presence of a building at Machu Picchu with three large windows in one of its prominent walls. There was an old Incan legend that the last of the pre-Incan kings who had ruled Peru for sixty generations had been killed during a battle with a band of savage raiders. His surviving troops had taken his body to a hidden cave in the inaccessible city of Tampu Tocco. And it was from this city, the legend continues, that the Incas re-created their civilization before striking out to conquer their empire, led by three brothers. These men, the heads of three clans or tribes, are said to have begun the journey, which led them eventually to Cuzco, by passing through three caves or windows. Indeed, "Tampu" means a temporary shelter and "Tocco" or "Tococo" means window.

When the Spanish arrived in the sixteenth century, they were told that Tampu Tocco was a small village one day's journey southwest of Cuzco in the Apurimac Valley, a place called Pacaritampu. "The chroniclers duly noted this location," Bingham wrote, "and it has been taken for granted ever since that Tampu Tocco was at Pacaritampu."[5] Bingham later declared unequivocally that Machu Picchu was actually Vilcabamba, the long-lost capital, and had served both as the cradle of the Incan civilization and as its last, temporary, refuge from the Spanish. While modern historians are far from certain what role Machu Picchu actually played in Incan civilization, they do agree that the buildings are all of late-Incan design, which would mean that the city surely wasn't Vilcabamba. Most of the burial chambers Bingham uncovered contained the remains of females, and there is no physical evidence that any battles were ever fought there. Indeed, the city looks as if it were abandoned, not overrun by an advancing army.

Members of Bingham's 1911 expedition spent most of their time compiling an inventory of the site and laying the groundwork for the intensive investigation that would have to be done by future expeditions.

For Bingham's next expedition, in the summer of 1912, he asked the National Geographic Society to join with Yale, which it readily did. Grosvenor knew a good deal when he saw one. This project carried no element of risk, since Bingham had already found the lost city, and surely a larger number of articles would result for the *National Geographic Magazine,* no matter what sort of historical site Machu Picchu turned out to be. Yale and the Society each contributed $10,000 toward the expedition's costs, a true bargain. Further Society-Yale expeditions under Bingham's directorship were sponsored in 1914 and 1915, as he continued his mapping and excavation work. Bingham's later expeditions thoroughly explored Machu Picchu's remains, uncovering, among other things, the Inca methods of terrace farming, their complex irrigation system, and the remains of many stone-paved highways through the mountains, including one that connected the mountain city and Cuzco.

Bingham was just the sort of fellow Grosvenor and the Society wanted to glorify. Bingham was a man of relatively financially humble beginnings and patrician bearing much as Grosvenor himself, yet he was fully aware of his place in the world; he knew how an explorer should look, and he played the role quite well, and photogenically. Indeed, one writer is convinced that Bingham—

with his riding britches and shirt, midcalf leather boots, and a battered khaki hat—was the inspiration for the character Indiana Jones, the explorer-professor hero of recently popular Stephen Spielberg films.

Today, when the Society lists its accomplishments, it nearly always reports that it sponsored the Bingham expedition that discovered Machu Picchu. In fact, of course, the Society agreed to fund his work only after he had already located the lost city; and while this is not exactly a grand-scale lie, it certainly is a misrepresentation. But it reflects what became under Grosvenor the habit of endless self-promotion, to generate positive publicity and garner new members.

Bingham returned the favor. To honor those who helped him, he named many of the glaciers in the area for officials from Yale and the American and Peruvian governments and his other sponsors. Today on maps one can find the Gannett Glacier, named for the Society's then president, and, of course, Grosvenor Glacier, in honor of the *National Geographic Magazine*'s editor.

In his exploration of Machu Picchu, Bingham was unable to find any gold objects, even though the Incas were reputed to have possessed vast quantities of gold. In 1915, however, the Peruvians, now more suspicious of American explorers, accused Bingham and his party of smuggling gold out of the country. Bingham was aghast. "For his part," wrote his biographer Daniel Cohen, "Bingham was incredulous 'that our statement [to the Peruvian government] that we were members of the National Geographic Society . . . was no claim in consideration.'" Deeply wounded, he abruptly departed, explaining to Teddy Roosevelt that he had decided there were "pleasanter activities for an American citizen than exploring Peru."[6]

Bingham next became interested in aviation, and had an illustrious career in the air; this interest also kept him connected to Grosvenor and the Society. In 1922, he was elected the Republican lieutenant governor of Connecticut, and in 1924 he was elected governor. Before he was even sworn in, one of the state's U.S. senators committed suicide, and Bingham won the ensuing special election to replace him. So Bingham served two days as governor in January 1925, and then resigned to take the seat in the Senate; he was reelected to a full term in 1926.

He was censured by the Senate in 1929 for allowing an employee of the Connecticut Manufacturers Association, who also worked for him, to help draft a new trade bill. Bingham was the first senator so punished in almost thirty years. He was defeated for reelection in 1932, although he ran far better than the rest of the GOP ticket did against Franklin Delano Roosevelt and the Democrats. A known womanizer, he was divorced by his wife, Alfreda, in 1937; his relations with his seven sons were distant. Bingham's last role in the political scene of Washington came during the hysterical McCarthy days of anticommunism. In 1951, Bingham was named chairman of the Loyalty Review Board of the Civil Service Commission. In that post, he declared that government workers should be fired not only based on their current disloyalty, but on the basis of any past beliefs that were contrary to the nation's best interests.

He died in Washington in 1956. Ironically, one of his grandsons, Stephen Bingham, was accused in 1971 of having smuggled a gun into San Quentin Prison for George Jackson, a jailed black activist. In the subsequent jailbreak attempt, Jackson, two other inmates, and three guards were killed. Facing multiple counts of murder, Bingham disappeared; he surfaced in 1984 and denied any role in providing the pistol. He was tried for murder in California in mid-1986 and was acquitted of all charges.

*　*　*

As the Society's business continued to boom, the organization constructed a new building next door to Hubbard Memorial Hall on Washington's 16th Street, scarcely more than a decade after having moved into that first full-scale home. The business and editorial offices moved into the new building in 1914, and Hubbard Memorial Hall became the Society's "scientific" headquarters.

In 1913, Grosvenor was vacationing in Europe when he was caught in a war scare in France and found himself unable to withdraw any funds from local banks until the public mood calmed.

Upon his return to the still generally isolationist and insular United States, Grosvenor ordered that 300,000 copies of a colored map of Europe be printed and stored in the Society's basement awaiting what he was now sure was the inevitable outbreak of a major war on the Continent.

On July 28, 1914, Austria-Hungary declared war on Serbia; in the August 1914 issue of the *National Geographic Magazine*, the map appeared, along with a note from Grosvenor saying, "The eyes of the civilized world are now focused upon Europe, and the stupendous war there beginning. The map will prove of much value to the members of the Society who wish to follow the series of military campaigns that it is feared will be without parallel in history." Also in the magazine were tables listing the sizes of the various armies and navies of Europe.

The war in Europe became a parlor game for many members of the Society. Each issue of the *Geographic* would summarize the preceding month's highlights and plot the positions of the combatants. The magazine was now getting so thick that Grosvenor decided to issue two yearly volumes of six issues each, as opposed to the single volume of twelve issues up to then. The change made it easier to handle the volumes physically and to meet the increasing demand for bound copies of the magazine.

The War to End All Wars became the *National Geographic*'s own. When America's draft law was passed, the Society offered the use of its stencil machines to help mail out the ten million notices, and its employees volunteered to run the machines. As volunteers, its "young ladies . . . have made innumerable sweaters, neckpieces and socks for our sailors and soldiers. . . ."[7] Its members were mailed an appeal for the first Liberty Loan drive, while the Society itself pledged $100,000 from its reserve fund to the drive. The Society established the National Geographic Society Ward at the American Ambulance Hospital in Neuilly, France. The *National Geographic Magazine* was sent free to all army bases, camps, and YMCAs and to the soldiers fighting in Europe.

In 1918, the Society published a map showing where the various armies were bogged down along the Western Front. That map was soon in demand around the world. American men and boys were fighting and dying in places that most Americans had never heard of and few could pronounce. The *National Geographic Magazine* worked hard to make some sense of the hostilities to parents and wives and brothers. And the message was surely getting through.

While other magazines were watching helplessly as their circulations nosedived during the war years, the *Geographic* was a house afire. When the war began in 1914, the National Geographic Society had 285,000 members; by the armistice of November 1918, membership had reached 650,000.

11. GLOBE-TROTTING

> *Geography is more than a thing of maps and charts. It is "the study of the other fellow." People . . . like what might be called the small-talk of geography. They enjoy human gossip about a race just as they enjoy gossip about their neighbors. . . .*
>
> Gilbert H. Grosvenor

By the end of World War I, the National Geographic Society was a staple of American life. When the war was over, things only got better for the Society; formerly generally isolationist, Americans, now residents of a first-rate world power, wanted to know more about their world.

By 1920, two years after the end of the war, the magazine's circulation had grown by another 100,000, and exceeded 750,000. The Society was the publishing industry's biggest success story; the Society and Grosvenor were news. For the first time, the industry was taking note, and Grosvenor was certainly enjoying his new celebrity.

People wanted to know how the Society was doing it, and Grosvenor was ready to talk. In the May 1922 issue of *American Magazine*, Grosvenor explained why the Society was such a smashing success. After reminding the readers how nearly all children seem to hate geography lessons in school, while at the same time adoring such things as adventure stories, he wrote: "Adventure! That was what you yearned for then [in school]. And no matter how commonplace your life may be now, you are only grown-up boys and girls in at least one respect—you still have a secret long-ing for adventure and romance."

He said, "Geography is more than a thing of maps and charts. It is 'the study of the other fellow.' People would be more interested in a tribe of men 10 feet tall than in a mountain 30,000 feet high. They like what might be called the small-talk of geography. They enjoy human gossip about a race just as they enjoy gossip about their neighbors. . . ."

Grosvenor said that he and his staff had learned that Americans were most interested in America, and that articles on the United States "always bring a special response from our readers." They are, he reported, followed in reader interest by nature studies. And as to the Society's particular success, he said, "Other nations have similar societies; but their membership is confined to a few scores of high-browed gentlemen, who would be amazed, possibly annoyed, if a great army of outsiders wanted to join their exclusive little circle.

"But here in America, this army of rank outsiders was wel-comed. Among them are bankers and barbers, financiers and farm-ers, railroad presidents and station agents, preachers and plumbers, children and centenarians."[1]

During this same period, Grosvenor was also discovering some other things about the tastes of his readers. The leaders of the Society realized that while they themselves might be seriously in-terested in the statistical and scientific side of geography, there was another side of this science that appealed to every man, namely the vicarious globetrotting that its readers were doing. And having discovered the keys to building reader and media interest in the Society and the magazine, Grosvenor moved to increase that inter-est. Now the things that interested his ever-growing constituency interested him; Grosvenor was the group leader on the world's largest around-the-world tour group.

And Grosvenor was also learning that a little money could go a long way. Aside from a few wealthy men and well-endowed univer-sities, hopeful explorers had few sources of funding; unless vast riches were at stake, governments were generally uninterested in sponsoring such work. Now Grosvenor, with a ready budget for exploration, could pick and choose from among the brightest lights on the scene, could make explorers' dreams come true, if he believed they would make good copy for his *National Geographic Magazine.*

Any lingering doubts about Grosvenor's complete control of the Society were dispelled in August 1922, when Alexander Graham Bell died at his beloved summer estate, Beinn Bhreagh, in Nova Scotia. During his burial ceremony on a mountain there, all the telephones in North America were silenced in his honor.

*   *   *

Grosvenor, in his search for people and causes for the Society to back, such as Peary and the North Pole and Bingham and Machu Picchu, found himself fascinated by one of the oldest living things on earth, the astounding giant sequoia trees of California.

Little in nature prepares one for the sight of these gnarled and ancient beauties, rising above the forest floor seemingly out of proportion with this world. Fossil finds of trees closely related to the sequoia have been discovered below the ancient lava flows of Mount Shasta in northern California and in rocks of the Jurassic and Triassic periods. While some eucalyptuses in Australia have been known to grow taller, the sequoias are considerably wider and live much longer.

The booming American economy at the turn of the twentieth century had sent lumber companies into the great giant sequoia and redwood forests of California to provide rot-resistant material for roofing, railroad ties, and vine stakes. The soft white wood is easy to cut and shape, and it turns an attractive shade of red when dried.

The lumber companies' feverish tree harvesting had led to one of the first murmurings of a nature conservation movement in the United States just as World War I ravaged Europe. "Nations have risen, reached their prime, and passed on to the decay and oblivion that is the ultimate fate of all things temporal, and other nations have succeeded them, in their turn to be followed by still others, since the great trees began their existence," editorialized the *Na-*

tional Geographic Magazine. "World powers have arisen, run their course, and disappeared—meteors as it were—in the sky of history, and the big trees still live on."[2]

One of the trees endangered by feverish harvesting was the largest known remaining specimen, the "General Sherman," 103 feet in circumference and 280 feet high. Sequoia National Park, a 166,000-acre preserve, had been established in California to protect these trees and surrounding redwoods, but the ground that they actually grew on remained in the hands of private owners. Alarmed by the rapid depletion of these great trees, Congress in 1916 had appropriated $50,000 for the Department of Interior to purchase the land.

The land's owners, however, while being relatively cooperative with the efforts of the government, insisted that some surrounding land—which they would not need if they couldn't harvest the sequoias—also be purchased, making a total of 667 acres. The owners agreed to sell all of the land for $70,000, well below its estimated timber-harvesting value of $156,000, but $20,000 more than the congressional appropriation.

The U.S. Department of the Interior secured an option on the land, but since Congress was not in session, the department was unable to come up with the additional money. But then, announced the *National Geographic Magazine* in a later issue, nearly breaking its corporate arm slapping itself on the back, "one of the officials of the department recalled the splendid work which has been done for a number of years by the National Geographic Society in stimulating public interest in the preservation of the nation's playgrounds and in safeguarding our song birds and wild life. Why not appeal to this Society, whose more than half a million members represent every state in the Union . . . ?"

The magazine continued, "The cutting of a Sequoia for grape stakes or railroad ties (and an 18-foot tree along the new state highway was cut a few months ago for that purpose), is like breaking up one's grandfather's clock for kindling to save the trouble of splitting logs at the woodpile, or lighting one's pipe with a Greek manuscript to save the trouble of reaching for matches." The Society's board of directors, at Grosvenor's urging, quickly voted to appropriate the $20,000, in what the magazine told its members was "a unique cooperation of a great national scientific society with the national government."[3]

This episode is quite typical of the view of Grosvenor and the Society toward nature and natural resources. The speedy success of Grosvenor and the Society's campaign seemed to show Grosvenor just how much political clout he was developing as the head of a thriving organization with far-flung and influential members. He was in favor of conservation, but in a general, old-fashioned, "Keep America Beautiful" way. The Society, in further application of Grosvenor's famous "Seven Principles," avoided the unseemly side of nature, and what man was doing to it, as much as it avoided bedbugs and cockroaches. That view of nature remains largely unaltered at the Society today.

The giant sequoias saved, conservationists next turned their attention to preserving the dwindling supply of redwoods, cousins of the great trees. The giant redwoods grow only along the California coast in a thin strip from the San Francisco area to the Oregon border, and only as far inland as the reach of the legendary heavy nourishing fogs, which bring moisture to the tops of the trees.

Redwoods live from about five hundred to thirteen hundred years, and at the time were thought to grow as high as 340 feet, an estimate that would prove conservative. However, they are substantially thinner than the sequoias. At this time, nearly all the redwoods were privately owned and faced virtual extinction.

In 1919, concerned private citizens donated money to purchase options on redwood-covered land, Humboldt County approved a bond issue with which to buy such lands, and the Save the Redwoods League was founded in San Francisco.

In 1920, three National Geographic Society members, stirred by Grosvenor's campaign in the magazine to finish the job of protecting the giant trees, gave the Society $21,330 to acquire three tracts containing sequoias and redwoods located within the confines of Sequoia National Park, totaling 609 acres, to be donated to the federal government. The next year, other members of the Society donated $50,000, and the Society itself came up with $5,000, for the purchase of another 640 acres, the last major private holding within the park's boundaries. In all, the Society eventually donated with its own funds, or that of its members who were inspired to help by the articles in *National Geographic Magazine*, a total of 2,239 acres.

The successes in Sequoia National Park seemed to inspire the supporters of the redwoods, including the Save the Redwoods League and the Sierra Club. Through the efforts of these groups and the National Geographic Society, many of the redwoods' homelands were saved and established as federal and state parks, most notably Redwood National Park, which includes some of the largest redwoods known to man; the world's tallest tree is believed to be a redwood in that forest that is more than 367 feet high.

* * *

In the January 1924 issue of the *National Geographic*, the Society gave its members a first look at the dark and mysterious netherworld of Carlsbad Cavern, a complex series of caves hollowed out of the Guadalupe Mountains in New Mexico. The caves, whose primary value up to that point had been to provide vast quantities of commercially mined bat guano for use as fertilizer, had been mostly unexplored until the efforts of Willis T. Lee of the U.S. Geological Survey began to reveal the spectacular beauty within the pitch-black environs of the caves.

The photographs that accompanied the article sparked so much interest that Grosvenor agreed to have the Society sponsor an expedition to explore the mysterious caves further under Lee's guidance. The expedition, Lee reported in a September 1925 article in the *Geographic* about the expedition, had profound effects on his men.

"The darkness of the cavern, its unbroken silence, and its unearthly aspect affected the workers in different ways," Lee wrote. "Some feared the dark and frankly confessed it; others feared and were ashamed of their weakness. Some were attracted by the mysteries of the unknown and were ever peering into dark corners;

others clung tenaciously to the beaten path and were persuaded with difficulty to leave it. It was obvious that all who worked regularly in the cavern were under a mental strain."[4]

For six months the crew probed the caverns. In Tom Sawyer fashion, the group weaved countless patterns of white kite string through the caves, guides back to the world of sun and sky in a place where most of man's senses were useless. The photographs are spellbinding, even sixty years after the fact. The Dome Room, the Nectar Fountain, and Shinav's Wigwam are no less mysterious and beautiful today than they were initially to the *National Geographic Magazine*'s audience then. Stalactites, like icy frozen fingers, drip from the ceilings; stalagmites shoot up from the floor like miniature mountains. Everything out of the range of the special high-intensity lights that were used to illuminate the caves is inky black, a backdrop for the illustrated treasures, which look like clubs, veils, organ pipes, and an Indian abode.

As undeniably interesting as the fruits of the Society's expedition were, again the organization moved to sponsor Lee only after the success of the project had been assured. Lee's first article in the *National Geographic* appeared three months after President Calvin Coolidge had proclaimed the caverns the Carlsbad National Monument.

* * *

Despite the great amount of attention Grosvenor was paying to domestic issues, he had hardly ignored international events. In each issue of the magazine, faraway places were still being explored and new attractions were being displayed for the readers. A few old favorites were still very much at the center of things, especially the North Pole.

Despite the apparent conquest of the North Pole by Peary or Cook, or both, much remained to be learned about the Arctic region, and about the much less studied Antarctica. In 1925, Grosvenor provided for the Society to join with the U.S. Navy in sponsoring the MacMillan Arctic Expedition. Grosvenor was, of course, ever ready to invoke the name of his beloved Peary and to revive the tale of how the Society had sponsored the man who history now said had "discovered" the North Pole.

The primary goal of this expedition was to study parts of what is now called the Arctic Ocean, specifically the area northwest of Alex Heiberg Island, which Peary had mistakenly claimed to have discovered in 1906 and called Jesup Land. Here was a chance for Grosvenor both to invoke Peary's name and to gently correct one of his errors. But this expedition had still another special appeal to Grosvenor. The project would employ airplanes, which were now beginning to acquire a reputation for dependability, working in tandem with a team of earthbound explorers.

Thus the Society had at least two compelling reasons to sponsor the work: its history of involvement in the North Pole and desire to reinforce Peary's status (one of MacMillan's two ships was called the *Peary*), and the expedition's benefit to the aviation industry, one of Alexander Graham Bell's longtime interests. And on top of all this, Grosvenor would acquire a new hero of the frozen wastes who would carry the Society's tricolored banner.

While the expedition was under the command of Donald B. MacMillan, the three airplanes and the eight men who ran them were headed by a young navy lieutenant commander, Robert E. Byrd, Jr., of the U.S. Navy's Bureau of Aeronautics, and a member of one of Virginia's richest and most powerful families. Byrd had become an aviator after graduating from the U.S. Naval Academy in 1912.

Byrd and his men easily proved that they could regularly operate airplanes in the Arctic summer. Quite excited by his exploits, when Byrd returned home he asked the navy for a leave of absence. After it was granted, he called upon Edsel Ford, president of the Ford Motor Company and an avid aviation buff, to sponsor a new expedition for a much more daring exploit, flying over the North Pole.

Edsel Ford was Henry Ford's only son; he had been thrust into the presidency of the car company at the age of twenty-five by his father, who had put his son to work in a factory at the age of nineteen. Under Edsel Ford, the company thrived and was the world's dominant auto maker for many years. He also combined his love of flying with business by moving Ford into aircraft manufacturing, most notably of the Ford Tri-Motor. However, airplane manufacturing was not profitable for the firm, and he later abandoned it.

After getting Byrd's request, Ford and some of his friends quickly came up with the necessary money to attack the North Pole by air. In April 1926, Byrd's expedition left New York Harbor on a reactivated steamer with fifty men, six months' worth of food, enough coal to carry the ship fifteen thousand miles, and a three-engine Fokker monoplane capable of flying on only two engines. The group landed at Spitsbergen, part of a group of Norwegian-controlled islands off the east coast of Greenland and now called the Svalbard Islands, on April 29.

After setting up camp, Byrd made some preliminary flights. And finally, on May 9, 1926, Byrd and Floyd Bennett, another young navy pilot, took off for the North Pole. Byrd was carrying a religious medal given him by a friend, a horseshoe, and a little coin, one which had been "taken by Peary, pinned to his shirt, on his trip to the North Pole," Byrd later wrote.

Off the two men flew into uncharted territory in the Fokker monoplane, the *Josephine Ford*, named after one of Edsel Ford's children. After a bout of disorienting snow blindness, Byrd looked "down into jagged regions never before seen by man. Ages of glacial ice had chiseled the land into grotesque, stupendous formations. An Arctic gale had sprung up and tossed the plane about with sickening jolts." He continued his account, in, of course, the *National Geographic Magazine*: "We were again getting into areas never before viewed by mortal eye. The feelings of an explorer had superseded the aviator's now, and I had that extraordinary exhilaration that comes from looking into virgin territory. At that moment I felt that we were repaid for our risk."

But an hour before he and Bennett should have been near the North Pole, Byrd spotted oil leaking from the plane's starboard motor. Bennett, after warning that the motor would soon stop, suggested they land and try to fix it. But Byrd, knowing that "too many expeditions fail by landing," decided they should keep flying for as long as they could. "We would be in no worse fix should we come down near the Pole than we would be if we had a forced landing where we were," he reasoned.

"At 9:02 A.M., Greenwich civil time, our calculations showed us to be at the Pole! The dream of a lifetime had at last been realized."[5] They circled the pole, took photographs, and were quite likely the first non-Eskimos ever to set eyes on this invisible top of the world. Their journey covered 1,360 miles and took fifteen and a half hours.

That the Peary controversy hadn't by any means faded is evident in the very first words Byrd used to describe his flight in an article in the September 1926 issue of the *Geographic*—published six years after Peary's death: "On May 9, 1926, Floyd Bennett and I looked down upon the North Pole from our monoplane, completely verifying Peary's observations, and demonstrating the feasibility of using airplanes in any part of the globe," he wrote.

Byrd never went on to explain what the comment meant, in light of the fact that many of Peary's few observations were found to be inaccurate. But from here on, Byrd was to be one of the favorites of Gilbert H. Grosvenor and the National Geographic Society. Byrd was always ready to invoke the name of Peary and to praise him; Grosvenor was already ready to provide funding to Byrd for his latest adventure.

In late June 1926, Byrd was awarded the Society's highest honor, the Hubbard Gold Medal; he was the seventh man to receive the award, after Peary—who had received the first medal—and explorer Roald Amundsen. Byrd's medal was presented by President Calvin Coolidge.

Soon after their North Pole expedition, Byrd and Bennett were preparing for a transatlantic flight to Paris when their plane crashed, seriously injuring Bennett and breaking Byrd's arm. Bennett's injuries kept him from joining Byrd in the later flight, which ended in the water off France when fog obscured all airports.

Two years later, the Society gave Byrd $75,000 as he turned his sights to Antarctica and the South Pole. Byrd helped map vast stretches of the continent and made the first flight over the South Pole. For thirteen months, from December 1928, the intrepid explorers in their camp known as Little America, kept the outside world informed of their progress by radio, providing their listeners a closeness to events that foreshadowed today's instant video communications.

To honor him anew for his many South Pole successes, the Society created a new award, the Special Gold Medal of Honor. At the banquet to honor Byrd, Grosvenor told the assembled crowd that while that night the explorer "can only summarize the geographic information he and his associates have accumulated . . . his first concern, the first day he set foot on American soil [after returning from the Antarctic], was to begin writing for his and our National Geographic Society a complete account of the discoveries and activities of his expedition."

In presenting the medal, President Herbert Hoover said, "Every hidden spot of the earth's surface remains a challenge to man's will and ingenuity until it has been conquered. . . . Great explorers . . . do not merely add to the sum of human knowledge, but also they add immensely to the sum of human inspiration."[6]

In an earlier address, Byrd said, "Other than the flag of my country, I know of no greater privilege than to carry the emblem of the National Geographic Society."[7]

12. PHOTOGRAPHY BLOSSOMS

> *People prefer pictures in which this
> element [of human interest] is present.
> But perhaps more than anything else, they
> want to see something that stirs the
> imagination.* [1]
>
> Gilbert H. Grosvenor

Ever since Gilbert Grosvenor's fateful decision to fill the eleven
empty pages in the January 1905 issue of the *National Geographic*
with photographs of Lhasa, Tibet, which had earned him overwhelming praise, he had been convinced of the great value photography could have in increasing the circulation of the magazine. In
those early years, when most of his competitors were still pooh-
poohing Grosvenor's use of photoengravings to reproduce his photographs and were stubbornly continuing to use only a few costly
steel engravings in each issue, Grosvenor embarked on a path that
was to revolutionize the magazine business.

But where was Grosvenor to get new and interesting photographs? Serious photography was still a hobby mostly restricted to
dabblers with the mechanical dexterity to operate the equipment
and the money to pay for it. Large, bulky, balky cameras mounted
on tripods had to be lugged into place; the images required heavy
and fragile glass plates; a darkroom full of dangerous chemicals was
necessary to coax the grainy images off the plates. It was very expensive, and the entire field was still in its infancy, even though
the rudiments of photography could be traced to the twelfth cen-

tury. It wasn't until 1840 that an American college professor, John William Draper of New York University, improved on the French daguerreotype etching process and produced the first human image on a photographic plate.

While photography remained as a carnival attraction to many Americans, the U.S. government became an early and important client for the emerging field. As already noted, the government became an important source for Grosvenor, who took advantage of the high-ranking positions held by his cousin, William Howard Taft, and the influence of several of the Society's principals; through them, he had access to all the government photographs he could find. To supplement the photographs he could borrow from the government, Grosvenor took up the hobby and encouraged the explorers who wanted to publish articles in the National Geographic to include photographs of their journeys and discoveries. But given the restricted capabilities of their equipment, the published photographs often illustrated only the explorers' trip to the site, or the camp used by the expedition's members, and not what was found in caves or under water or in the air. However, cameras were soon added to the supply caches of all the world's explorers; no longer would the world have to debate which explorer had made a discovery, as in the Cook-Peary fiasco. An early example was the National Geographic's article on Hiram Bingham's discovery of Machu Picchu; it was well illustrated, mostly with photographs taken by Bingham. Even Bingham in that article remarked that despite the many bogus claims others had made of important Inca discoveries, he was lucky to have had a good camera and a sunny day.

The next frontier was the use of color. In 1906, the National Geographic Magazine had started to use a little color to brighten up some of its maps, including one of South America in the August issue, and one of Cuba in the September issue. For many years, while color photography was still being perfected, most of the color plates in the Geographic were illustrations, not photographs. But even in this area, Grosvenor proved himself a resourceful marketing expert. After learning from his twin brother, Edwin Prescott Grosvenor, that all 100,000 copies of a U.S. Department of Agriculture pamphlet containing full-color portraits of fifty common birds had been gobbled up by the public in two weeks, and that the department still had orders for thousands more that it couldn't meet, he borrowed the color plates and published the portraits in the *Geographic*'s June 1913 issue, and at the very least inherited as customers the heretofore frustrated buyers.

Earlier, in 1910, as the Society expanded, Grosvenor opened the organization's photographic laboratory to do the Society's own film and print processing and to begin experimenting with new techniques. Also in 1910, the Society published the first series of "color photographs" in the November issue of the magazine, "Scenes in Korea and China." A twenty-four-page series, it was the largest collection of color photographs that had ever been printed in a single issue of any magazine. However, since color film was still an experimental process, the "color photographs" of the series were actually hand-tinted, using notes taken by the photographer on the actual colors of things. This technique was adopted from the practice used to color engravings of the period. For this series, the hand coloring was done by a Japanese artist employed by the photographer. Despite this hand coloring, "Scenes in Korea and China" was still a breakthrough, a harbinger of what would become the magazine's trademark.

In 1911, Grosvenor introduced what would become another *National Geographic Magazine* staple, the large panoramic photograph, an eight-foot-long, seven-inch-high foldout of the Canadian Rockies.

When it came to selecting publishable photographs, Grosvenor learned early in his tenure to respond to the tastes of his audience. Of one of the Society's continuing series of lectures in Washington—this one on the explosion of Mount Pelée on the island of Martinique in 1902, which killed forty thousand people—Grosvenor later wrote: "Though the lecturer had picures of the explosion's dramatic aftermath, he would not show them, thinking them too grisly. Yet, behind me, during the lecture, I heard several young society belles complain: 'Why doesn't he show exciting photographs? That's what we want.'"

As a result of this and other incidents, Grosvenor said, the lesson of what the *Geographic* should contain became clear: "Lucid, consistent writing; material of general, not academic interest; an abundance of pictures." And, of course, photographs that involved "human interest," no matter how gory. [2]

From the time that the Society opened its photography lab, each succeeding issue, it seems, had more photographs than the preceding issue and was as likely as not to contain some photographic "first." In 1906, the *National Geographic* published the first flashlight photographs of animals in the wild, which were caught behaving naturally. By various devices, including a boat rigged to take night flash pictures, deer and other animals were caught feeding and drinking, while others were caught in various pursuits, including a porcupine invading a houseboat in search of a meal to steal.

In a second series, in 1913, the magazine carried photographs "taken" by the animals themselves, when they tripped a wire on an automatic camera. All these photographs were taken by George Shiras III, a former member of Congress who became a pioneer in "camera-hunting," a sport that he said brought the primary thrills felt by the person who hunts with a gun—such as stalking a wild animal in its habitat and relying completely on one's wits—but left the prize alive for others, and provided a prize that many could enjoy: photographs.

Shiras, scion of a wealthy family, had walked into Grosvenor's office one day lugging a box full of flashlight photographs of animals in the wild. He had invented the technique employed to take the shots, and had won several awards for his work. Shiras explained to Grosvenor that he had offered the box of photographs to a large New York magazine, which had chosen to use only three of them. Grosvenor reported that Shiras was astounded when he published seventy-four of the photographs in the July issue, with only three pages of text.

By publishing Shiras, the National Geographic Society allied itself with photography as a means of conservation. In an early plea for such conservation, Shiras wrote, "Every true sportsman will admit that the instant his noble quarry lies prone upon the earth, with the glaze of death upon the once lustrous eye, the graceful limbs stiff and rigid, and the tiny hole emitting the crimson thread of life, there comes the half-defined feeling of repentance and sorrow."[3] During his brief stay in Congress, Shiras had authored legislation to provide federal protection to migratory fish and birds. He went on to serve as a trustee of the Society's board for thirty-one years.

After the World War, which had led to the further development of another National Geographic Society favorite, the airplane, Grosvenor opened a very successful era by putting photography and aviation together, just as he had earlier united photography and the conservation movement. Only the few aviation buffs in the world had ever seen the earth from the sky, until Grosvenor and the magazine took to the heavens. Even the most mundane topic took on heavenly wonderment when viewed from a few thousand feet up in the air.

Indeed, in 1922, the magazine took its readers aloft to fight bugs in "Fighting Insects with Airplanes: An Account of the Successful Use of the Flying-Machine in Dusting Tall Trees Infested with Leaf-Eating Caterpillars." Aerial photographs of Mount Everest, the Alps, the Andes, the Amazon, Canada, and Palestine were breathtaking wonders to behold.

Then, after having taken its readers around the world in black-and-white photographs and color paintings, the *National Geographic Magazine* soon took them on a return visit as color photography became a reality. In 1926, the *National Geographic* revisited the Arctic and returned with natural-color photographs of life at the North Pole and environs. Taken during the MacMillan Arctic Expedition of 1925, the photographs showed the rest of the world the natural beauty of the western coast of Greenland during the summer months, blue skies meeting blue waters and snow-white clouds and, indeed, snow-white snow. Also well photographed were many native women wearing colorful garb—a taste of the old *National Geographic* in a new latitude—and villagers performing many everyday tasks of life such as preparing halibut for canning, all of it looking downright elegant in color. The next MacMillan Arctic Expedition the following year led to Robert E. Byrd, Jr.'s, historic overflight of the North Pole, and more photographs.

In January 1927, the magazine went to the bottom of the ocean in an expedition that provides an interesting glimpse into the measures required to obtain color photographs with the technology of the day. The undersea expedition was to the Dry Tortugas, a cluster of small islands off the western Florida Keys, and was led by Dr. W. H. Longley, an ichthyologist from Goucher College, and Charles Martin, from the Society's photographic lab. The type of film available required strong light and long exposure times under normal conditions; because of the reduced light under the ocean, and since the inhabitants of the underwater world were uncooperative in maintaining poses, new techniques had to be developed.

"It was necessary to hypersensitize all [photographic] plates used in shallow depths," the magazine explained when it presented the expedition's results, "so that the undersea exposures might be reduced to a twentieth of a second." Because of the dampness in the Dry Tortugas, the heat, and the lack of power to operate an electric fan, the plate sensitizing had to be done each morning at five o'clock "to prevent the emulsion on the glass plates from melting."[4]

But when the divers tried to take pictures under more than fifteen feet of water, they discovered that even the hypersensitive plates needed more light in order to record an image. Martin then created a flash mechanism utilizing a pound of magnesium powder for each exposure. Divers would ignite the magnesium and simultaneously open the camera lens—which led to an arrangement out of Rube Goldberg, whereby two men tending the necessary equipment, a battery to spark the explosion, the flashlight powder, and a reflector, in a dory floating above had to follow the movements of the diver with the camera below and be ever ready for the diver's detonation of the charge. The process, the National Geographic later explained, "was more than human nerves could stand. Especially was this true when it sometimes happened that the men in the boat had to wait for two or three hours, every moment anticipating the blinding and deafening detonation. They could never know at what instant the diver would find his quarry in the desired position with respect to his lens."

Finally, a small floating device that the diver could handle himself was constructed; it carried the necessary dry-cell battery, the flash powder, and a reflector. During the expedition, Longley was seriously burned when one ounce of the magnesium powder exploded prematurely. The injury incapacitated the zoologist for six days, and was a grim reminder of what could happen if a full charge, sixteen times more powerful, went astray.

The camera used on the mission was placed in a watertight brass case with a glass window for the lens. Another hood was placed above the camera's reflector, and an acute-angle mirror was employed to allow the diver to focus while looking straight ahead and not have to bend over the reflector, as was usually the case. The results of the journey were eight full- and natural-color photographs, the first glimpse below the sea for millions of readers.

Around 1930, about three years after Longley's hard-won underwater success, Grosvenor began to take advantage of further improvements in the field, and the *National Geographic* turned its color eye upward. Color aerial photography had never been successfully achieved because the color film of the era required exposures fifty or sixty times longer than those for black-and-white photography. With such requirements, it was impossible to achieve sharp photographs from swift-moving aircraft or even from slower lighter-than-air vehicles.

But Grosvenor, after hearing about a new technique that was being employed in Europe, sent Charles Martin, the chief technician of its photographic laboratory who had assisted Longley in the underwater work, to study the process abroad. The photographic plates that Martin brought back turned out not to be suitable for taking pictures from airplanes, since they still required longer exposures than airplanes could manage. But the Society was able to adapt them for use in dirigibles. And in the September 1930 issue of the magazine, the Society published nine natural-color photographs, including what it said was the first ever natural-color photograph taken from the heavens—a shot of the U.S. Capitol taken from the Goodyear-Zeppelin dirigible *Mayflower*.

The nine shots, of Greater New York and Washington, were all taken by Melville Bell Grosvenor—Gilbert Grosvenor's son, who had joined the *National Geographic*'s staff in 1924, one year after graduating from the U.S. Naval Academy, and was then the assistant editor of the magazine. Melville Bell Grosvenor had begun in the Society's illustrations department, where he worked with a photographer and a clerk. Not long after starting there, he was himself experimenting with photography.

Of these historic aerial photographs, young Grosvenor wrote: "When the photographer was in position for the proper composition, the pilot in charge of the *Mayflower* was given a signal, the motors were momentarily cut off to eliminate vibration, and the big bag floated quietly while the brief exposure was made."[5]

Much time was spent gathering those precious few photographs, because, as Grosvenor explained, "Sometimes, after scurrying over Washington at express-train speed [in anticipation of the sun's reaching the location to be photographed], the ship would arrive at the desired spot just in time to have a wisp of cloud form between the scene and the sun, and thus make the attempt futile." Pollution was already taking its toll, as Grosvenor found much of the New York area looking as though it were covered by "a gossamer veil, a condition which the Navy's air skipper assures the writer is frequently encountered."

Through the work of Capt. Albert W. Stevens, the Society published the first photographs to show laterally the curvature of the earth. Also from the sky, the Society published Stevens's photographs of the moon's shadow on the earth during a solar eclipse in November 1932, and the first color photographs of the sun's corona, taken during a total solar eclipse four years later. Yet another Stevens mission illustrates that the Society could be swept overboard in its desire to claim a "first." The cover of the March 1937 issue promised the reader the world's first natural-color photograph ever taken in the stratosphere. Indeed, inside, above the caption headline "The color camera conquers the stratosphere," is a picture of the bottom of the balloon that was used to lift Stevens off the earth, which was taken by shooting straight up from the gondola.

The result looks like a fluttering round bedsheet with a series of garters flying off in myriad directions to connect to some mysterious contraption. Absent the caption, it is unlikely many of its readers would ever have guessed what it was, not to mention that it might have been taken at an altitude of some eight miles above sea level.

As the technology of photography improved, it opened up the range of material that could be presented in the *National Geographic Magazine*. In 1936, Kodak produced the first color film in rolls, 35-millimeter Eastman Kodachrome. The film was portable and had a faster emulsion, meaning it could be used in lower-light situations, freeing photographers to take more action shots and to travel anywhere. No longer did photographers have to be musclemen. On one trip to China in 1931, according to W. Robert Moore, then chief of the *National Geographic*'s foreign editorial staff, the photographers had to carry 150 pounds of fragile glass plates, in addition to the camera and plate holders, which weighed a total of 50 pounds.

By now the Society was able to send its technicians to work with the leaders in the industry in Rochester, New York, and in Europe, to learn the latest techniques and to work to overcome the obstacles that remained. But in photographs, as in words, the National Geographic Society moved to be as technically proficient as possible, but never interpretive or openly subjective.

* * *

As the *National Geographic* evolved into more a picture book than a serious text-filled geographic magazine, Grosvenor paid increasing attention to the reactions of its ever-expanding number of readers. He wanted to know what his masses liked and what they disliked, what topics or scenes excited them to sit down and thumb through the latest issue when it came through the mail slot—and what topics were to be avoided at all costs.

In a 1922 article in *American Magazine*, then a thriving general-interest publication, Grosvenor answered a question he said he was often asked—which one of the *National Geographic*'s photographs was the most popular. "I wonder if you could guess," he said. "It is a picture of a Mussulman [Moslem] praying at sunset, beside a camel, among the interminable sands of the Sahara.

"The fact that this picture has had the widest appeal to the public is very interesting. It shows that people in general have a true sense of the beautiful and a genuine instinct for what has artistic merit; for artists themselves have declared that this picture is remarkable because of its composition, its 'values' in light and shadow and the pose of the figure." Grosvenor said another important factor of the photograph, which the *National Geographic* called "The House of Prayer," is that "the kneeling Mussulman furnishes the element of human interest. People prefer pictures in which this element is present. But perhaps more than anything else, they want to see something that stirs the imagination."[6]

Writing in 1936, Grosvenor said one of the most popular issues ever of the *Geographic* was the March 1919, one "devoted entirely to 'mankind's best friend,' and splendidly illustrated from paintings by Louis Agassiz Fuertes." Fuertes, an American artist and naturalist, was one of the nation's best-known illustrators of birds. His work was praised for, in addition to its superb technical detail, what critics called his "sensitive understanding of the individual characteristics of the bird species portrayed."[7] In years following the dog issue, Grosvenor gave similar treatment to horses, cattle, deep-sea fishes, birds, wild animals, and what he called "other interesting creatures."

The *National Geographic* published the first of its flag issues in October 1917; its second flag set, in September 1934, reproduced in color the standards of 808 nations. In 1917, an article on state flowers, which was accompanied by color paintings, was published, "with the result that nearly a score of states have since [in 1936] adopted state flowers by legislative action. . . ." Grosvenor said.[8]

But what has become the National Geographic's best-known trademark, much to its great chagrin as it tried to maintain at least the veneer of a serious scientific magazine, is nature of a different feather.

Even before Grosvenor decided to use unprecedented numbers of photographs to grace the pages of the magazine, he had crossed another bridge in 1903. From his cousin, William Howard Taft, who was then the governor-general of the Philippines, Grosvenor had been supplied with several photographs. One of these pictures was of two scowling, bare-breasted aboriginal women who were working in a rice field.

Grosvenor was unsure what to do. "Should we publish them?" he wondered. "The women [usually] dressed, or perhaps I should say undressed, in this fashion; therefore the pictures were a true reflection of the customs of the times in those islands."[9] This, of course, was a time when in Western culture no lady would dream of showing much of her neck in public, let alone an arm or a knee, and when publications that contained reproductions or drawings of breasts were, if anything, sold quietly under the counter. Grosvenor himself was quite the prude, but he quickly grasped the potential of running these semiscientific photographs and, for a man who abhorred tobacco, alcohol, and harsh language, was quite willing to see his magazine populated with at least a few half-naked women.

As was usually the case in ticklish situations, Grosvenor turned to Bell. "'Print them,' advised the distinguished scientist, agreeing with me that prudery should not influence the decision," Grosvenor later wrote. "Since then the *National Geographic* has published many similar pictures of women in Africa and elsewhere," Grosvenor continued in genteel understatement.[10]

History was made. The picture was published and admired, and there was little adverse reaction and no doubt lots of private lusting.

". . . So patently pure its anthropological interest," one writer said in the *New York Times Magazine* in 1970, "that even at a time when nice people called a leg a limb, it never occurred to anyone to accuse Grosvenor of impropriety. . . . Since that time, many pictures in the magazine have shown women of the world in true native dress."[11] Said *Esquire* magazine in 1963, "Its use in a family magazine at a time when the female form was concealed from neck to ankle was a daring decision."[12]

Breasts of the world have become a major product of the *National Geographic Magazine* ever since. And although the Society's management takes vehement exception to comments about the sexual attraction or eroticism of the photographs, it seems, based on personal observations and the number of reminiscences one hears whenever the name of the *National Geographic* is introduced into conversation, that more young men and boys have gotten their first sight of the unclad female form from the *National Geographic* than from *Playboy*.

Indeed, as the *Times* writer continued, "during the grim 1930s and '40s, curious youth turned to the *Geographic*. Certain pictures were burned deep into the brain of countless thousands of men who were adolescents in those years. Staff members say it's the first thing that they hear when they introduce themselves."

Grosvenor himself, in *American Magazine* in May 1922, said, "Some of the reactions we get from our readers are rather amusing. For instance, an article describing some savage race almost invariably brings two or three letters from troubled members who feel that the ladies in the illustrations are rather insufficiently clothed. But very often the same mail brings an enthusiastic epistle from a college professor, calling for more close-ups of savages, as invaluable records of those dying races. . . ."

Since that rice-picking photo, according to *Esquire*, "to the everlasting joy of its readers, the magazine has shown women all over the world in true native undress, with no trouble from the U.S. mails." While there actually had been a similar photograph (of a "married Mangyan woman, wearing typical costume"—i.e., none) in the June 1898 issue, those were the early, technical-journal days of the magazine, when its readership was at its lowest point.

"My own favorite, for what it's worth," wrote the *Times* writer, "was a photograph of an exceptionally nubile, perhaps Nubian, young woman who was identified as a Sudanese slave girl, 'the property of an Arab merchant in Mocha . . .' in 1937. I looked her up in a dusty bound volume of the *Geographic* not long ago. She was still there, head erect, hands on hips, shoulders thrown back in proud servility, the stuff of multidimensional sexual fantasy beside whom the girls in *Playboy* are poor plastic things indeed."

Grosvenor's policy of running photographs of scantily clad natives met with much favor, and not from just the Society's male readers. *The New Yorker*, in 1943, found, "Moreover, to judge from their letters, *Geographic* readers look with favor upon Grosvenor's policy of running a good many pictures of lightly clad young people, generally of the colored races of far-off lands. Grosvenor knows that the *Geographic* is read by a great many ladies, so, in addition to pictures of girls, he makes a point of running occasional photographs, or paintings, of handsome young men, some of whom, being natives of tropical regions, are dressed in next to nothing. 'One of the Chief's hobbies in the magazines is to see that both sexes are well represented on looks,' a Grosvenor associate once said."[13]

For generations of pubescent boys and girls the *National Geographic* has been an anatomy primer, since the magazine is readily available and being caught reading it evokes no censure even in the strictest of households. And many bookstores still keep old copies of the magazine in basements for use in school research projects and for closet ogling.

Indeed, breasts of the *National Geographic* seem to hold a universal appeal, judging from the jokes one hears, or the winks and leers passed by men of all ages. One modern writer discussing Grosvenor's use of the Lhasa, Tibet, photographs wrote, "Even the fact that the men and women were warmly dressed in quilted robes, yak-fur capes and felt boots could not detract from their interest."[14] *Playboy* itself did a parody of the magazine, entitled the *National Pornographic*, in which grand *National Geographic* discoveries were shown being made by naked, or nearly naked, people. The *National Geographic* itself, however, at Grosvenor's strict orders, while permitting an occasional buttock or two, does not depict frontal nudity.

But for all of the frivolity and seemingly innocent sexual fantasy the photographs inspire, they also seem to underline the thinking in the executive offices of the Society, especially its subtle racism. While the *Geographic* has been highlighting breasts of the world since 1903 (not including the one earlier shot before Grosvenor took over) the only color of breasts that haven't been seen in the *National Geographic* are white ones—unless one counts the fully mud-covered woman shown during a supposedly healing mudbath, or a recent thumbnail-sized picture of a Las Vegas showgirl.

"On one occasion," reported a magazine writer in 1970, "a

frolicking Polynesian girl appeared suspiciously fair-skinned. The problem was taken care of in the *Geographic*'s photographic laboratories. 'We darkened her down,' said Melville M. Payne, the [then] president of the Society, 'to make her look more native—more valid, you might say.'"[15]

13. THE CHIEF

[*The National Geographic Society's*]
quarters reflect some of the rewards of the
Grosvenor policy of freeing geography
from its shackles. The Chief's two-room
office is a good deal larger than, say, the
ballroom in the old Peter Cooper house on
Lexington Avenue, and his four or five
chief assistants . . . occupy rooms almost
as spacious. . . .

The New Yorker, *1943*

In the early, tenuous days of the National Geographic Society, Gilbert Grosvenor had been its only employee. But in 1905, when membership had risen to 11,479, the Society reached a monumental plateau: financial solvency. Although it was far from rich, it had finally achieved black ink in its ledgers, and the Society's directors decided that it was no longer necessary for Alexander Graham Bell to pay his son-in-law's salary out of his pocket. In a gesture of outright generosity, they also agreed to Grosvenor's request that he be allowed to hire an assistant to take over some of his less enjoyable chores as a reward for his efforts.

At the recommendation of Bell's personal secretary, a twenty-five-year-old man went to see Grosvenor about the newly authorized job. The man, then employed as the chief telegrapher for Western Union at the U.S. Capitol, was named John Oliver LaGorce. "The word 'John' appealed to me very much," Grosvenor later explained. "It was a most honored name in the Bible. The name 'Oliver' was one of the magic names of chivalry. I didn't know at the time what 'LaGorce' stood for, but I soon found that his father was a colonel of artillery in a very distinguished

145

French family. I also learned that his mother was Irish, and I thought the combination of Irish and French would be very suitable. He was sure to be a good mixer, and practical." [1]

That Grosvenor, even at this early stage in his life, believed he could judge a man's character, social characteristics, and work habits solely by his name provides some insight into the antiblack and anti-Semitic hiring practices that have marked the Society's choice of employees throughout its history.

The first thing Grosvenor turned over to his new assistant—who agreed to work for $75 a month, less than Western Union had been paying him as a telegrapher—was the addressing machine Grosvenor had purchased as soon as he had taken over the moribund magazine. After a few months of operating the pedal on the manual addressing machine, LaGorce told Grosvenor, "You know, addressing all these thousands of envelopes is pretty hard on my foot. My foot's lame. I think we ought to have a boy in here to do this work." Grosvenor replied, "A-1 right." [2] And so began the empire.

John Oliver LaGorce, later known to all around the *National Geographic* as JOL, turned out to be just the sort of dedicated fellow Grosvenor was looking for. During his first ten years on the job, he is said to have never taken a vacation, unless, of course, one counts the trips to exotic lands he took on a regular basis in order to entertain the readers of the *National Geographic* and research the delights of the world for them. And LaGorce was as dedicated to Grosvenor as an employee could be. He even named his only son Gilbert Grosvenor LaGorce.

As the Society's membership grew by leaps and bounds, so too did its staff, and all under the firm control of the abstemious Grosvenor. Just as the Society instituted its policy of refusing, at Grosvenor's instigation, to accept advertisements for alcohol, tobacco, or patent medicines, so Grosvenor also tried to hire people in his own puritan image. The Society's halls were smokeless for many years. Finally, in 1925, Grosvenor hired Frederick Simpich, a former magazine writer and State Department official. Simpich, "who smokes inexpensive cigars by choice but thoughtfully carries more costly ones in his pocket for friends," according to one writer, was the first employee to dare challenge Grosvenor's anti-smoking policy. On his first day of work, he simply pulled out a cigar and lit it. ". . . A few days later, Grosvenor, whose avoidance of tobacco had, in office hours, been followed by his associates as a matter of course, quietly placed ashtrays on the desks of his more important male assistants."[3] It took about forty years more for women to earn the right to smoke on the job.

Here is Grosvenor's idea of an afternoon cocktail, a daily ritual that he played out between four and five in the afternoon, just before he left the office for the day. He would pour some Ovaltine, a powdered drink mix, onto a shoehorn, deposit it "in a Lily cup filled with water, stir . . . it with a penholder and drink . . . it down with a pleased expression."[4]

Grosvenor, known as the Chief to all who worked for him, but almost always addressed as Dr. Grosvenor, took his job, and his place at the head of the Society, very seriously. His pince-nez firmly in place, his suit coat always on, he ruled his growing flock of minions with a firm, albeit fatherly, hand.

Now that the Society was starting to make money, Grosvenor quickly showed the ability to spend it well on himself and his flock. For while the Society was "nonprofit," Grosvenor quickly learned that the tax classification hardly prevented him from lavishing the latest in creature comforts on himself and his fellow directors and upper-level workers. By 1920, the Society's staff had grown so large that the recently expanded headquarters building downtown was bursting at the seams. Two hundred office workers were moved to a building in another part of Washington, where five years later a new four-story building was constructed and filled with the latest technology available in order to handle the membership rolls, dues, and address changes of its legion of readers. In 1932, a major addition was constructed at the downtown Washington headquarters on 16th Street.

By now, the Society had become known as a perfectly respectable place for young Southern women to work for a few years while they searched for a proper husband. Women employees weren't allowed to smoke, were required to dress "properly"—which meant wearing stockings all year round, including during Washington's oppressive summers—were expected always to act like "ladies," and had to eat in a dining room by themselves. Likewise, the "gentlemen" who worked at the Society were expected to keep their coats on and their ties high whenever they were in public view and never to use harsh language near the Society's ladies.

Grosvenor's bright-side-only editorial policy "existed in tandem with a quaint atmosphere at Society headquarters, variously described by oldtimers—of which there are many—as resembling a 'gentlemen's club,' a 'Baptist church' or a 'finishing school,'" noted the *Washington Post* on July 17, 1977. "Hiring practices were always backward toward blacks and women, some say, adding that segregated dining rooms—for men, women, blacks, blue-collar workers—abounded." These practices, established and perpetuated by Grosvenor, seemed hardly out of place in a segregated, Southern-thinking city like Washington and in a white Anglo-Saxon Protestant organization like the Society, and they continued in force for many years. But one might have expected different behavior from an organization that specialized in geographic exploration, much of which involved research in lands populated by brown- and black-skinned people. But then, Grosvenor usually referred to natives as "savages" in his early writings.

Outstanding food at greatly subsidized prices was now being offered to all Society employees, but in hardly equal surroundings or on identical menus. Until well into the 1960s, most of the female employees ate in a large cafeteria maintained by the Society specifically for them. A smaller dining room nearby fed most of the middle- and lower-level male staff members. There were also two executive dining rooms (and since all the executives were men, they were all-male) and a very special smaller dining room "where two places and the day's menu are always set for the senior Dr. and Mrs. Grosvenor, whether or not they happen to be in Washington," according to *Esquire* magazine. Next to Grosvenor's private dining room was his majestic executive bathroom, with two marble shower stalls.

Whenever top *National Geographic* staffers were asked about the segregated dining facilities, they invariably offered the explanation given by Grosvenor over the years, that separate dining halls were really maintained as a service to the female employees, to protect them from the men, who might lose their heads and utter an obscene word or two in the course of their masculine lunchroom talk. This practice ended only after the Chief had given up the reins of the Society; the change came with the construction of new main headquarters in 1963. Tying the policy shift to the move to the new building allowed it to occur without drawing much attention or implying a criticism of the Chief.

As for the rest of the surroundings the now-prospering *Geographic*'s employees faced, *The New Yorker* reported on September 25, 1943, "These quarters reflect some of the rewards of the Grosvenor policy of freeing geography from its shackles. The Chief's two-room office is a good deal larger than, say, the ballroom in the old Peter Cooper house on Lexington Avenue, and his four or five chief assistants . . . [including LaGorce and Grosvenor's son, Melville Bell Grosvenor, then a middle-level employee] occupy rooms almost as spacious. . . .

"The twenty or so editors of the *Geographic*, all of them notably polite individuals who are forever bowing one another through the sculptured bronze doors of their elevators, move in a leisurely welter of thick rugs, bookshelves stocked with British and American *Who's Who*'s, encyclopedias, [and] bound volumes of the *Geographic*. . . . The editors freshen up in rooms where the towels are hung under a hierarchy of name cards. . . . For business errands around town . . . the editors have a fleet of five chauffeur-driven cars. . . ."

As the postwar boom continued unabated throughout the United States and much of the world, membership in the Society mushroomed, exceeding one million by 1935—with an estimated monthly readership for its magazine of five million, according to Society figures. To service these members, by 1936 the Society employed more than seven hundred workers.

Grosvenor continually invoked his "Seven Principles," painting a rosy view of the world and blue-penciling any mention of the distasteful side of traveling, such as bedbugs, oppressive dictatorships, or poor hotel accommodations. If a place was in such turmoil that the negative simply couldn't be ignored, the Society simply didn't write about it. Thus, what might be called the Marie Antoinette school of geography was institutionalized. While some might praise the lack of ethnocentric criticism of less-developed lands, what was really developing was the geography of omission. Nations that Grosvenor and the Society approved of could be lavishly covered in pretty pictures and words; what was not so nice about those lands could be ignored. The Society could excuse its failure to carry articles about nations that weren't in its political favor by pointing to their instability or economic turmoil.

The Society continued to find endless inspiration in, and fascination with, nature. Nature always scored high in reader interest, could be written about relatively close to home, and rarely raised much controversy. The entire March 1919 issue was dedicated to dogs, and another to cows. Birds, Grosvenor's personal favorite, were a perennial fixture; fish, ants, jellyfish, seashells, and turtles all had their day in the magazine.

He explained to one interviewer in 1943, "Our interpretation of geography [at the Society] is very wide. When I see a subject that I think would be interesting to our 1,200,000 members, I don't scrutinize it to see if it's geographical."[5] In other words, there was and is hardly anything in the world that the Society can't decide is proper fodder for the magazine, if it wants to run an article. Thus it has featured such things as "The FBI, Public Friend Number One," and a piece by LaGorce's wife on her Christmas cookies: "You have to put a lot of love into it," she revealed to the readers.

All the time, in Grosvenor's words, "the Society has sought to present articles and pictures of a type to interest and inform the average intelligent man and woman."

In practice, authors were all instructed to use the first person singular—unless they were willing to take along the wife and kids, in which case the first person plural was quite acceptable—and to construct their tales as a slightly longer postcard home to Aunt Martha, a wonderful lady, but lacking a vocabulary more advanced than early high school.

To the often-heard criticism of the *Geographic*'s topics and dull writing style, one of the Society's, and Grosvenor's, defenders replied, "The texts, naturally, are not meant to appeal to 'sophisticated' readers . . . but the complaint is that the articles lack a certain vitality that could only be obtained by adopting a very critical viewpoint. One can say in answer to this that the eminent success of the *National Geographic Magazine* all over the world proves the appeal of its style."[6]

Indeed, wrote a proud Grosvenor in 1936, "One member's copy travels first by train, then by mighty ocean liner, by upriver sampan, by coolie courier, and finally by camel caravan to interior China. Other prosaic stencil record cards [of the Society's addressing machines] are magic keys to a monarch's gold-bedecked palace in India, a South African ostrich farm, a tea plantation in Malaya, a jungle settlement among wild rubber trees of tropical Amazonia."[7]

As much a guiding light as Grosvenor's "Seven Principles" were to the Society and the magazine, he acknowledged that there were some exceptions to be made even to those iron-clad rules. "Some subjects I have regarded not as controversial, but as sound, plainly evident facts deserving the support of all thoughtful men and women," he said.[8] When a debate was raging throughout the country over the importance of aviation in military tactics, the Society supported Gen. Billy Mitchell, air power's chief lobbyist in America, and published a long paper of his in support of that position.

But most of Grosvenor's exemptions involved Britain and things British. "Long before World War I, and always since that cataclysm, I have sought to promote mutual understanding and good will among English-speaking people," he later wrote. And he recalled that in 1918, he had written in response to a contributor's letter, "I intend to use the *Geographic Magazine* to the best of my ability to promote a better understanding between Great Britain and the United States."[9] Grosvenor that year also wrote, "Let us hope the American people and the British people will be smart enough to learn the principal lesson of this war, that the two nations must stand absolutely together hereafter."[10] And there has been a steady stream of articles on England, including the entire April 1949 issue, entitled "The British Way."

In return for providing money and a forum to explorers from

throughout the world for the adventures, Grosvenor quickly piled up an astounding number of monuments to himself. By the late 1930s, there were named after him a fish in southern Peru; a sea-shell off the coast of Greenland; Gilbert Grosvenor Island off the coast of Alaska, a repayment from its discoverer for the book title suggested by the *Geographic*'s editor, *The Friendly Arctic*; a lake in Alaska; a glacier in Peru named for him by Hiram Bingham, discoverer of Machu Picchu; the Grosvenor Trail and Gilbert Grosvenor Mountain Range, both named for him in Antarctica by Richard E. Byrd; Mount Grosvenor, near the Tibet border in China; Grosvenorfjellet, a mountain on the Arctic island of Spitsbergen; Grosvenor Arch in Utah; an elementary school near his home in Bethesda, Maryland; a Nepalese thrush named after him by S. Dillon Ripley, longtime direcor of the Smithsonian Institution; a warbler in America; and a plant discovered in China, which—oddly enough, considering its namesake's straight-laced views—is thought to possess aphrodisiacal qualities.

How strongly Grosvenor felt about these tributes is illustrated by an event in 1925, when the U.S. Board on Geographic Names, a part of the Department of the Interior charged with standardizing the names and spellings of geographical features on official government maps, moved to change the names of Lake Grosvenor and Mount LaGorce, which were also located in Alaska. The board's feeling was that topographical features shouldn't be named after living persons. According to *The New Yorker*, "Grosvenor got wind of this scheme and, accompanied by LaGorce and [Robert F.] Griggs [the botanist who discovered and named Lake Grosvenor], took the matter up at the White House with President Coolidge, who had been two classes ahead of him at Amherst. Coolidge instructed the board to leave the names alone, and moreover he chided the board, tersely, for even thinking of making the changes. Grosvenor is a modest man and he usually can't recall all of the things named after him. . . ." But, the magazine quoted Grosvenor as saying, "We felt that the suggested changes constituted a reflection on the Society"; he believed that the board was conducting a vendetta against the Society. [11]

To make up for the insult, the Society was eventually allowed to name its own representative to sit on the Board on Geographic Names. In grateful appreciation for his services in keeping Grosvenor and LaGorce on the maps of America, the Society named Coolidge to its board of directors in 1929.

*   *   *

During the Society's first years of enormous growth, Grosvenor—despite what must have been tremendous temptation to do otherwise after the organization abandoned its original scholarly objectives—still required that all new members be sponsored by existing members and that the magazine remain a premium of membership in the organization. This sponsorship requirement was finally dropped in the 1950s, but it had never truly affected the growth in membership. "Should you be in the unthinkable position of not having a sponsor," said one writer, "your application goes before the Membership Committee. No one whose check has cleared the bank has been known to be refused."[12]

In 1938, a writer for *Scribner's Magazine* explained the Society's membership process: "If the applicant lives in a city with an address that suggests neither a prison nor other suspicious circumstances, he is quite certain to gain admittance into the Society. . . . And even if the applicant does reside in prison, he can pay an extra 50 cents a year and receive the magazine without becoming a member of the Society."[13] Indeed, when Al Capone was sent to Alcatraz, he was shifted from the Society's membership list to its subscription list.

"Most people think our membership principle is phony," Grosvenor once explained, "but it is perfectly sound. The members really own the Society and, in addition to receiving the magazine, and the maps, which we publish separately, share in the responsibility for the scientific expeditions which we sponsor."[14] And Grosvenor continued to remind the members, in every issue of the magazine, that the Society belonged to them. But, of course, the members of the Society actually had nothing to do with the organization's focus or how it was run.

As the organization grew, so did Grosvenor's influence and his ego. By now he had acquired a large country home, which he called Wild Acres, in Bethesda, Maryland, a wealthy, then-rural suburb of Washington. One of his proudest accomplishments, according to his listing in *Who's Who*, was that his country house held a record from the Audubon Society and the U.S. Biological Survey for the largest number of nesting birds ever discovered in one acre of property adjacent to a house in the United States— fifty-nine pairs counted in 1915.

In addition to the Bethesda estate, Grosvenor owned at the time a winter cottage in Coconut Grove, Florida, and his wife had inherited the magnificent Bell estate from her parents on Cape Breton Island in Nova Scotia. At Cape Breton, Grosvenor spent much of his time with his son and four daughters, sailing his fifty-seven-foot yawl, given to him by his famous father-in-law and named the *Elsie*.

One morning, as he was driven from his Bethesda home to his office by his Society-paid chauffeur, the car was stopped by a local policeman for speeding. "The president of the National Geographic Society leaned out of the window and beckoned to the officer. 'I'm Dr. Gilbert Grosvenor,' he said. The policeman waved him on," reported *The New Yorker*.

A former staff member recalled, "You were aware that he [Grosvenor] was the squire and you were the yeoman. A feeling of peasanthood in the staff was what they wanted. Sometimes he seemed to have a God complex. I remember once at one of the Society's [continuing series of] lectures . . . that it seemed like every fire engine in Washington was screaming by. You couldn't hear a thing. Dr. Grosvenor, who was sitting down front as usual, turned in his seat and beckoned to the man in the booth who operated the projector and the sound equipment. The man—his name was Rideout—ran downstairs and crouched alongside him. 'Mr. Rideout,' Dr. Grosvenor said, 'go outside and make them stop.'"[15]

In 1939, Grosvenor co-edited *The Book of Birds* with a world-famous ornithologist and Society trustee, Dr. Alexander Wetmore. The title pages of the book, which was really a compilation of many of the bird articles Grosvenor had ordered for the magazine, and which was published by the Society, read: "Edited by Gilbert Grosvenor, L.L.D., Litt.D., D.Sc., and Alexander Wetmore, Ph.D., D.Sc." Grosvenor's name was in slightly larger type, even though Wetmore was the professional bird expert. "Grosvenor is regarded with considerable veneration in his office," *The New Yorker* explained on October 2, 1943, "and, according to those who know the Society well, the title pages were simply a reflection of the National Geographic state of mind, in which the Chief's name just naturally seems larger than anyone else's. . . ."

In fact, all of Grosvenor's doctorates were honorary. His first such degree came from Georgetown University in Washington, followed by degrees from Amherst, William and Mary, Lafayette, the University of Maryland, and the South Dakota School of Mines.

In the Society's cumulative index from 1899 to 1940, Grosvenor's name appears 371 times. The index reported that the *National Geographic* carried 269 pieces of text, including speeches and captions, by Grosvenor; two hundred photographs by Grosvenor, and twenty-eight photographs of Grosvenor.

Perhaps it is easier to understand the numerous citations of Grosvenor when one knows Grosvenor's role in the scheme of things, as viewed by the Society. LaGorce once explained: "Behind the term geography is exploration. Behind that is adventure and just over the hill is romance. . . . Under Dr. Grosvenor, these three elements are stepped into closer focus. The Chief has removed the technical padlocks from the science of geography."[16]

*　*　*

Throughout Grosvenor's reign, the Society worked hard at maintaining superb relations with the world's press. Inquiries from the press were handled cheerfully, quickly, and abundantly. As a result, critical mentions of the Society are just about impossible to find in any newspaper or periodical.

"If the Society should ever be the target of unfriendly investigation," commanded *Esquire* merrily—although no doubt accurately—in 1963, "a life membership and a map case should silence its harshest critic." Another magazine said the Society "is frequently considered equally as unassailable as motherhood and the flag."[17]

The closest thing to a critical view of the Society was presented in a three-part series by Geoffrey T. Hellman in *The New Yorker*, published in 1943. It was one of the few examinations of the National Geographic Society as a business, which, of course, it was. He reported: "In view of the magazine's current circulation of 1,200,000, its continuing tax-free position as an educational institution, and its success in building up a reserve fund of some $10 million, Grosvenor's insistence on the membership principle appears to have been sound."

Hellman found that the membership principle not only made the readers of the National Geographic feel as though they belonged to a club, but had also been a factor in bringing the Society several unsolicited legacies, which by then already totaled more than $100,000.

Hellman reported that the first bequest was from Miss Jane M. Smith of Pittsburgh, who left the Society $5,000 in 1911. Miss Smith wanted the income from her donation to be used to create life memberships, which then cost $100, "in cases where worthy and competent persons are not able to pay for such memberships."

With his tongue apparently buried deep within his cheek, Hellman reported that Grosvenor's "disinclination to inquire into people's finances" has led the organization to award Smith Life Memberships to "a number of persons who perhaps did not strictly belong in the category outlined by their benefactor," namely wealthy explorer Hiram Bingham; a former wealthy congressman from New York; André Citroên, founder of the French automobile empire; and King Leopold III of Belgium.[18]

Four years later, Hellman was awarded a Jane M. Smith Life Membership, which he accepted.

14. MARCH TO THE RIGHT

As a substitute for Scout training, German youngsters now join an institution known as the Hitler Youth organization. Its emblem is the swastika, and its wide activities and political training are enormously popular with all classes.

National Geographic Magazine, February 1937

As the world was being pulled into the bloodiest conflict in the history of mankind during the 1930s, several of Grosvenor's policies combined to create a dismal chapter in the National Geographic Society's history. Grosvenor's see-no-evil "Seven Principles," together with his extreme case of Anglophilia and his rising social and financial station, led the Society and the magazine into a strongly pro-fascist point of view, which supported Britain's appeasement policies by showing the fascists in the best possible light.

Grosvenor was very proud of his and his wife's British origins. He and Elsie had even traveled to London in order to be married in a chapel that was located just off Grosvenor Square. Early in his stewardship of the Society, Grosvenor had said that one of his stated goals for his administration of the Society and the magazine was to foster better relations between the United States and Great Britain. He had even gone so far as to exempt stories about Great Britain from the strictures of his "Seven Principles."

As the new global conflict approached, Grosvenor, now in his fifties, had a strong case of the anticommunist fervor that was rampant among moneyed Europeans in the wake of the Russian Revolution and was perhaps most common among the British upper classes. Many citizens of the United States, especially the capitalists and industrialists, were at least mildly pro-fascist, anticommunist, and antilabor. And many of them saw the nation's new president, Franklin Delano Roosevelt, as an enemy, because of his alleged liberal leanings and interventionist ideas in Europe. Even though Grosvenor's own family had been far from rich, he and Elsie had inherited much of the Bell family estate, and Grosvenor now clearly allied himself with the wealthy ruling class; he brought to the National Geographic that class's policy of encouraging the fascists to beat back the communists in Europe, somehow always sure that if and when the time came, Grosvenor and his ilk could certainly control the fascists.

The Society, under Grosvenor's leadership, had weathered the Great Depression in good shape. Although it lost circulation in 1931, 1932, and 1933—the only years it has ever failed to increase its membership—the losses were minor, compared to the economic devastation that engulfed the world. And as the world recovered from the depression, its economy fed primarily by the rearming of Europe, the Society once again prospered greatly. By its fiftieth anniversary in 1938, membership was up to a record 1,132,079, advertising revenues from the magazine were close to $1.5 million, and the staff had grown to eight hundred.

* * *

The first real notice of European turmoil Grosvenor provided to the readers of the National Geographic, "Turbulent Spain," an article in the October 1936 issue, mentioned the goings-on since the end of the Spanish monarchy, when King Alfonso fled the country. Civil war had since broken out in July 1936 between the generally left-wing loyalists and the right-wing rebels who were pushing for a return of the monarchy.

The article was a peculiar mix of travelogue and war report, with the war news couched in the understated tones for which the National Geographic is noted; the entire story was written in the past tense, even though the civil war would rage on until 1939. "The top end of the Gran Via [in Madrid] is becoming a Times Square, with its crowds, bright lights, moving signs and din of motor homes," wrote Ruth Q. McBride. "Traffic is worse here than at the corner of Pennyslvania Avenue and 14th Street in Washington. Picture palaces blaze with electric lights and show American films. The Puerta del Sol, the very heart of Madrid, is an oval-shaped plaza into which debouch six of the principal streets. Surrounded by cafés and advertising signs, it is full of hurrying crowds, street-cars and taxicabs. Colorful announcements of bullfights vie with advertisements of soccer games.

"This spot was a scene of wildest disorder in the civil war, with thousands of troops and armed civilians, even women and girls, shouting 'Viva la Republica!' All motorcars were requisitioned, communications cut and troops rushed out the north road to defend the capital. . . ."

At the end of her stay, and her article, McBride reported that while traveling on the train, she and her fellow passengers learned that the city of Córdoba had been captured by the advancing rebels. "How much more this war may change Spain nobody knows," she concluded.

Five months later, in February 1937, Grosvenor was prepared to show just how much. In an article by a young American tourist, Gretchen Schwinn, a nineteen-year-old who was traveling with her mother, the *Geographic's* readers were shown a horrific picture of a crude and oppressive loyalist government that was seen to be collapsing from within. "We Escape from Madrid" opened with a clear violation of Grosvenor's "Seven Principles" of objectivity and good news only, with no upsetting events or snide put-downs: "Stewed cat cost mother and me a dollar a plate in Madrid. We were Americans, and still had money. Two aged Spaniards, less fortunate, watched us through the restaurant window."

The article went on to describe the deprivation caused by the war and the harsh measures adopted by the Spanish government to deal with the rebel threat. Finally having had enough of the inconvenience and the danger, the pair decided to leave, long after conditions had led to the evacuation of most foreign nationals. But by then, the last American evacuation ship had departed. What were they to do? Fortunately for them, the British embassy agreed to take them out on the next rescue mission of their own nationals.

Their "escape" actually had few thrilling aspects. While the author tries to pour on the terror and danger, the facts belie the tale. And the article contains glaring omissions, such as mention of the major assistance that was being provided to Franco by Hitler and Mussolini.

British consular officials placed the travelers on a train. After their baggage and their bodies were searched—they expressed incredulity over being strip-searched; the Spaniards failed to locate their hidden traveler's checks, which were secreted in the young woman's hair—they were allowed to board the HMS *Despatch*.

"A little motorboat took us to the *Despatch*, where all the officers—at least, it seemed so—and five other refugees were on the deck to greet us.

"Dinner was waiting in the messroom. I'm afraid I made a pig of myself, particularly with the meat and butter, but there seemed to be plenty."

* * *

Turning from those distasteful doings in Spain, Grosvenor's *National Geographic Magazine* found things much more to its liking in Nazi Germany.

In "Changing Berlin," in the February 1937 *National Geographic*, the writer Douglas Chandler was most impressed with Germany's public-works accomplishments under Hitler and with the varied nature of her people. He wrote, "Behold the anomaly of an urban agglomeration [Berlin] with a total population of some 4,220,000, a city that can boast one of the most highly perfected transportation systems in the world, with every convenience contributed by science—and yet that contains within its limits the following: Twenty thousand cows providing a third of the milk supply, 30,000 pigs, 10,000 goats, 700,000 chickens, 180,000 rabbits, 5,800 people keeping bees, only three or four buildings that I could find as much as 10 stories high [and] 12 windmills still functioning. . . ."

Chandler continued, "As I walked through the streets of the Old City, I found myself humming a line from a Princeton Triangle Club play way back in the dim ages of the Wiley Pure Food Act [which was approved in 1906]: 'Renovate, rejuvenate, and incidentally change the date,' it ran. This jingle describes aptly the evolution taking place today in Berlin."

The article waxed poetic about Berlin's four-a-day mail deliveries, her thirteen universities, 147 high schools, and 503 grade schools. Chandler wrote that he had spent two days in search of how the "other half" lived. "Nowhere," he reported, "did I find a spot which measured up to my conception of a 'slum.'"

The blood-red Nazi flags and pennants dangling from street lights made for dramatic color photographs in the middle of the long *Geographic* feature, carrying captions such as "Banners Over Berlin—A Bright, Sunshiny Day, With Unter Den Linden in Gala Dress," the gala dress, of course, being the swastikas that were everywhere in the photograph of a busy street in front of the Zeughaus (armory), which contained weapons and memorabilia from battles from the Middle Ages to World War I.

Chandler was very much taken with Germany's mandatory "labor camps" where all boys between the ages of seventeen and twenty-five were required to spend six months giving service to the state, mostly in the building of public works. "To develop boys and girls in body and mind," Chandler wrote, "and thus insure a sturdy race to defend Germany in the future, is a policy of the present government. . . .

"As a substitute for Scout training, German youngsters now join an institution known as the Hitler Youth organization. Its emblem is the swastika, and its wide activities and political training are enormously popular with all classes."

Chandler spent so much effort assembling the details that he was able to inform the *Geographic*'s readers that on an average day, Berliners consume 720,000 loaves of bread; that each year, eleven thousand tons of coffee made from malt "and only two-thirds as much real coffee" are consumed; and that some fifty million people attend Berlin's four hundred movie houses each year. This maddening stream of disconnected facts, so typical of *National Geo-*

graphic features, takes on a more sinister meaning here, where it is used to mask the reality of life in Nazi Germany and to present a picture so mundane as to reassure the politicians who favored appeasing Hitler.

Chandler found it significant that the city's beer consumption had shrunk 40 percent in the previous eight years, "a fact of much significance as foreshadowing the physique of the future Berliner."

But what Chandler didn't report to his readers was that Hitler had opened many concentration camps for the employment of Jews and other undesirables as slave labor for Germany's resurgent economy after initiating the practice at Dachau, just outside of Munich, in 1933; or that in 1935 Germany's infamous Nuremberg decrees, which severely restricted the rights of Jews, had been imposed; or that Hitler had illegally reoccupied the Rhineland in March 1936; or even that Hitler had abrogated the Versailles Treaty in January 1937, clearly setting the stage for what would be called World War II, the deadliest conflict in the history of man.

Rather than depress his readers with those facts, Chandler wrote of his last day in beloved Berlin: "Across the bridge, returning from an outing, marches a group of small boys wearing the uniform of the Hitler Youth—short black trousers, brown shirt and black neckerchief slipped through a braided leather holder. They are singing in accurately pitched, youthful treble that moving modern national song, the 'Horst Wessel Lied.'"[1]

Horst Wessel was a pimp who also served as a neighborhood leader of Hitler's SA (storm troopers or "Brownshirts"). The son of a Protestant chaplain, he had devoted his life to Nazism. He was reportedly killed by communists in February 1930, and "would have passed into oblivion along with hundreds of other victims of both sides in the street wars [as Hitler was coming to power] had it not been for the fact that he left behind a song whose words and tune he had composed," according to Nazi historian William L. Shirer. "This was the Horst Wessel song, which soon became the official song of the Nazi Party and later the second official anthem—after 'Deutschland über Alles'—of the Third Reich."[2] Wessel, under the skillful manipulations of Hitler's propaganda chief, Dr. Joseph Goebbels, became one of the Nazi's greatest he-roes, thanks to the popularity of this song.

Chandler completed his piece with: "A faint chill creeps over the dusky, shimmering water. Winter is not far away. I shall hie me back to my Schwarzwald eyrie and my skies."

Chandler also wrote articles in the *National Geographic* in the crucial prewar years 1938 and 1939 on Belgium, the Baltic states, Turkey, and Yugoslavia. At a time when the American right wing was trying to secure national support for the Nazis, or at least the nation's neutrality toward the Nazis and its fascist allies in Italy and Japan, Chandler was one of several right-leaning writers who appeared regularly in the *National Geographic*. Hitler invaded Po-land in September 1939, and then ravaged Europe—all the while liquidating Jews, liberals, communists, homosexuals, gypsies, and anyone else perceived as an enemy—but it was only after the bombing of Pearl Harbor on December 7, 1941, that there was sufficient public support to push America into the war.

Chandler was a native of Chicago who grew up in Baltimore and had been a writer for the Hearst newspaper chain, during its most reactionary period, at the company's *Baltimore Sunday American*. He eventually became a stockbroker in New York but was wiped out in the crash of 1929. He moved to France in 1930, after telling friends his wife's income would support them abroad. He traveled through Europe and the Balkans for several years, spending much of his time in Vienna and Berlin.

In July 1943, Chandler was indicted by the U.S. Department of Justice, which charged that he "knowingly, intentionally, felon-iously, traitorously and treasonably did adhere to the enemies of the United States . . . giving to the said enemies aid and comfort" by making propaganda broadcasts that were designed "to persuade citizens of the United States to decline to support the United States in the conduct of the war." [3]

Chandler was indicted along with seven other Americans, in-cluding the anti-Semitic poet Ezra Pound. All the indicted Amer-icans, except for Pound, were accused of aiding the Nazis; Pound was working for Mussolini.

At the time of Chandler's indictment, the government released a short dossier on him to the press:

A musical and literary dilettante . . . [who] from time to time . . . wrote articles about his travels for American magazines. Several were published in the *National Geographic Magazine.* This publication dropped him, however, when the editors learned that Chandler was receiving monetary favors from the Nazi government. Later, an elaborate home in a Berlin suburb which had been confiscated from a "political prisoner" was placed at Chandler's disposal by the Nazis.

By 1938, Chandler's conversion to Nazism was complete, and he made a lecture tour through England and Scotland on behalf of the German government, extolling the virtues of National Socialism. . . . In 1940, the virulence of his anti-Semitic and pro-Axis views caused the Jugo-Slavian government to withdraw a temporary residence permit it had issued him. [4]

The Nazis, the Justice Department said, had established a program to beam radio broadcasts to the Allied nations featuring former Americans who "intended to weaken the morale of the American people; to dissuade them from making war on the Axis powers; [and] to destroy their faith in their own government. . . ." [5]

The Justice Department said that when Chandler began broadcasting for the Nazis in the summer of 1941, he showed a "polished and caustic manner. . . . He was billed as 'Paul Revere,' and the program was introduced to the strains of 'Yankee Doodle,' with the sounds of galloping hooves in the background. What followed was a harangue on the old themes of 'international Jewry,' the warmongering of the Roosevelt administration and the serenity of life in German-controlled Europe." [6]

When Grosvenor learned of Chandler's indictment for treason, the Society told the news industry's trade magazine, *Editor & Publisher,* that Chandler "was dropped from the staff of contributors when it was found that he was receiving money from the Nazis." [7]

In the popular weekly newsletter *In Fact,* famous antifascist writer and gadfly George Seldes wrote, "It is apparent [Chandler] was not dropped by the *National Geographic* because the stuff they printed by Chandler was outright Nazi propaganda, but because the magazine discovered that Chandler was getting double pay—from it and from Hitler." Seldes added, "The best evidence on whether or not the traitor Chandler published Nazi propaganda in the *National Geographic* may be obtained by any person looking through the file of the magazine."[8]

Chandler was arrested by the Americans after the Germans were defeated, and he was returned to the United States. Attorney General Tom C. Clark hired a special prosecutor to handle the trial, and Chandler was convicted in July 1947. He was released from the federal prison in Lewisburg, Pennsylvania, in August 1963, at which time he planned to return to Germany. From here, he disappeared from the pages of history.

* * *

Europe after World War I was a fomenting, seething place with the unhappy working classes struggling to find ways to better their lot, while the ruling classes tried to protect their holdings. Particularly in Italy, labor unrest had led to violent confrontations and to a ready acceptance of communism as a solution by the populace. Into this out-of-control society came Benito Mussolini, who obtained power when he demanded it, brought an end to many of the manifestations of the unrest, and beat back the communists.

In the eyes of the ruling classes of the world, at least, Mussolini was to be applauded. Thus, as exemplary as Grosvenor and his *Geographic* found Germany, Italy was treated as a home away from home—after England, of course. Indeed, Grosvenor and the *Geographic* seemed to find unending interest in Italy during the Fascist reign. While Benito Mussolini was trying desperately to rejoin the world of nations after his ostracism for the invasion and occupation of Ethiopia, the *Geographic* fell all over itself trying to find nice things to say about his regime and his accomplishments, no doubt as a reward to glorify this successful anticommunist.

Said one former *National Geographic* staffer, "Of course the old man liked Mussolini. Il Duce brought order to Italy and threw out the Communists. He built roads and protected the museums. . . .

Italy was where people like Grosvenor went to look at art and to wallow in culture . . . and Mussolini was only too happy to have them."[9]

And it was Italy that was to get the *National Geographic* "treatment" next: "I stood under Benito Mussolini's office window after Addis Ababa [Ethiopia] fell. I saw him throw up his strong right arm and say, slowly and distinctly: 'The war is finished!' The Roman Empire was reborn that night."[10] So began "Imperial Rome Reborn" in the March 1937 issue, a rhapsodic portrayal of Fascist Italy, glowing beyond belief, even by *National Geographic* standards.

"Empires have fallen," wrote John Patric. "This one—and this one alone—has risen again. More than 26 centuries ago the wolf-suckled twins quarreled and Remus was slain for leaping scornfully over the wall of Romulus' new town. Far from having been 'built in a day,' the Eternal City is unfinished even now; and to her seven hills more and finer roads than ever lead from far places."

Grosvenor's *National Geographic* found that even poverty was quaint and admirable in Fascist Italy. "There [outside a restaurant in Rome] shuffled from the street a wrinkled old violinist. He seemed to play even more for love of it than for the battered coppers, worth about a cent, every diner gave him—even the gnome-like little man who had brought his own bread and cheese and ordered only wine. The poorer the Italian the more generous he seems."

And life was grand for more than just the bona fide citizens of Rome: "In three months," the author reported, "I did not see one animal badly fed or ill-used. I did not see a child punishd corporally. Laws are stern and strictly enforced. Yet I cannot believe, even after visiting Roman prisons, that political prisoners suffer physical cruelty in Italy today." Indeed, Rome was even "haven for many an alien. I talked with Jews running busy auto wrecking shops and wondered how many old cars America would scrap if metal jumped to war prices and four gallons of gas cost $5.

"'There are perhaps 25,000 of us [Jews] in Rome,' remarked the father of a large family whose younger members watched him melt babbitt from bronze bearings. 'Many of us fought in Ethiopia. We are free to worship as "Judea," but we are Romans, too.'

"Another Jew, a retired clothing merchant, said he lived in Rome because 'here I feel more equality than I ever knew.'"

In fact, although Mussolini was far less a fanatic than Hitler, by August 1938 he ordered all Jews who had come to Italy since 1919 out of the country within six months, removed all Jews from public office, fired all Jewish teachers, removed all Jewish students from schools and universities, and banned Jews from marrying Christians.

Even though Italy is still the only country in Western Europe in which Jews have lived continuously since before the Christian era began, by the early 1940s the nation was helping feed Hitler's death machinery. In all, about eight thousand Jews, some 20 percent of the forty thousand that were believed living in Italy at the time, were killed, and thousands of others were sent to concentration camps.

Meanwhile, Patric made clear that he wasn't afraid to ask the hard questions: "I asked about jury trials.

"'We believe in them. But we don't think judgment by "12 of a man's peers selected by lot" is fair either to the accused or to the state. A jury of masons, housewives and shopkeepers cannot examine evidence dispassionately. Our jurymen are especially selected by the court for their knowledge of its subject, their scientific fairness and legal training.'"

The author did find the fact that Italy had tried 209,959 people for crimes in 1933 a trifle peculiar. "That is a surprisingly large number in a country so heavily policed, so thoroughly locked and barred." But rather than give his readers cause for concern, he went on to interview a quaint carpenter who was in an Italian prison.

"I asked him what he'd done. 'I stole some railroad iron,' he replied, a bit shamefacedly.

"'When I was a kid, I did that,' I told him. He brightened, said he could live and eat on what he earned here, and explained that, like the Wolf of Gubbio, he was bad only when he was hungry."

Another time, the author was walking around the Flaminia district north of Rome when a sheepherder asked him to take a picture of himself and his dog.

Because I did, two policemen took me to the station. While I was waiting there the priest came, blessed it [the station], and passed on.

"There are well-dressed people in the Flaminia, and new apartment houses with beautiful entrances. There are automobiles. There is even a park with statues in it. Why not photograph these?" they asked.

At last a note arrived from the Ministry of Newspapers and Propaganda, "Well and favorably known." I was released.

Plainclothes men have halted me on Rome's busiest streets to "see my papers." I was awakened in a hotel early one morning in a town unfrequented by tourists. Officers asked what I was doing there. Sometimes I was questioned on the street, sometimes in the police station. Four official papers explained who and what I was, and I soon learned not to fear consequences of being a well-documented foreigner with a pocket camera.

The custom of "controlling the population" became, to me, merely a time-consuming annoyance.

The article spoke glowingly of the sacrifices Italy's women and children were willing to make, giving up gold wedding bands and steel pan covers and tin toys for the war effort. 'Sons of the Wolf' [Mussolini's equivalent of the Hitler Youth] at 6, young Italians are never thereafter outside Fascist organization. Schools increase, instilling childhood beliefs that individual freedom and private rights are always subordinate to duty and sacrifice to the state. The younger generation is devoted to Fascism with all the passion of its Latin blood."

Patric did not take note of what an inspiration Mussolini had been to Adolf Hitler during some of the Nazi leader's darkest hours during his climb to power. Mussolini's successful 1922 "March on Rome" to demand control of the nation emboldened Hitler and inspired him with an example of what a fascist party, with the proper leadership, could accomplish. Mussolini was also playing a

The National Geographic Society was instrumental in saving the remaining sequoia and giant redwood trees in California. (*National Archives*)

Well-illustrated articles in the *National Geographic Magazine* helped build the American public's interest in Carlsbad Caverns, a series of caves in New Mexico's Guadalupe Mountains. Visitors are dwarfed by rock formations in the Hall of Giants; top photograph is of the Big Room. (*National Archives*)

Richard E. Byrd inherited the Society's interest in Arctic and, later, Antarctic exploration. In 1926, he flew over the North Pole; in 1929, he flew over the South Pole. He is shown taking a sighting at his Little America camp in Antarctica in 1930. (*National Archives*)

Byrd visiting the grave of President Theodore Roosevelt in Oyster Bay, Long Island. *(National Archives)*

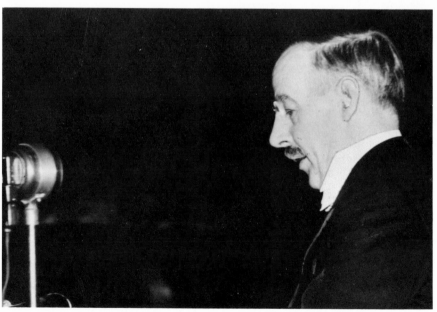

Gilbert H. Grosvenor addressing a meeting of the Daughters of the American Revolution. *(Washington Post)*

The senior Grosvenors as they prepare to depart on a three-month voyage to Africa in 1952. (*Pan American World Airways*)

Melville Bell Grosvenor holding a copy of his favorite magazine in 1974. (*Washington Post*)

Gilbert Melville Grosvenor sailing below Bell's Beinn Bhreagh estate in Nova Scotia in 1984. (*Washington Post*)

The headquarters of the National Geographic Society has grown from the small building in the center of this photograph, Hubbard Memorial Hall, built in 1903, to include the 1914 building *at left*, the 1932 building *at far left*, the 1968 structure *at far right*, and the newest edifice, *center right*, dedicated by President Reagan in 1984. *Photo by author*.

The 1984 building houses new and lavish executive offices in over 500,000 square feet of office space and has been compared to a Mayan temple. It was built at a cost of more than $35 million. The Society paid cash. *Photo by author*.

major role in the Spanish Civil War, supplying the monarchist forces.

As did Chandler in his article on Berlin, Patric makes even the terror and militarism of fascism seem quaint and acceptable. Again, it seems part of a concerted effort to lull the American public into accepting fascism as a reasonable way of fighting communism.

John Patric was a right-wing, antilabor writer who quickly became a favorite of Grosvenor's. In addition to being a regular contributor to the then rabidly conservative *Reader's Digest*, Patric wrote glowing articles for the *National Geographic* on two of Hitler's earliest targets, Hungary and Czechoslovakia.

Indeed, according to Seldes, "Grosvenor offered Patric $15,000 to continue to write his articles about the glories of fascist nations in the *Geographic*, but Patric saw bigger money in the kind of reaction the *Reader's Digest* spreads every month."[11]

For nearly ten years before the outbreak of World War II, it appears that Grosvenor couldn't get enough of Fascist Italy. In February 1930, the *National Geographic* featured an article titled "Beehive Homes of the Italian Heel"; in October of that year it devoted many pages to the president of Georgetown University, who was revisiting the land of Virgil and the Roman Empire; in August 1934, the magazine was exploring the Pontine Marshes; in January 1935, the Italian Riviera attracted the *Geographic*'s attention; in September 1935, *Geographic* readers went on a trip to hunt castles in Italy; the September 1936 issue featured "Sojourning in the Italy of Today"; Patric's "Imperial Rome Reborn" was run in March 1937; the October 1938 issue featured "Augustus—Emperor or Architect?"; and just two months later, the attraction that brought the magazine to Italy was the treasure to be found in some of her gardens.

While most of these articles carefully avoided outright political commentary, the articles no doubt fostered tourist travel by portraying Italy as a nation reborn. And in this glorification came, to at least some degree, acceptance.

In "Sojourning in the Italy of Today," Mrs. Kenneth Roberts explained that in the spring of 1935, most Italians had looked upon

Mussolini's preparations for the invasion of Ethiopia "unemotionally. . . . Little was known about the country, except that it was a place where bananas grew. Bananas, to the mind of a resident Italian, are perhaps the most desirable of all fruits. He regards them as a truly regal dish, just as some people regard caviar. He has almost the same feeling toward them that colored people are supposed to have toward fried chicken." It is in fatuous comments like these that the folksy cuteness of the *National Geographic* pales and one is better able to see that point of view that the Society advocates.

In March 1940, John Patric—who had had so much praise for Mussolini's Rome three years earlier—and the *National Geographic* were back in Italy, again gushing about the public-works projects of Mussolini in "Italy, from Roman Ruins to Radio." By the time this article ran, Hitler and Mussolini had announced their formal alliance, "the Pact of Steel," almost nine months earlier; Hitler had annexed Czechoslovakia and defeated and annexed Poland; Britain, South Africa, and Canada had declared war on Germany while the United States and Italy were officially neutral; Finland had been defeated by the Soviets; and work had begun on the Auschwitz death camp.

Scarcely more than three years later, Allied military men would be fighting and dying throughout Mussolini's scenic, historic, and hospitable land, and utilizing the many public works of Sicily and Italy in their own way.

The *National Geographic* also found space to let Patric write a wonderful travelogue about a journey through Japan. Unlike the Mussolini piece, this one was mostly a glowing vacation piece about the happy oriental countryside, but it was designed, as many of the other pieces were, to paint a picture of the tranquillity, or at least normalcy, of life in totalitarian countries.

While Grosvenor was perfectly happy to run articles about life in lands under Hitler's thumb, he was prepared to ignore American foreign policy when it ran counter to his stance. One example concerned the Society's handling of Czechoslovakia. Despite the American government's refusal to accept Hitler's annexation of the country, and despite the protests of Czechs in the United States, the Society insisted on showing Czechoslovakia as part of the German Empire on its maps.

Seldes, editor of the newsletter *In Fact,* seems to have been the only writer willing to challenge the right wing's hold on many of the country's publications, including the *National Geographic.* His newsletter was published during the 1940s, and although it reached a circulation of almost 200,000, he eventually closed it because of monetary difficulties. I. F. Stone later revealed that it was Seldes who inspired him to begin his own little newsletter.

Seldes, who received a Polk Award for his journalistic work in 1982 and published a book in 1985, when he was ninety-four, offered this view of Grosvenor's politics in late 1943, at the conclusion of an article about Patric and his articles and DeWitt Wallace, then owner and publisher of *Reader's Digest:*

. . . Wallace denies that he is a fascist. No one, however, denies Wallace is a reactionary, and again it is useful to quote the only honest thing Mussolini ever said, that reactionary and fascist are one and the same.

The same definition explains why the *Geographic* has published articles by pro-Fascists. Editor Dr. Gilbert S. [sic] Grosvenor is about as deep a reactionary as they come. At one time Wallace and Grosvenor worked together. A Washington correspondent writes that Grosvenor broke with his fast and bosom friend Wallace because Grosvenor gave Wallace permission to reprint an article about the South Sea island where they grow potted palm seeds and everyone shares in the proceeds fairly and equally, according to the time worked. In the *Geographic,* this part was played down, only briefly mentioned, but in the *Digest* it was played up. Thus the *Reader's Digest* made the *Geographic* appear to be a follower of the principle of cooperative industry and fair division of the product of a worker's daily toil. . . .

Grosvenor married the daughter of Alexander Graham Bell of telephone fame—and many millions. Like DeWitt Wallace, Dr. Grosvenor is interested in money. Grosvenor is so upper-class conscious that when one of his writers sent him a piece which was mostly a travelogue on Nova Scotia, but which included a favorable mention of the great Nova Scotian cooperatives, he was fired. Grosvenor is heir to the Bell fortune, has a large investment in American Tel & Tel, and is scared to death about possible public ownership of public utilities. . . . [12]

PART THREE

15. WORLD WAR, COLD WAR

The [National Geographic Society's] maps are to be found at the front, in the air, in our embassies and consulates, in business and newspaper offices, in schools. As a whole, they constitute the most complete atlas and gazetteer ever compiled. . . .

New York Times, 1945

Despite the National Geographic Society's earlier pro-fascist sympathies, when the war actually began in the fall of 1939, Grosvenor had no doubts about which side he and the National Geographic Society were on. But then, Britain was under attack. When the Japanese attacked the American naval fleet at Pearl Harbor, Hawaii, on December 7, 1941, the Society threw itself wholeheartedly into what many Americans had up until that time called "Europe's war."

As during World War I, Grosvenor was ready to have the Society help in the war effort against all the enemies of the United States in any way it could. The American armed forces needed the help; the United States was woefully ill prepared for a growing global war. The Society, with its storerooms full of maps and photographs, had much to offer to the nation's war machine. Despite Grosvenor's prewar antipathy toward Franklin Delano Roosevelt and the President's "liberal" policies, political concerns were secondary to the welfare of the nation when it was at war—as they were for many who had opposed Roosevelt and his New Deal.

Two weeks after the Pearl Harbor bombing, an aide to President

Roosevelt visited Grosvenor at the Society's downtown Washington headquarters, in search of a map that included a small town located in the vicinity of Singapore, in Malaysia, which was at that time under attack by invading Japanese forces. The aide explained to Grosvenor that he had come at the request of the President, who liked to spot on a map the location of places that were in the war news. Grosvenor later wrote that the President had been unable to find one headline-making little town on charts available in the White House.

So that afternoon, he said, he sent President Roosevelt a special cabinet containing National Geographic Society maps mounted on rollers. Grosvenor was later informed that within an hour of its arrival at the White House, the cabinet had been mounted directly behind the President's study chair so that it was within easy reach.

The President was hardly the only government client for the Society's maps. The U.S. armed forces were in a very low state of readiness and had an entirely inadequate supply of maps and photographs of the world. So the military turned to a logical source and neighbor for assistance: the National Geographic Society. And long before Pearl Harbor, according to Grosvenor, army and navy officers were given access to the Society's huge collection of photographs of the entire world. These pictures, which included roads, public works, topography, railroad networks, manufacturing plants, and the like, had been taken for the *National Geographic*; now they became a gold mine for the intelligence sections of the American military. Thirty-five thousand prints of photographs selected by government experts from the National Geographic Society collections were reproduced in the Society's photographic laboratory.

The U.S. armed services also drew heavily on the Society's collection of fifty-three thousand maps of every part of the globe, many of which were large-scale charts of strategic cities, harbors, railroads, airplane routes, and even caravan trails, Grosvenor recalled. Grosvenor opened the Society's cartographic library and files to the navy's Hydrographic Office, the army's Map Service, and the U.S. Coast and Geodetic Survey, which was preparing maps for the air force.

Very quickly, events showed that World War II, like World War I, would be great for the National Geographic Society's business. Following World War I, America had slowly sunk back into a generally isolationist point of view. Protected from Europe's troubles by the Atlantic Ocean, most Americans had again turned their concerns inward after the troops returned home victorious, oblivious to the glowing embers that would reignite the world only a few years later. Now, however, the actual outbreak of fighting rekindled the kind of curiosity that had swept the nation when the first war had begun. Once the United States actually entered the battle, Europe was America's primary topic of interest once again. To meet that interest, every issue of the *National Geographic Magazine* contained at least one major article on the war.

As it had during World War I, Grosvenor—no doubt remembering his great successes—directed the Society to publish for its readers as soon as possible a new map for every new battle zone of the spreading war. When Hitler seized Austria in March 1938, the Society gave its readers a map of Europe and the Mediterranean. Soon after the Nazis invaded Poland in September 1939, Society members received a new map of Central Europe and the Mediterranean. In September 1941, as Grosvenor tried to put his readers into front-row viewing stands to observe the unfolding war—a task now carried out with more efficiency and immediacy by television—the *National Geographic* issued a map of the Atlantic Ocean, spanning all the areas of German U-boat activity. In July 1942, members received a map encompassing the war zones of Europe, Africa, and western Asia. The Society's 1944 map of Japan was actually created at the suggestion of the army, which was searching for a more comprehensive map than any it had. Officials of the Army Air Forces were so impressed with this new map of Japan that they immediately borrowed the original drawings and made five thousand 50-by-65-inch enlargements for the planning of the air offensive against the Japanese.

During one of his many wartime visits to the White House, British Prime Minister Winston Churchill saw Roosevelt's elegant map cabinet, presented to him by Grosvenor, and was quite taken with it. Roosevelt then asked Grosvenor to send one to Churchill, which Grosvenor readily agreed to do. Interestingly, after the war, Grosvenor asked Churchill to return the cabinet, because of its association with the great English leader and with Roosevelt, but Churchill refused. In his graceful reply, Churchill told Grosvenor that while he appreciated the Society's desire to preserve the cabinet, he felt that since it had been a gift from his devoted friend Roosevelt, he wished to keep it with his family possessions. Roosevelt's map cabinet had been moved to the family estate in Hyde Park, New York, after the President's death.

Another time, Grosvenor received an urgent request from Dwight David Eisenhower, who was then in northern Africa, asking, without explanation, that the Society immediately send to him copies of the two-volume *Book of Birds* that Grosvenor had coedited with Dr. Alexander Wetmore, a noted ornithologist and Society trustee, in 1939.

Throughout the war, Grosvenor said in his 1957 history of his tenure, he remained curious about the incident. Years later, when Eisenhower was in Washington, Grosvenor met with the future President, who explained that he liked to be on a first-name basis with all of the Allied military leaders under his command, but had been unable to penetrate the reserve of Gen. Sir Alan F. Brooke, chief of the British Imperial General Staff, who was later named Field Marshal Lord Alanbrooke.

During a conversation he had with Brooke, Eisenhower explained to Grosvenor, Brooke had confided to him that he had been unable to locate a copy of the *Book of Birds*. Eisenhower told Grosvenor that from the moment he presented Brooke with the volumes Grosvenor had supplied, they were on a first-name basis.

The U.S. government's appetite for the Society's maps continued unabated throughout the war. Nine times in one early war year the Society put back on the presses its large ten-color wall map of Europe that had first appeared in the *National Geographic*, so great was the demand from the army, navy, and federal agencies. In addition to the map of Japan that the Army Air Forces had put to work, the Army Corps of Engineers used the Society's "Map of Germany and Its Approaches" to make thousands of enlargements, copies of which were later posted at all major road intersections in

Germany to act as reliable guides for the American ground forces as they advanced toward Berlin. A traditional wartime tactic for a retreating army was to remove all roadside directional signs to confuse the invaders.

In a letter to Grosvenor after the war, Lt. Gen. Eugene Reybold, who directed the army's mapmakers, said, "Our dependence upon the National Geographic Society for the type of map it issues has, in fact, led us to consider the Society an integral part of our military mapping establishment."

For the navy, the Society published ten thousand copies of a book on the South Pacific. It also extended map-copying courtesies to various Allied governments and gave excess copies of old magazines to the armed services for distribution at Allied military facilities around the world.

After the war, Grosvenor received a letter from Fleet Adm. Chester W. Nimitz revealing a heretofore unknown service that the Society had performed in 1942. The letter, Grosvenor told his readers, explained how the Society's map of the Pacific Ocean enabled Nimitz's B-17, which was lost over the Coral Sea in a driving rain, to reach Henderson Field on Guadalcanal, on a flight from Espíritu Santo in September 1942. Studying the big map's Solomon Islands inset, Grosvenor related, the commander-in-chief of the Pacific Fleet and his ten American and New Zealand aides were able to identify the shoreline of San Cristobal Island and thus put the plane back on course.

In late 1942, Grosvenor received a letter from a man who lived in Yorkshire, England, respectfully requesting that he be sent a copy of the November 1942 issue of the National Geographic. He reported that the ship carrying that issue across the Atlantic had sunk with all its cargo. The man in Yorkshire explained that he needed the November number before he could have the latest six-issue volume bound. Grosvenor sent the man a copy and then ordered the November issue put back on the presses. Another thirty-five thousand copies were printed and shipped to subscribers in England.

Grosvenor was very proud that the Society's maps also found many other wartime uses. Among them, the American Red Cross used Society-issued maps to locate Japanese prisoner-of-war camps, and the Canadian Postal Corps used them to expedite the delivery of letters to troops stationed overseas. Also, Grosvenor recounted several years after the war, many Filipino and Chinese members of the Society in Manila had kept their files of *National Geographic* maps throughout the Japanese occupation, even though being found with one such map would have meant severe punishment or even death. Dog-eared copies which survived the occupation are prized mementos in many homes in the Philippines today, he said.

In early 1944, America's three largest news-gathering organizations, the Associated Press, United Press, and the International News Service (which would later be merged with United to form United Press International), were looking for a way to reduce the confusion caused by the lack of uniformity on spellings and usage of foreign place-names, especially in nations that use other alphabets, such as in the Middle East, which required the adoption of phonetic spellings in English. The three organizations agreed in April 1944 to adopt the spellings followed by the Society, a practice still generally followed by many news organizations, including the two remaining American wire services and the *Washington Post.*

A few months later, on January 15, 1945, in a compliment Grosvenor was quite proud of and one that he often repeated, the *New York Times* referred to the Society's mapmaking division as

"probably the most ambitious cartographical undertaking on record. . . . The maps are to be found at the front, in the air, in our embassies and consulates, in business and newspaper offices, in schools. As a whole, they constitute the most complete atlas and gazetteer ever compiled—no mean achievement at a time like this. . . . The Society deserves thanks for having undertaken voluntarily an important task in education. Its maps not only enable us to follow the war's progress, but convince us, as never before, that China, Australia and Europe are our next-door neighbors."

After the war was won, the Society had a new task—to remap the world to correspond to the new realities, charting the demise of the Axis empire, the birth of the East-West Cold War, and the emergence of the noncolonial Third World.

*   *   *

When the smoke had settled and relative peace had returned to the world, it became even clearer that once again war had been good to the National Geographic Society. Its membership, one million in 1935 and 1.1 million by America's entry into the war in 1941, increased to 1.6 million by 1947, when most of the members of the armed forces had returned to civilian life. As a result, another addition was constructed at the Society's downtown Washington headquarters complex, and its employee force rose to close to nine hundred.

During the war years, Grosvenor himself seemed to have acquired a new maturity, just as the United States itself went from being the new world power on the block to the dominant leader of what was now called the "free world." His administration of the Society reflected that maturation. The *National Geographic Magazine* was no longer just a wish book of never-to-be-fulfilled fantasies for the great American middle class; it was one of the best windows on America's large new oyster: the world.

Now that the Great Depression was finally over—thanks in large part to the production requirements of the war—the American economy rapidly expanded, creating and responding to new markets and new commercial needs. So did the National Geographic Society. Up until this time, the *National Geographic Magazine* was the only real major retail product put out by the Society. Now, however, Grosvenor, better aware of the Society's strengths and its potential as a marketing company, was beginning slowly to explore new avenues for the organization, as well as to strengthen its hold on its current membership.

The magazine was printed on one of the highest-quality papers used in the publishing industry, a coated stock that had been supplied to the Society since 1913 by the Champion-International Company in Lawrence, Massachusetts, a firm that traced its roots to 1846. Soon after World War II ended, the Society acquired full ownership of the paper firm. The Society began publishing an oc-casional book on a geography-related topic, but it was at first a minor, tentative effort, and the books were available for sale only at the Society's headquarters or through the mail. The Society also sold bound copies of its six-issue volumes, and by the 1940s, more than 200,000 members a year were purchasing them and putting them on their bookshelves.

While schools were in session, the Society was now publishing a weekly bulletin for teachers, covering geography-related topics and suggested areas of instruction. But it charged only 25 cents a year for the service and ran it more for the goodwill and the potential customers it generated than for the added revenue; the effort was fundamentally a further extension of Grosvenor's belief in, and penchant for, positive publicity and salesmanship.

It was this same desire for publicity and goodwill that had led Grosvenor to establish a daily news bulletin for newspapers during World War I. The bulletin was created, Grosvenor said, because of the large number of questions that kept coming into the Society's headquarters from individuals and from newspapers. The bulletins, between five hundred and a thousand words long, were sent with-out charge to 550 newspapers during World War I. When the armi-stice was signed, according to Grosvenor, the Society's officers felt that the bulletins probably would not have any special interest to newspaper readers. But just to make sure, a questionnaire was sent to the newspaper editors, and the Society was surprised to learn that practically without exception, they asked to have the service continued. During World War II, Grosvenor proudly reported, the Society's daily bulletins were sometimes published by as many as two hundred newspapers.

Now, as the Society's business acumen improved, these bulletins were used to perform several tasks for the Society simultaneously. First, each helped establish the Society as a geographical authority in the eyes of the many newspaper readers, since each issue promi-nently mentioned the Society as the source of the material. The bulletins also provided the newspapers with a convenient expert to go to with questions and to rely on for information. They also created a link to the various newspapers and newsmen with the Society, which was very helpful in sustaining the Society's aura as a benevolent, helpful educational institution.

The bulletins, which were first issued on a regular basis in 1919, eventually led to the creation of the Society's News Service Division, formalizing the links established by the bulletins. In just a few years, the news service was sending out two Society bulletins a week to 2,250 newspapers, magazines, and broadcasting stations free of charge. Grosvenor was delighted by the number of newspaper editors who were willing to publish National Geographic Society news releases. But one of his most cherished compliments was from the *New York Times*, which reported, "It is highly reassuring, when such place names as Staryi Oskol and Zivotin crop up in the communiqués to be able to ask somebody what and where they are—and get the right answers. The National Geographic Society hasn't failed us—yet."[1]

Grosvenor also found still another use for a map cabinet of the type that he had given President Roosevelt and Prime Minister Churchill. When the *Washington Post* moved into new headquarters soon after the end of the war, Grosvenor supplied a cabinet for the new newsroom. In a story celebrating the presentation, the newspaper reported glowingly that the gift was "placed within arm's length of the paper's news editors."[2]

In the years after World War II, a period of unprecedented newspaper consolidation began in the United States, which was one of the causes of a drastic reduction in the number of foreign news bureaus that were maintained by U.S. newspapers. As fewer sources of foreign news were available, the National Geographic Society's influence on the press grew proportionally and the use of the Society-produced "news" increased greatly.

Another indication of Grosvenor's new understanding of the Society as a marketing organization was his ordering in 1941 of an analysis of its readers in order to impress potential advertisers with the reach of the *National Geographic Magazine*, and to help better understand for just whom he was running the magazine. When readers were asked how heads of families earned their livings, the Society found they belonged to 529 different categories, among them 53,514 physicians and surgeons, 39,543 housewives, 36,816 farmers, 32,518 clerks, and 27,843 clergymen. There were also 15,084 bankers, 13,710 executives, and 11,715 dental surgeons. And there were also 3 tropical-fish raisers, 9 philanthropists, 15 poets, 33 roll-turners, 114 members of royalty, 159 senators and former senators, and 228 other assorted politicians.

* * *

During the war, Geoffrey T. Hellman in *The New Yorker* described Grosvenor as "a kindly, mild-mannered, purposeful, poker-faced, peripatetic man . . . with the sprightly air of an inquiring grasshopper, with a clear, pink complexion and with the mixture of business sagacity, intellectual curiosity, regard for tradition and tolerance of temperate innovation that is sometimes found in the president of a fairly wealthy college."[3]

Despite the fact that Grosvenor was now around the age that most men retire, he was having an even stronger personal influence upon the Society, as if the organization was finally broken in, like a good leather chair, and was beginning to take on the shape of his body. During these years, the Society reinforced some of Grosvenor's trademarks, such as continually finding good news to report and voluptuous females to pose half-naked in photographs despite the incalculable death and destruction that continued throughout the world. At the same time, the Society and the *National Geographic* adopted another Grosvenor pastime: a strong fondness for numbers and statistics, which the Society quickly made into an art form.

For instance, when writing about the Society itself, Grosvenor informed readers that just one month's issue in 1936, when membership was slightly more than one million, "would form a pile more than five miles high, rivaling Mount Everest; 50 piles each as tall as the Washington Monument. The ink alone used in printing each issue weighs 5¼ tons—as much as 70 men could carry."

In the early days of the Society, it had been customary to print the names and addresses of the members. "To do so today in small type allowing 50 names to a page would require 20,000 pages,"

Grosvenor continued, "filling solidly more than 12 years of *Geographics*, without another word or a single picture." [4]

And the magazine's contributors were encouraged to do likewise with statistics, details, and comparisons, which is how we learn that the Louvre has forty-five acres of masterpieces and that the male Australian lyrebird has sixteen tail feathers, two lyrate, two fine and whiplike, and twelve filamentary, and that the female carries the family's droppings and dumps them in nearby streams, presumably to destroy the scent.

"In one case," *Esquire* reported, "one editor distinctly told a writer who handed in some (he thought) sprightly copy: 'What do you say we brighten this up with a few statistics?'" [5]

Statistics used this way did bring the strangeness of the wide world into homely terms average Americans could understand and appreciate. To announce that the Louvre has forty-five acres of art, however, is to quantify that phenomenon rather than qualify it—and stands as a good example of the way the National Geographic Society appealed primarily to culturally middlebrow Americans with a growing, but uninformed, taste for the world's wonders and complications.

*   *   *

As the Society prospered, it developed operating procedures that were quite different than those that the Chief had been able to use in the early days. Lack of material for an issue had led to Grosvenor's important decision to publish the pictures of Tibet in 1905 that marked the most significant publishing decision ever made by Grosvenor and the *National Geographic*, but that was a situation never again to occur at the Society. By the mid-1940s, the Chief had some 350,000 unpublished photographs in the Society library, along with several thousand unused manuscripts. He once estimated that if he chose only to run the material he already had on hand, he could put out the *National Geographic* for fifteen years.

This bountiful store affected the entire operation. No longer was a printer's deadline, such as the one faced by the Chief in 1905, something to be feared. Now the Society was the master of time. With its warehouse of backed-up material and its increasingly high production standards, lead times between events and publication lengthened. In disseminating the finds of the missions it had sponsored, the *Geographic*'s publication schedule took precedence over the public's need to know.

But even in his lean years, Grosvenor never let a need for timeliness interfere with his editorial decisions. In 1903, Joseph C. Grew wrote an article entitled "Waimangu and the Hot-Spring Country of New Zealand: The World's Greatest Geyser Is One of Many Nature Wonders in a Land of Inferno and Vernal Paradise." When it was written, the author was one year out of Harvard and traveling the world. At the time, the Waimangu geyser was very active, providing breathtaking displays to visitors. Grosvenor bought the manuscript and put it in a drawer for later use. When next he pulled it out, however, he was advised by staff members that Waimangu had cooled off and was no longer performing the spectacular feats described in Grew's article.

But Grew was hardly a bashful man. By 1906, he was third secretary of the U.S. embassy in Mexico City, and he wrote Grosvenor asking when the article would be published. He received no specific commitment from Grosvenor. So, for the next twenty years, Grew continued to send Grosvenor letters every so often, postmarked from Grew's latest diplomatic assignment, asking when the piece would run. In 1925, Grew, now undersecretary of state, sent Grosvenor a harsher note.

Finally, Grosvenor spied an Associated Press dispatch from New Zealand that reported that Waimangu had regained much of its former strength and was once more performing its geyserly duties. Relieved, Grosvenor set Grew's article in type and ran it in the August 1925 issue, just as Grew had written it in 1903, with the simple addition of this editor's note: "Members of the American Fleet, now enjoying the sights of Australia and New Zealand, will upon their return to the United States in September, have wonderful stories to tell of the antipodes. They are especially fortunate in that Waimangu (Black Water), the world's greatest geyser, for many years quiescent, has resumed activity, although not on the magnificent scale observed by the author." Gilbert M. Grosvenor could turn even unruly natural phenomena to his advantage.

*　　*　　*

Owing to Grosvenor's efforts to make the *National Geographic* and the Society a part of the war effort and a tool that could explain graphically what was going on in the battle theaters around the world, the Society had been able not only to weather the war years in healthy condition, but to grow and prosper. But even that war-time growth paled compared with the boom years in the United States that followed World War II. In that period, in what became Gilbert H. Grosvenor's golden age at the helm of the Society, by 1954, some sixty-six years into its existence, Society membership was up to 2,150,000, and advertising pages were fattening each issue of its magazine. The man who had piloted the organization for more than fifty-five years, and many of them almost single-handedly, Gilbert H. Grosvenor, had turned seventy-eight and was still going strong. While he had for some time been cutting down his involvement in the day-to-day workings of the Society, he was still the undisputed ruler of the organization, and he still made every important decision.

By the time the Chief began even to consider turning the reigns of the National Geographic Society over to someone else, the Society had become a prestigious enough institution to inspire an interesting tempest-in-a-teapot article in one of America's most sophisticated publications, *The New Yorker*. Geoffrey T. Hellman, who had written the earlier series on Grosvenor and the Society in 1943, had pointed out in those articles, among other things, that Grosvenor had converted a member's bequest to present life memberships in the organization—which then cost $100—to poor but otherwise worthy persons into a fund with which to present such awards to rich and famous persons.

But in the September, 27, 1952, issue of *The New Yorker*, Hellman wrote of "How to Get a Rather Bad Case of Paranoia." He recalled the 1947 letter from Grosvenor reporting that four other members of the Society hierarchy were "present and most enthusiastic at my suggestion that we tie you thus [by making Hellman a life member] permanently to the National Geographic Society."

"I was pleased," Hellman now wrote. "My services in diffusing geographic knowledge had consisted of writing a number of articles on ornithologists, archeologists and explorers, but I had never dreamed that these would produce a compliment more serious than an editor's fleeting encomium." Hellman went on to describe the Smith Life Memberships, this time omitting the explanation that they were established for "worthy and competent persons . . . not able to pay" for them.

"Well," he continued, "Nemesis has overtaken me. Last week, I received from the Society, my Society, a letter that read, in part: 'I have the honor of advising you that you have been nominated for membership in the National Geographic Society. . . . With membership now at an all-time high, The Society can serve only a limited number of new members in 1952. . . . To avail yourself of your friend's nomination, please sign the enclosed application and return it PROMPTLY with your annual dues of $5. . . .'

" . . . Have I received a dishonorable discharge . . . ?" he wondered. "I have never felt so lonely in my life. I keep wondering if I have done anything wrong. . . ."

While at least partially tongue-in-cheek, Hellman's "Bad Case of Paranoia" was testament to Grosvenor's life work, his success in converting the National Geographic Society into a pillar of American life, and one as ubiquitous and as American as Coca-Cola and McDonald's.

16. GROSVENOR II

> *When I was a youngster . . . [my father]*
> *never told me that he wanted me to join*
> *the Geographic staff. But he whetted my*
> *interest in geography by taking me all over*
> *the world. He bought me a little Eastman*
> *Kodak, and we would have competitions*
> *in photography. . . .*
>
> Melville Bell Grosvenor, 1957

Giving up sole control of "his" National Geographic Society was a very difficult task for the aging Chief. While he had brought his son and heir apparent, Melville Bell Grosvenor, into the organization in 1924, after Melville had graduated from the U.S. Naval Academy, the Chief had retained firm control of the Society's activities for more than fifty years, as president of the Society and editor of *National Geographic Magazine.*

But finally in May 1954, Gilbert H. Grosvenor "retired" to the post of chairman of the Society's board, a job created for him, at the age of seventy-eight. He retired with accolades, fanfare, and comment from many quarters, for the National Geographic Society was now an important American institution, known to all, and far removed from the obscure, moribund club it had been at the start of Grosvenor's reign in 1899. "Dr. Grosvenor once said that he would take his readers around the world, and that he would take them first class," according to *Scribner's Magazine.* "He has done it and, most remarkable of all, he has done it without letting his fireside travelers have a drink, a smoke or a bicarbonate of soda."[1]

And even when Grosvenor relinquished the titles of president and editor, he did so only halfheartedly. At his direction, the responsibility for running the daily operations of the Society was turned over not to his son, who was already fifty-two, but to the Chief's longtime assistant, surrogate, and alter ego, John Oliver LaGorce. LaGorce would run the Society Gilbert Grosvenor's way, and heed Gilbert Grosvenor's suggestions. At the same time, Melville Bell Grosvenor was named a vice-president of the Society and associate editor of the *National Geographic*. LaGorce served as caretaker for the elder Grosvenor from May 1954 until January 1957, when the Chief was apparently finally convinced that Melville was ready to take over the ship, or perhaps more accurately, that the Chief was finally ready to relinquish actual control.

*   *   *

On January 8, 1957, at the age of fifty-five, Melville Bell Grosvenor, who had been the heir apparent at the National Geographic Society for thirty-three years, was finally the boss; LaGorce stepped aside, and Melville, known around the Society as MBG, became the magazine's editor. LaGorce, who retired when he relinquished control, was named vice-chairman of the Society's board of directors, where he was once again the Chief's number two.

By the time he took over, Melville Bell Grosvenor was already a white-haired, round-faced man deep into middle age. Having served so long in the shadow of his father made Melville much more an implementer and a refiner than an innovator. He was far less the creative dreamer than his grandfather, Alexander Graham Bell, who had sketched the outlines of the Society in broad theoretical strokes for the Chief to fill in, and far less the driven aide following the general orders from the president to win, no matter what the cost, as his father had been.

In his speech to the trustees following his formal selection, Melville spoke glowingly of how his father and grandfather had prepared him over the years to take over the Society. In his talk, the second Grosvenor let the trustees in on a secret. "This is not the first time I have been editor of a magazine." Under Alexander Graham Bell's tutelage, he revealed, "I founded and was the editor of the *Wildacres Weekly* [Wild Acres was the name of the Grosvenor family estate in Bethesda, Maryland], a little paper patterned after the *Geographic*. I had a typewriter, and I wrote the stories. Some related my adventures on a raft; others described physics experiments which I conducted under Dr. Bell's wise supervision. . . .

"Then, of course," he told the board, "there is my father, Dr. Gilbert Grosvenor, whom you know as a great editor and a great president. But he is also a great father—indeed, a brilliant one. When I was a youngster," Melville explained, "he never told me that he wanted me to join the Geographic staff. But he whetted my interest in geography by taking me all over the world. He bought me a little Eastman Kodak, and we would have competitions in photography, just between the two of us. . . .

"He would also drill me in spelling and synonyms. While I was in the Naval Academy, and later, I had to write every week a 250-word composition. If I failed to write it, I didn't get my allowance, and the story had to be on time. He didn't care what I wrote about. . . ."[2]

These comments, from a fifty-five-year-old man, shed some light on the relationship between the two Grosvenors and give an idea of the iron hand with which the Chief must have ruled the domestic roost, and how Melville could have remained in his father's professional shadow for thirty-three years.

Gilbert H. Grosvenor's "Seven Principles" remained as the guiding light in the *National Geographic Magazine* under Melville, and the articles retained their folksy informality. Photographs were still the magazine's primary emphasis, and the membership aspects of the Society, which Bell had devised and the Chief had strengthened, were reinforced. Indeed, in the middle of the second Grosvenor's reign, one writer found, "If the magazine has changed through the years, the changes have been of the head and not the heart. War, pestilence, starvation, revolution and natural disasters have not shaken its conviction that the world is a beautiful place. Buttressed by this faith, even old discoveries can be rediscovered with fresh bloom."[3]

*   *   *

If Melville Bell Grosvenor made his personal mark anywhere in the Society, it was in its mapmaking division. Grosvenor "hated blank spaces on any map," according to one Society cartographer. "Antarctica really bugged him—no cities, no roads. He insisted on more map notes, more information."[4]

At the time Melville began his administration, the Society's mapmakers had redrawn the world's boundaries in the wake of World War II—new nations were carved from old, European colonies were now independent, former Axis territories were realigned and reassigned by the victorious Allies. Now the Society's cartographers were at work recording the changes inspired by events during peacetime, which ranged from newly discovered geographic features worthy of inclusion on maps to more accurate placement of others as a result of technological advances.

Earlier, the Chief had explained some of these discoveries and advances—ranging from iron mountains discovered in Utah and in Labrador, to a 1,068-mile pipeline across a desert in the Middle East to fill tankers near ancient Sidon on the Mediterranean coast of Lebanon, to engineers tunneling a mountain, reversing the course of a raging British Columbia River, and creating the enormous hydroelectric aluminum-processing center of Kitimat. Each of these discoveries and man-made projects required the addition of new place-names and symbols on the Society's maps.

The death in 1953 of Soviet Premier Joseph Stalin sent the Society's cartographers poring over some ten drawers full of Soviet maps, Grosvenor explained. The cartographers located more than a hundred places and features that were named for the Soviet leader, and noted on the Society's new maps that they may all be destined for change. And, of course, they were.

Then, as always, there remained plenty of military battles to spotlight, which often resulted in new names or boundaries to draw. While not on the scale of the world wars, they too attracted reader interest and, eventually, changed the lines of the globe. National Geographic Society members received their color maps of Korea in June 1950, the month the North Koreans invaded the south. Near the end of 1956, a map of the "Land of the Bible Today," showing Israel and its Arab neighbors, was sent to readers as the Suez Canal crisis—involving Israel, Egypt, England, and France—was at its peak. And there were, of course, countless coups and brush wars that made only the inside pages of the *New York Times,* but had to be reflected on the Society's latest maps.

And what was good for America was good for the National Geographic Society. Melville Bell Grosvenor's National Geographic Society benefited greatly by the most significant result of the World War II for America—the assumption of the mantle of leader of the free world, and the ready acceptance of that role by her people. At the same time, a revolution in mobility was radically changing the nation; everyone was driving everywhere. Now, Americans craved more practical information about the United States, and places that they were likely to visit. The airplane, stalwart servant of the military during the war, was beginning to play a major role in commercial travel, turning what had been a four- or five-day ocean journey to Europe into a voyage measured in hours. And Melville Bell Grosvenor was going to give his readers every fact about every spot on the globe that they wanted, foreign and domestic.

The Society's entire foreign staff had consisted only of two writer-photographers before World War II; the organization had relied on diplomats, vacationing educators, and businessmen for most of its stories from around the world. But as a result of America's new preoccupation with the rest of the world, and as the Society prospered from its ever-increasing popularity, Melville Grosvenor directed that more and more employees be added around the globe. Ten years into his administration, the Society employed some fifty full-time writers and fifteen full-time photographers to cover the non-American part of the earth for the *National Geographic,* the news service, and the school bulletin.

On the domestic front, Melville Bell Grosvenor's *National Geographic* waxed poetic on American national parks and natural treasures, on its quaint regions and its booming cities, forever tempting Americans to travel over their new interstate highway system, which, under President Eisenhower, was beginning to connect everyplace with everywhere. For example, in successive issues in 1955, the *National Geographic* offered its readers "Cruising Florida's Western Waterway," "Cities Like Worcester [Massachusetts] Make America," "Ohio Makes Its Own Prosperity," "Grand Canyon: Nature's Story of Creation," and a special supplement on New England, including a large map.

Melville Bell Grosvenor was as much a man of his age as his father had been of his own. America was getting used to being the leader of the Western world, settling into its new role with a measure of righteous comfort, and adopting its practices and attitudes accordingly. The tone of the *National Geographic Magazine* reflected those new attitudes. Melville Bell Grosvenor was reshaping the Society's own sails for the new winds it would be encountering as a major force in world publishing.

The new Grosvenor sharpened the tone that his father had adopted before World War II; the magazine's longtime strongly nationalistic, anticommunist viewpoint fit in well with the world's new confrontation, the "Cold War." However, owing to the "Seven Principles" and its good-news-only presentation, the only way that Grosvenor and the Society could really be anti anything was to simply ignore its existence, a tactic it was certainly prepared to use.

Thus, the Soviet Union failed to make the pages of the *National Geographic* from the end of World War II until 1959. When that breakthrough article finally appeared, Grosvenor included a full-page preface that began, "No matter how you and I may feel about the Soviet Union—about the policies and practices of its political leaders, about their often avowed determination to destroy or subvert the United States of America and all free nations, about the whole doctrine of Communism with its denial of religion and even of God—the fact remains that the Union of Soviet Socialist Republics covers one-sixth of the world's land surface and contains more than 200 million people."[5]

The article was primarily a travelogue, and barely mentioned the Soviet Union's political system. Rather, it used ethnocentric stereotypes to gently ridicule the Soviets, going to great lengths to point out the lack of consumer goods in Russia and the major role women played in jobs Americans at the time viewed as male-only.

And, as if to make sure that no one mistook the Society's loyalties, the cover story of the issue was "Good-will Ambassadors of the U.S. Navy Win Friends in the Far East," an in-depth look at the navy's carrier-based airplane fleet and submarine-based missiles.

From the end of World War II, Grosvenor determined the magazine's coverage of Eastern European countries by the ups and downs of each nation's relationship with the Soviet Union. After Tito broke Yugoslavia out of the Soviet orbit in 1948, the Chief saw to it that the country was featured in the *National Geographic* in 1951. Melville Grosvenor saw to it that Poland made the magazine in 1958, in the aftermath of an anti-Soviet uprising. In the late 1960s, after Romania showed signs of increasing independence from Russia, the *Geographic* carried an article on that nation. But hardline satellites were ignored for many years; Hungary failed to make the magazine even after its abortive anti-Soviet revolt in 1956 and had to wait another ten years for "Hungary: Down the Danube by Canoe."

Reported one writer, no doubt only half-jokingly, "Czechoslovakia had the bad luck to become a *National Geographic* subject in February, 1968. Conceivably, the Kremlin realized at that point just how mutinous the Czechs had become and sent its troops in a few months later."[6]

* * *

Melville Bell Grosvenor spent much of his efforts in solidifying the Society's empire. First, he moved to refine and institutionalize the organization as it had been established by the Chief, and then he moved to expand it to a scale that even his father had probably not believed possible.

By the early 1960s, the *National Geographic Magazine*'s renewal rate was at 90 percent, an unheard-of percentage in the commercial publishing industry, especially for a publication that offered no special rates or premiums. And on top of this renewal rate, Melville Grosvenor instituted one of the most amazing policies in the publishing business, and one that is the envy of all the Society's competitors: the "Summer Renewal Program." Under this plan, members receive one mailing in the summer from the Society asking them to immediately renew their memberships in order to save the Society bookkeeping expenses and effort, even though all memberships actually expire at the end of the calendar year.

While other magazines spend months inundating their subscribers with renewal notices, hoping to keep 60 or 70 percent of them for another year, by the early 1960s, half of the Society's members were gladly paying their fees a half year in advance, and another 40 percent were resubscribing at the usual time. In addition to keeping their readers, the Society was reaping a bonanza of interest on the money its readers were sending it during the Summer Renewal Program. In 1962, with a membership of three million, this practice alone netted the Society $100,000 in interest on the $10 million its readers voluntarily paid in advance.

Under the new Grosvenor, the Society retained its full-scale and ongoing campaign of self-promotion—and its good luck. The Society's three-millionth member was enrolled on December 8, 1961; in order to pick out that milestone membership, the Society's already computerized logs were slowed. While officials of most publications might have fretted, wondering what sort of crackpot would win the award, sorely testing their public relations department, the National Geographic Society had nothing to fear. As the Society's computers were slowed to allow the selection of the three-millionth member, the fates again protected the organization. Member number three million was a schoolteacher from Nebraska, whose students had banded together to pay her dues. As a reward, she was brought to Washington for a celebration, written up in the *National Geographic*, and given the classic Society present for all special occasions: a life membership.

Under the Chief, the *National Geographic* had become the only magazine "with promotion tied to the President of the United States," according to a 1938 article in *Scribner's Magazine*, by regularly getting American chief executives to bestow the Society's Gardiner Greene Hubbard gold medals for geographic distinction. In addition, the first Grosvenor had gotten several Presidents and Vice-Presidents to write about their travels for the magazine.

But Melville Bell Grosvenor quickly outdistanced his father in this category as well. In addition to getting Presidents to award medals, he got Vice-President Richard M. Nixon to describe his trip to the Soviet Union and his famous July 1959 kitchen confrontation with then Soviet Premier Nikita S. Khrushchev in the pages of the Society's capitalist standard-bearer, the *National Geographic.*

The article on Nixon's trip was guaranteed a large audience. Nixon was in Moscow to open the American National Exhibition, and while walking through what was said to be a replica of a typical American house, Nixon and Khrushchev became embroiled in a debate over the relative merits of capitalism and communism, and what each held as rewards for its workers. While the dialogue of the discussion seems naive by today's standards, coming as it did when the Cold War was still young, it was newspaper banner-headline news. The July 25, 1959, *New York Times* lead headline stated: "Nixon and Khrushchev Argue in Public as U.S. Exhibit Opens; Accuse Each Other of Threats."

In his article in the December 1959 issue of the *National Geographic,* Nixon told the Society's members that he had told the Russian people "that we do not object if Premier Khrushchev expresses his belief that our grandchildren will live under communism—we only object if he attempts to bring this result about by interfering in our internal affairs. As for us," he continued, "we do not say that his grandchildren will or ought to live under a system of free enterprise. The very essence of our belief is that every nation should have the right to choose for itself, free of all coercion, free of outside force, and with full awareness of all the alternatives, the political, economic, and social system under which it wishes to live. . . ."

The Society under Melville Grosvenor was just as happy to publish the exploits of—and make friends with—Democrats as Republicans. As evidence of the Society's nonpolitical air, coupled with its educational aura, President Lyndon B. Johnson dedicated

197

the Society's major new headquarters building that it opened in downtown Washington on January 18, 1964, and Republican Ronald Reagan presided at the Society's next major dedication two decades later. The $8.5 million architectural monument that LBJ dedicated in 1964 was designed by the noted architect Edward Durell Stone, who was later responsible for the John F. Kennedy Center for the Performing Arts among other major projects.

The Society's new building attracted a lot of favorable media and high-society attention in the 1960s, since it marked a move away from the austere functionalism of most modern government buildings in Washington. For the new building, which was built on Washington's 17th Street, just behind its cluster of other headquarters buildings and all within the same block, the Society paid in cash.

*   *   *

Melville Bell Grosvenor was convinced that there was a ready, untapped market for products related to geography, so he ordered that the Society produce its first atlas and its first globe. These were added to the maps that the Society was already offering for sale and the occasional books it published. The new products were instantly successful with a public ravenous for general geographic knowledge. Eventually, the Society produced a breakthrough globe of the world that has no axis rod to interfere with its workings or to cover up part of the world. In two years, 200,000 of the globes were purchased, sight unseen, through the mails by Society members. Very quickly, the Society became the world's larest purveyor of globes and atlases.

Much of Melville Bell Grosvenor's tenure at the Society's helm was spent streamlining the organization's operating procedures and putting the finishing touches on the quality of its products; he was harvesting the seeds that the Chief had planted.

The paper the Society used to print the magazine was among the finest ever used by a periodical; the manufacturer of its color inks claims the hues will retain their brilliance for two hundred years;

the magazine's thick yellow covers and glued binding testify to its quality. Near the end of the Chief's reign, the Society bought the paper mill; when Melville became head of the Society, he also became chairman of the board of the paper mill, the Champion-International Company. One writer said that when a reader picks up a copy of the National Geographic, he knows immediately that it "is obviously a quality product, built to last, like a horsehair sofa or a Pierce-Arrow. . . ."[7]

Copies of the National Geographic seem never to be thrown away. And the editors obviously expect that they aren't discarded, since features in the magazine commonly send readers scurrying back to articles that appeared years before on the same, or similar, topics. This has made the National Geographic a collector's item, and sets are often advertised in the classified sections of newspapers throughout the country, being offered at high prices. And because readers keep them, at least one member reported an additional, unexpected benefit: In 1963, a woman wrote that since she had started storing the back issues of the National Geographic in her attic, her heating bills had gone down. "Printed on some of the heaviest-coated paper stock used in publishing," reported one writer, "the magazine is not only indestructible, it insulates."[8]

The National Geographic's factual errors were so few—the staff checks every fact and every quote in every story—that the errors that got through have made history with its readers. One press run was stopped to correct the middle initial of a man mentioned in an article. And the most noted error occurred in an article on Dag Hammarskjold, a Swedish diplomat who was then the secretary-general of the United Nations in New York City, in the January 1961 issue. A caption on an accompanying photograph identified the wrong peak as Mount Everest. Some thirteen astonished readers wrote to the editors, leading, two issues later, to one of the few corrections in the National Geographic Magazine in recent history.

Under Melville Grosvenor, his father's "Seven Principles" continued to reign supreme. In a 1962 feature on Burma, "Burma, Gentle Neighbor of India and Red China," the magazine happily delved into the lives of people in this faraway nation. Conspicuously absent from the article was mention of the fact that Burma's leader, Gen. Ne Win, had abolished parliamentary government and had thrown many key government officials into jail.

As the Society's printing and photographic techniques evolved, an old problem was reinforced, that of presenting harsh reality without glamorizing it. Reported *Esquire* during the young Grosvenor's reign, ". . . The *Geographic* has achieved such jewel-like tones in its reproduction of pictures on the rich glossy stock of its pages that even the suppurating sores of the filthiest betel-nut-chewing street urchin are somehow glamorized. It takes the murky smudge of newsprint to convey some forms of ugliness."[9].

The young Grosvenor was so successful at satisfying the Society's ever-growing membership that his accomplishments began to get in his own way. Readership surveys continued to show that upward of 90 percent of the Society's members were so satisfied with the publication that they wouldn't change a thing. This delighted Grosvenor and his staff, but one result of such an approval rating is that it can make change a very painful process.

Melville had decided that it was time to modernize the *National Geographic*'s stodgy cover, which consisted each month of an oak-leaf border surrounding the type that detailed what was inside the issue. Grosvenor wanted to display on them what had become the magazine's trademark: photographs.

"I had grown tired of looking at the same cover," Melville Grosvenor said during an interview with the *Washington Post* after he had retired to the board of directors, just before he was honored for fifty years of service to the Society. "The staff was against my change. My son, Gil, then a very junior member of the staff, opposed it. One day I called them into my office and tossed ten magazines on the floor and asked them to pick out the latest issue. They had to sort around.

"Then I tossed ten sample covers with photos on the floor and said, 'O.K., pick out the Japanese issue.' Gil immediately picked up the one with the geisha girl on the cover. So I said, 'That's what we're going to do.'"[10] Pictures became a regular feature of the *National Geographic*'s covers in 1959.

Grosvenor also decided that the next way to modernize the magazine's cover was to remove the trademark oak leaves that had adorned its borders since the Chief's early days. The decision sparked a flood of angry letters. "I guess they consider it a part of the magazine," MBG said later.[11] To counter this opposition, the staff decided on a plan to slowly and quietly remove the offending foliage leaf by leaf, by covering some of the greenery with a photograph or some type each month. According to one staff member, it became a game the editors played. Sitting around in an editorial meeting while an issue was being planned, an editor would shrug and say, "Hell, let's drop off two or three for September."[12]

But the entire pruning operation was done on *National Geographic* time, that is to say, slowly. By the early 1970s, the foliage had been reduced to a small box at the top of the cover surrounding its logo. It wasn't until the July 1979 issue that only the logo and the yellow border remained as constant fixtures.

Explained William Garrett, the magazine's associate editor at the time of the project's completion: "Actually the cover's been quite fluid, if you want to call molasses fluid. The cover has really been evolving since 1957, when we started putting pictures there. . . . There's no real thought process there. . . . We're just trying to open the book up, make it more readable. There are some people who've said we've killed the golden goose, but reader response has been very good."[13]

The ever-expanding membership's happiness with the status quo also infected the *National Geographic*'s staff. In 1963, of its thirteen hundred full-time employees, twenty-five had been with the Society for more than forty-five years, and 268 had been there for more than twenty-five. "I can't tell you much about the place," one editor reported to *Esquire* at this time, "I've only been here ten years."

Under Melville Bell Grosvenor, some of the Society's discriminatory hiring practices were eased, although more so for women than for blacks. However, even now, few blacks, women, or non-WASP white males are allowed to hold positions of power in the Society. While the top editorial employees weren't as coddled as they had been in the Chief's day, life was still good and the Society was still a refuge from the harsh outside world. Courtesy and decorum still reigned supreme; the fleet of limousines remained; expense accounts abounded; and while the intimate dining rooms had been lost when the Society moved the focus of its operations into the new headquarters building, there was still a private "masthead" restaurant for all employees whose names appeared on the inside cover of the *National Geographic*.

One editor, a former newspaper employee, said when he began working at the Society, "I felt as though I had died and gone to heaven." But another, disturbed by the Society's stodgy, insular, clublike atmosphere, quit, saying, "I just felt I was too young to die."[14]

17. GOLDEN TOUCH

I was told to be downstairs at four-thirty the next day in sailing clothes. It never occurred to anyone that you might not want to go. . . . Sailing with the Grosvenors was forced labor, of course, but in the nicest possible way. . . .

Former employee of the National Geographic Society, 1970

Melville Bell Grosvenor was a much easier man to work for than his father; he was less reserved, much less formal and unapproachable—although he was still unmistakably a member of the Society's royal family. While he worked hard, Melville was much less the workaholic than had been the Chief in his prime years.

Grosvenor II's greatest love outside the National Geographic Society was sailing his forty-six-foot yawl, the *White Mist*. And many times, staff members were shanghaied to round out the necessary crew. A former staff member recalled, "I was told to be downstairs at four-thirty the next day in sailing clothes. It never occurred to anyone that you might not want to go. As it happened, I was working against a deadline, but when I told my boss about the invitation, he decided that we could put off whatever it was for a couple of days. Sailing with the Grosvenors was forced labor, of course, but in the nicest possible way. MBG is really an awfully nice fellow." And as a result of the entire Grosvenor family's enthusiasm for sailing, almost all the top staff at the Society avowed a love of the water, whether they meant it or not. Indeed, one executive reported: "Around here we say, 'Thank God that MBG didn't take up fire walking.'"[1]

Melville B. Grosvenor, who joined the National Geographic Society's staff in 1924, one year after he graduated from the U.S. Naval Academy, was also viewed by some as naive and unworldly. "The 40 sheltered years he has spent on the *Geographic* have given MBG . . . a rather odd and whimsical outlook," reported one magazine. "A senior member of the staff recalled the time that MBG was studying the photographs that accompanied an article on refugees. 'Look at those poor devils,' he said, or words to that effect, 'they're carrying everything they own—their clothing, their keepsakes, their stocks and bonds.'"[2] Another popular quip that made the rounds of the Society's headquarters during Melville Grosvenor's early reign concerned a time that he, his son Gilbert, and the *National Geographic* staff member who wrote the articles that appeared in the magazine under MBG's byline were seen together walking down a hallway, and someone said, "Here they come, father, son and holy ghost."[3]

One positive social aspect of MBG's having had to toil under his father's strict hand for so long was that the apprenticeship removed his desire to be a world-shaking business executive. Melville wanted to succeed, and to improve the Society and its performance, but he also wanted to enjoy himself. One former longtime employee said, "MBG was easily the nicest of them. He was always pleasant, always a gentleman. He worked hard, but never too hard. And he well knew how to enjoy himself."[4]

* * *

Under Melville Bell Grosvenor, his father's art of never being pushed into hurrying a story into print was perfected. While the elder Grosvenor had been known to hold on to some stories for years, the Society now released its discoveries—including those that it knew would make news or history—only when it served the Society best.

One memorable example of the Society's unhurried attitude under Melville involved the discovery of the wreck of the HMS

Bounty, the famous British armed merchant ship that the crew, under the leadership of love-struck Fletcher Christian, had seized from Capt. William Bligh off the coast of Tahiti in April 1789. Following their mutiny, and after sailing the *Bounty* around for a time as they searched for a home, the mutineers burned and scuttled the ship in an attempt to prevent the British from finding the island on which they had chosen to settle. The events on the *Bounty* had inspired a famous court-martial for Bligh—at which he was cleared of the charges—and the story is told in several successful books and at least two major motion pictures.

In 1953, Luis Marden, a forty-four-year-old writer-photographer for the *National Geographic,* was in the Fiji Islands covering Queen Elizabeth's empire tour after her coronation. When he visited the Royal Museum at Suva, the island group's capital, he saw what was described matter-of-factly as the rudder of the HMS *Bounty.* The museum display reported that the rudder had been accidentally dredged from the ocean bottom by a fisherman off Pitcairn Island. Excited by this key to the location of the lost ship, which historians had long sought, he asked the Society's headquarters in Washington for permission to launch an expedition to find the rest of the ship. And, Marden later told the *Washington Post,* "Melville Grosvenor, bless his soul, said, 'Let Marden do it.'"[5]

"His bosses were enthusiastic," reported *Newsweek* magazine on December 9, 1957, "but in the manner of the *Geographic,* unhurried." It was three years before Marden and his crew arrived at Pitcairn Island.

After receiving permission from the governor of Fiji to search for the ship in 1956, Marden spent six weeks scouring the Pacific Ocean bottom—despite large swells, and warnings from the natives that he would die if he dived in that area—on a line between Ship Landing Point and the spot where the fisherman had found the rudder. "There was only one place to anchor [at Pitcairn Island]," Marden said. "I knew the *Bounty* was there. . . ."[6]

Finally, in mid-January 1957, Marden found an oarlock far off the line between the rudder and Ship Landing Point; he then concentrated his search in that area. "Then I came on two long, sandy-brown trenches. I stuck my face within six inches of the bottom. It was covered with white-chalk squiggles, looking like white worms." Marden said he thought they might be sheathing nails, so he shoved a chisel into the sand around them. ". . . A puff of black smoke came up," he said. And he knew that he had the remains of history; from his undersea search experience, he knew that the "smoke" that he was stirring up was actually the carbonized wood of the *Bounty*, which had been on the bottom of the ocean for more than 165 years. [7]

Marden, in many ways the quintessential National Geographic Society writer-photographer-adventurer, now needed to inform his superiors in Washington of his find without alerting the rest of the world, since the Society was, of course, going to save the *Bounty*'s discovery for the pages of the *National Geographic*. Harking back to a famous earlier moment in the Society's history—the 1948 discovery in Alaska of the nest and eggs of a rare bird—Marden, using a ham radio, contacted a man in New England who forwarded a cryptic message to Society headquarters in Washington: "Have found the curlew's nest."

When, months later, he finally made his triumphant return to Washington, he asked how his surreptitious message had been received at the Society. An editor told him, "We got some garbled cable about a bird." But the scoop was intact. Still, fully aware of the historical significance of Marden's find and of the interest it would inspire, it took the Society until the December 1957 issue to reveal that the HMS *Bounty* had been located. When Marden was asked why it had taken so long to publish the article about his discovery, he replied: "The gestation period of one of our stories is even longer than a man's." [8]

In the years since Melville Grosvenor's reign, articles are often planned as much as five years in advance, and are many times in active preparation for two years. During his administration the magazine's editorial committee would meet only monthly to discuss possible articles, many of them proposals for stories that were advanced by local governments or chambers of commerce, lobbyists, and other booster organizations, all seeking to harvest the unfailingly favorable national and international publicity that would result from a feature in the *National Geographic*.

*   *   *

The Society had been publishing books on a sporadic basis for many years, but had never put any emphasis on them. Sales were restricted, since they were available to the public only at the Society's headquarters or by mail order. And, for the most part, the early books had simply been compilations of articles that had appeared in the *National Geographic,* or expansions on articles that had been printed, incorporating material too detailed or lengthy for the magazine.

But in October 1955, after the successful publication of "Indians of the Americas," Melville Bell Grosvenor, while still officially only the second-in-command at the Society under John Oliver LaGorce, made his first major move. He ordered the creation of a formal book service to plan and print a steady flow of publications on topics judged to be of special interest to Society members.

"Book publishing, like the other 'educational arts,' came along almost inevitably as a spin-off of the magazine's immense popularity," wrote *Publishers Weekly,* an industry trade journal. "As membership grew, questions poured in from the public: 'What is the biggest North American animal?' 'How did the ancient Egyptians build the pyramids?'" And Grosvenor said that he founded the book division in order "to answer some of the questions [the staff anticipated would be asked by members] in advance and to make fuller use of the Society's growing store of photographs and information. . . ."[9]

Publishing books on a regular schedule also allowed for better utilization of facilities, such as typesetting and printing, that the Society already had to maintain in order to put out the magazine. The book division's publications were a quick commercial success. By focusing on proven winners—as shown by reader reaction in the flood of mail that poured into Society headquarters every day, calling for articles on such topics as animals, American travel, and the Bible—the book division quickly became an important moneymaker for the Society.

When the Society's book division was in full swing, Melville's extensive political ties paid off again, and established a new direction for the division. Grosvenor's new executive-branch coup involved John F. Kennedy, the man who defeated Richard M. Nixon, whose trip to the Soviet Union had been prominently displayed by the Society just a few years before, in Nixon's attempt at the presidency.

In January 1961, after reading an article about the White House in the National Geographic, soon after she had moved in, First Lady Jacqueline Kennedy established the White House Historical Association to foster interest in the building and aid in its preservation. As part of her efforts, she called Grosvenor and asked for his help in producing an official guide to the presidential residence. Grosvenor, ever eager to help and obviously aware of the commercial, and social, potential of a connection with this new group, made an interest-free loan of $100,000 to the fledgling organization to help cover the production costs of the guide. He also offered the Society's staff to produce the publication, and supplied editorial assistance and quality-control experts at no cost.

When the books arrived, Jacqueline Kennedy turned to J. B. West, the White House's chief usher, and said, "Now, J. B., I want it understood that everyone must pay one dollar for the book. Even Ethel"—the wife of her brother-in-law, Robert F. Kennedy. [10] The initial printing of The White House: An Historic Guide was 250,000 copies; it sold out in less than ninety days. With the proceeds from these sales, the loan to the Society was quickly repaid and the book was reprinted. Later, the Society produced two other books for the White House Historical Association, and other books for the U.S. Capitol Historical Association and the Washington National Monument Association, which were sold through bookstores at those well-traveled sites.

The Society's political flexibility can be seen in the evolution of The Living White House, one of the other books done for the White House Historical Association. It was first produced in 1966 at the suggestion of Lady Bird Johnson, who had succeeded Jacqueline Kennedy as first lady; by the middle of Ronald Reagan's first term in office, the book's seventh edition, the "Reagan Edition," had a foreword by First Lady Nancy Reagan. By the time that edition was produced, almost 900,000 copies had already been sold; the proceeds were used primarily to purchase and maintain antique furnishings in the mansion.

Another breakthrough that resulted from Grosvenor's stated political neutrality and social ties occurred in 1965, when the Society published *Equal Justice Under Law,* a book offering both a history of the U.S. Supreme Court and a manual designed to explain to general readers just how the court works. Published under the auspices of the Federal Bar Federation, it became the first publication concerning the Supreme Court that the justices ever allowed to be sold in their Capitol Hill building.

Although these books didn't garner "profits" for the Society's treasury, since the proceeds went to the sponsoring organizations, each of them served to cement the relationship between the National Geographic Society and the federal government, and especially to cement that relationship in the eyes of the reading public. They helped the Society's stated position of political neutrality, despite the obvious rightward leanings of its ruling family. "Although the tone of the *Geographic* could reasonably be described as conservative, possibly even Republican, perhaps even a hangover from the Taft era," said the *New York Times* in 1970, "it is resolutely nonpartisan in politics, aside from an implicit belief in the capitalistic, free-enterprise system."[11]

Meanwhile, the Society's book division, under Melville's continued prodding, became a major source of revenue. It developed a policy of producing one "big book" and several smaller-scale projects annually. In the beginning, the Society took a book-club approach, asking members to sign up for several books a year in advance. The "big books" were divided into three categories: the history of man and civilization, natural science, and travel. By adapting much of the material from existing material in the Society's files, by primarily utilizing free lances when writers were required and thereby keeping its own staff small, and by taking advantage of the Society's tax-exempt status, the Society's book division was able to market its products with substantially lower prices than competitive products. The many detailed reader-preference surveys that became a staple of the entire National Geographic Society operation helped the book division develop a success record that is unmatched in the industry.

Of the first eighteen "big books" put out—between 1955 and 1973—all at least earned back the expenses incurred in production, in an industry where at least two-thirds of the books published generally fail to break even. By 1973, sixteen of the eighteen books were still in print, and a total of five million copies had been sold, an astonishing average of 275,000 copies each. By the end of 1972, the sales record was held by *America's Wonderlands,* a guide to America's national parks and monuments, which had sold 622,445 copies. The runner-up in this period was *Song and Garden Birds of North America,* which sold 429,409 copies through 1972.

As the book division prospered, it moved to lessen its dependence on the *National Geographic's* editorial warehouse. The aim of the book division has become to produce publications that will summarize a complete subject and at the same time be timeless enough in character to have a long commercial shelf life. "Ours may be the one book on the subject a family needs to pin down a particular subject for a long time . . ." explained Merle Severy, when he was running the division in 1973. Aided by its successes and by the financial backing of the Society, the book division didn't face the hardships of its publishing rivals. "Here, quality is a way of life," Severy said. "There is no cutting of corners." [12]

*　　*　　*

During this period, the *National Geographic* became probably the most sought-after assignment for photographers around the world. The Society paid well, sent photographers to the most exotic spots on earth, used photographs extensively, and, from early in Melville's reign, printed nearly every one in full color, at a time when the use of color in newspapers and on television was very rare, and even its use in magazines seemed exotic. But—perhaps even more of a lure to photographers—the Society developed a well- deserved reputation for never letting cost stand in the way of a good picture. Many are the tales of photographers—who are reimbursed for their expenses on a dollar-for-dollar basis—disappearing for months in search of the perfect setting, or lurking with cameras in hand for weeks in a spot waiting for the perfect shot.

According to a feature in the *Washington Post,* by the late 1960s the average *National Geographic* photographer was a thirty-five-year-old male, a former newspaper photographer who had won some regional prizes in the Midwest before moving to Washington to work for a newspaper or wire service. In Washington, he eventually garnered an important award for his work from the National Press Photographers' Association or the White House Photographers' Association before landing a job at the Society.

By this time, the photograghy staff was flying 500,000 miles a year and each photographer was spending a minimum of two three-month stints abroad each year, although some of them were away from home for up to ten months at a time—which led to a very high divorce rate among the staff. As a result, the Society eventually loosened up its policy about allowing wives to accompany their husbands on assignments and paying their expenses.

One photographer, Bob Sisson, spent such a long time away from his family while he was meandering along the Amazon River on an assignment that his wife didn't hear from him for six months. "Then she took a collect call from a San Diego dentist she had never talked to before. The dentist 'patched-in' her husband from a ham radio hook-up," the *Post* reported. "He was fine, she recalls, refusing to admit if she worried. 'When I hear nothing I know he's all right. If he's sick, I'll get a bill. If he's dead I'll get a box.'"[13]

That the *National Geographic* is prepared to go to almost any lengths to get its stories and photographs is reflected by the expense sheets of its staff members. These vouchers have included reimbursement requests from photographers for a $30,000 airplane, plus $6,000 for the pontoons that allowed it to float (it was sold when the assignment was completed); the purchase of an ambulance in India (it was sold at a profit after the story was done) and a snowmobile in Alaska (which caused a little fuss in the accounting department because the photographer gave the machine to his Eskimo guide at the end of the assignment; the guide had no use for cash); thousands of dollars for helicopter rental incurred by a photographer waiting for the precise light for a panoramic shot; and $8,000 in excess baggage charges on one commercial airline flight to Tanzania.

But perhaps the best *National Geographic* expense account story occurred years later, during a 1983 assignment by George Stuart, the magazine's resident archaeologist, to cover a rumored discovery of a Mayan tomb in Guatemala. Enlisting the aid of the Guatemalan government, which lent the Society's team an air force helicopter and crew, Stuart's group headed into the dense jungle in search of the tomb. The pilot lost his way. "The pilot landed his fully armed chopper next to a man on a bicycle and, in his guns and bandoleers, got out and said, 'Excuse me, but could you tell me where Guatemala is?'"[14] Armed with directions, the group headed off. But the helicopter ran out of fuel and they had to crash-land in a swamp. "All I had was my Eddie Bauer bandanna and a cowboy hat," Stuart recalled. "The soldiers were worried about guerrillas. They said they were going to set up a machine-gun periphery. We said, 'Whatever works.'"

The next day, another helicopter arrived and dropped food and tools with which to clear a landing pad for the ship. Stuart charged the unexpected costs involved in clearing the landing site on his Visa credit card.

During the average assignment for the *National Geographic*, photographers shoot between 250 and 350 rolls of 36-exposure color film, although more demanding assignments can require up to a thousand rolls. Of these shots—most of which will be well composed and properly exposed—about 150 will be seriously considered for the thirty to forty illustrations required for a major feature in the magazine.

Despite all this care and expense, and the Society's reputation for being in the forefront of photographic technology, its photographs are often pedestrian. They are beautiful, classic pictures of grand color and scale, to be sure, but they are unexciting and unimaginative. ". . . A not unfriendly observer, himself a recognized expert in photography . . ." reported the *New York Times Magazine*, said "that he doubted if a single 'memorable' picture had ever appeared in the *Geographic*. The pictures are influenced by the editorial content. They are sharp, clear and composed according to the classic laws. They're easy to look at; they don't startle. In many ways they are like the illustrations in a textbook. What they are not is interpretive, subjective or impressionistic."[15]

* * *

During his tenure, Melville brought two very different and important explorers into the National Geographic Society's tent: the world's premier underwater explorer, and the patriarch of a renowned family that is hunting for the origins of man in Africa.

French underwater diver Jacques-Yves Cousteau was already a quite successful, if still obscure, explorer. He had co-invented the Aqualung, the underwater breathing device that freed man from the bulky diving suits that had previously been required, and from the air-carrying lifelines from the surface to those suits. In an expedition sponsored by the Society, in 1952, using his converted World War II minesweeper, the *Calypso*, Cousteau located the wreckage of a 2,200-year-old Greek merchant ship in 140 feet of water off the southern coast of France. More than three thousand amphorae—Greek wine jars—were salvaged from the ancient ship, along with thousands of pieces of black-varnished Campanian pottery. In subsequent expeditions for the Society, Cousteau explored the Atlantic and Indian oceans and the Mediterranean and Red seas.

In many of these Society-sponsored projects, Cousteau was joined by inventor Dr. Harold E. Edgerton of the Massachusetts Institute of Technology. On one of those expeditions, in August 1956, Edgerton took what were then the deepest undersea photographs ever made, in the Romanche Trench, a depression in the Atlantic between Africa and South America.

In 1961, Cousteau was awarded the Society's Gold Medal for his efforts; the award was presented by President Kennedy. Unlike most of his colleagues, Cousteau eventually learned how to be commercially successful and to attract research funds and support from the public. This lessened his dependence on the Society and other public sources of funding.

It was a perpetual lack of funding that brought Dr. Louis S. B. Leakey to the National Geographic Society's doorstep. Leakey led his first African expedition in 1926; while the generally accepted belief at the time was that man had evolved in Asia, Leakey set out to prove that the cradle of civilization was actually Africa. He and his wife, Mary, struggled for years, perpetually short of money, until July 17, 1959, when Mary uncovered the skull of what became known as Nutcracker Man, at their dig site in Tanzania, an important step in their effort to show the link between man's evolution and Africa.

As soon as Nutcracker Man was discovered, the National Geographic Society was ready to publicize and to finance the Leakeys; this was an important link for both the family and the Society. While the *National Geographic* had turned down Leakey's suggestion that it do an article on the find, he got to see Melville Grosvenor, who arranged for him to address the exploration committee. The committee, after hearing the skilled Leakey's plea, awarded him $20,200. Leakey provided the Society a connection with an important scientist who, with other members of his family, would make several more historic discoveries, and the Society gave him money. Leakey was just the sort of man the Chief would have enlisted. "Louis was a great believer in popularizing science through the media," said Leakey biographer Sonia M. Cole in 1975, "above all in lectures. He was a showman and loved the limelight, and his seeking after publicity has been freely criticized. But to do him justice, he had to make the very most of each new find in order to raise the money to carry on."[16]

The Society wasted no time cashing in on its investment. Articles on the Leakeys' work appeared in the *National Geographic* in 1960, 1961, 1963, and 1965. Also in 1963, the Society sent a television crew to film their exploits. In 1966, an hour-long show on the Leakeys' work ran on CBS. The Society also sent Leakey out on several lecture tours. Leakey, meanwhile, was sending the Society other likely candidates for its largesse, including Jane Goodall. "By

1968, however, the National Geographic Society was beginning to lose interest, and Louis had to raise money elsewhere," according to Cole. [17] Leakey continued to work until his death in 1972; his wife and son Richard have continued on.

*   *   *

The winds of change eventually reach even the National Geographic Society, and the final leaves of its second chapter, the Gilbert Grosvenor era, began to turn.

On December 26, 1964, Elsie May Bell Grosvenor, whom her husband called "the First Lady of the National Geographic," died after a full and active life. She, as well as Gilbert Grosvenor, had played an integral role in the Society's evolution, from the days of their courtship when she had helped him address solicitation letters, and when she had stood by him as he and Elsie's father, Alexander Graham Bell, had done battle with the Society's board of directors while the Society's very existence hung in the balance. Elsie had also created the Society's flag and had taken part in much of her husband's globe-trotting.

She had been very active in the women's suffrage movement in Washington in the early twentieth century and in 1913 had participated in one of the major marches in the capital urging that women be given the right to vote. Elsie later testified at a Senate hearing after the march, at which she told of a group of angry young men who taunted the participants, and complained about the lack of police protection. "The crowd closed in on us and . . . began smashing the balloons out of the children's hands," she recounted.

In 1937, she flew to Hong Kong with her husband aboard a Pan American World Airways flight, and they thus became the first married couple to fly across the Pacific Ocean as paying passengers. Many times she was pictured in the *National Geographic* with her husband at some exotic location.

After her death, Gilbert H. Grosvenor wrote the eulogy in the *National Geographic* in mid-1965. "To her eighth child—the Society and its great family of members—she gave a lifetime of devotion. As so many of our members have said, she belonged to us all."[18]

Just months after writing the farewell to his wife, Gilbert Hovey Grosvenor, now ninety and in failing health, took an afternoon nap at the family estate in Nova Scotia on a cold February day. He never woke up.

* * *

In the years after his father's death, Melville Bell Grosvenor met with continuing success; the Society's business was booming. And now, at the top of his game, and apparently wanting to make sure that he didn't force his heir to wait, as he had had to wait, until well into middle age to take over the reins of the family empire, Melville stepped down as the Society's chief executive effective August 1, 1967, ten years after taking over as president and editor.

In his era, Society membership had skyrocketed from 2,175,000 to 5,500,000. By 1966, Society income totaled $48.3 million a year, including some $7 million from advertisements in the *National Geographic*; the magazine's renewal rate was an astounding 91 percent. By now, the Society employed more than two thousand people.

The death of his parents seems to have influenced Melville's decision to retire at the relatively young age of sixty-five. While his own son, Gilbert Melville Grosvenor, then thirty-six, wasn't quite seasoned enough to inherit the business, MBG divided the power in two and turned the organization over to a caretaker administration.

Melvin M. Payne, who was then the Society's vice-president and secretary and had been with the organization since 1921, was named president. Frederick G. Vosburg, vice-president and associate editor, became the *National Geographic*'s editor. Young Gil, as Melville's son was then known around the Society, was promoted from vice-president and senior assistant editor to the position of associate editor.

In turn, Melville replaced Thomas W. McKnew, the man who

had succeeded his father into the chairmanship of the Society's board after his death. McKnew, once discussing the Society's many successes when he was still vice-chairman of the board under the Chief after LaGorce had died, placed a hand over his heart and said solemnly, "Gosh, how they love us."[19]

18. BIG BUSINESS

As the National Geographic Society's coffers bulged with the fruits of its supremely successful efforts under the golden touch of Melville Bell Grosvenor, the Society underwent a fundamental change. No longer a lean eleemosynary institution begging the world for a chance to fulfill its stated task—"the increase and diffusion of geographic knowledge"—the Society began to be a big and lucrative business.

From Gardiner Greene Hubbard's dream of bringing educational knowledge to the upper classes of provincial Washington, to Alexander Graham Bell's ideal of popularizing geography among the upper middle classes, to Gilbert Hovey Grosvenor's appeal to the vast and growing middle class, under Melville Bell Grosvenor the Society became an institution of the masses, and a quite successful and wealthy one. But it was also, as a result of that success, far less a charitable, educational institution than it was a giant commercial publisher and mail-order house.

By the end of Melville Bell Grosvenor's tenure, the Society was selling magazines, advertising space, newsletters, maps, globes, atlases, books, and records to the tune of about $50 million a year, as measured in 1960-era dollars. Membership—already up to 5.5 million under Melville—was still swiftly growing. This membership was enough to give the *National Geographic Magazine* the third-largest circulation in the United States, trailing only *Reader's Digest* and *TV Guide*. As membership grew, so did the staff the Society found it necessary to employ in order to service the members, and to sell them more products.

On top of possessing a good product in an obviously desirable part of the publishing market, the National Geographic Society also had a handful of trump cards up its corporate sleeves. For the Society wasn't run according to the rules followed by most of its fellow successful corporations, or by all of its competition—the commercial book and magazine publishers, atlas and globe makers, record producers, and the like—because the National Geographic Society was deemed a "nonprofit" organization under the rules of the Internal Revenue Service.

*   *   *

In order to inspire altruistic endeavors, the federal government over the years had determined that certain organizations should be exempted from some taxes and regulations in order to help them survive. This has come to mean that "nonprofits" as a rule don't pay federal income taxes, are exempt from paying local property taxes, pay reduced rates for their postage to the federal government, and can offer those who make donations to them deductions on their own personal federal income tax returns.

The purpose of these exemptions is to make it easier for private citizens to fund altruistic operations, with the indirect assistance of the federal government. Part of the reasoning behind the federal help is that unless such aid is encouraged and given, the government would find itself in the position of having to provide all such funding, because, the logic goes, even organizations that provide great social good often find themselves unable to secure sufficient funding. In that case, the federal government would have to determine which charities were worthy; under the tax-refund system, individuals make their own determinations, and the federal government reimburses them for part of their expenditures.

Tax exemptions—at least for churches—are seemingly as old as taxes themselves, going back to ancient Egypt, Greece, and Rome; the exclusion of tax levies on secular properties, however, is a more modern, Western idea. Under this theory, exemptions were given on the premise that "if, in the absence of a private enterprise, taxation would be necessary in order to discharge a needed function, the state may properly subsidize the institution which performs the service."[1] Exemptions for institutions of higher learning apparently date from King Henry VII (1457–1509), who agreed not to tax the universities at Oxford and Cambridge. These tax benefits—which are, in fact, public subsidies over which the public has little control—have been quite helpful for many worthy organizations: colleges, hospitals, philanthropic charities, and others.

*   *   *

Early in the National Geographic Society's history, the taxing authorities in Washington had exempted the Society's holdings from the major local source of revenue-raising, property taxes, because of the organization's educational activities. While not paying taxes certainly assisted the Society, in its early years it in fact had little property to be exempt. But as the Society grew, the value of this property-tax exemption also grew.

The city of Washington was under increasing financial strains as World War II loomed; as the government grew in the city, so did the number of organizations that aimed to assist or lobby the government, many of which claimed tax-exempt status as religious or educational organizations. In 1941, Washington's board of commissioners, delegated by the national government to run the affairs of the federal District of Columbia, decided to take some action: Property belonging to several organizations, including the National Geographic Society, was ordered placed on the tax rolls. The commissioners decided to tax all of the Society's assets, except for the library it maintained in the headquarters building, because the Tax Exemption Board ruled that the Society was "not an educational institution within the meaning of the tax-exemption statute."[2]

The commissioners' move would restore properties assessed at that time for some $2.3 million to the city's revenue rolls, which would earn the District about $40,000 a year. The Society's properties represented more than half of the total, $1.27 million, that the commissioners wanted to put back on the books, and would yield some $21,000 a year at the existing tax rates.

The Society, then still being run by Gilbert H. Grosvenor, expressed immediate and loud outrage at this move, which was a direct threat to the organization's pocketbook. Grosvenor immediately appealed the decision to the board of commissioners. The appeal was rejected in January 1942, and D.C. Corporation Counsel Richmond B. Keech ruled that the Society's property was not used "for educational purposes" as defined by the applicable law. "On that ground alone," he ruled, "we conclude that the property is not entitled to exemption. Accordingly, it has become unnecessary to examine the question as to whether or not the property is conducted for private gain," which was Grosvenor's main line of defense.

But the city's commissioners obviously didn't know with whom they were tangling when they challenged Gilbert H. Grosvenor and his pride and joy, the National Geographic Society. With Grosvenor leading the way, an appeal for help was made directly to Congress, bypassing the local administration completely. Appearing before a Senate committee, Grosvenor informed the solons that the Society was in fact a tremendous educational and social asset to Washington, which more than compensated for any tax loss suffered by the city. Over the years, Grosvenor lectured the senators, the Society had published seventeen illustrated articles on the District of Columbia in the *National Geographic,* articles that had had a worldwide distribution of more than sixteen million copies. This also had to make up for the lost taxes, he said. And furthermore, Grosvenor added in his testimony, the Society's weekly school bulletins were sent out to more than thirty thousand public-school teachers in congressional districts all around the country.

On Christmas Eve, 1942, Congress presented Grosvenor, the National Geographic Society, and some other Washington-based tax-exempt institutions with a special gift from the taxpayers of the nation's capital, a federal law specifically exempting them from property taxes.

That issue settled, the Society returned to its business of making money and expanding. By the end of Melville Bell Grosvenor's tenure, the Society's Washington property was assessed at more than $16 million, a conservative figure considering that the building that opened in 1964 had alone cost more than half that amount. At the time, the city estimated its taxes lost by virtue of the Society's congressionally mandated exemption at more than $500,000 a year. The Society's headquarters complex now occupied about two-thirds of a prime city block; nestled between the buildings, the Society provided free surface parking for its workers on some of its tax-free land in the shadow of large magnolia trees, and thus the Society was said to be the only organization in Washington that could afford to offer its employees such an expensive perquisite.

The congressionally mandated tax exemption was actually a regressive subsidy: The larger the Society got and the more property it acquired, the greater the subsidy that was provided by the taxpayers of Washington. Indeed, by 1979, the Society's Washington holdings were assessed at $33 million, the largest assessment of any nongovernmental tax-exempt institution in Washington, and would have yielded at least $610,000 a year in taxes. These assessments were well below the fair market value of these properties. In addition to these Washington holdings, the Society by this time owned its enormous "Membership Building," where more than a thousand employees spearhead the Society's mail-order business, magazine billing, and endless stream of mailings offering memberships, books, films, records, and lectures. The 400,000-square-foot building is located in Maryland on a 150-acre tract overlooking an eleven-acre pond. That building, which cost some $6 million to construct, and its lavish grounds would have paid some $300,000 in taxes were it owned by a commercial publisher. Additionally, the Society has other holdings, such as the new high-tech printing plant it recently opened in Mississippi, to which it shifted much of its work away from private, tax-paying firms.

After Washington was granted limited home rule by Congress in the 1970s, a new move to limit the spread of tax-exempt institutions sprang up. Two members of Congress urged Washington to move in that direction, and the D.C. City Council, led by David A. Clarke, began to react. Clarke, who was later elected chairman of the city council, said in the spring of 1979 that he was encouraged by the support of the two congressman and hopeful of quick passage of legislation to harness the tax-exempts. The legislation hasn't been heard of since. And as valuable as the property-tax exemption was, it represented only the tip of this wildly expanding iceberg.

*　　*　　*

The corporate income of the Society, as well as that of its "nonprofit" brethren, was also excluded from federal income taxes, a potentially much more valuable exemption for an exceptionally successful nonprofit organization like the Society. For this exemption applied not just to the Society's substantial revenue from membership dues, but to the millions in advertising dollars.

The Society's gross income in 1968 was $60 million; membership at the time was up to 6.8 million, which kept the magazine in third place in the United States, still trailing only *Reader's Digest* and *TV Guide*. But the *National Geographic*'s readers were more affluent than the average readers of the other two magazines, and thus were more sought-after, especially by makers and sellers of upscale products.

And, as the Society competed with Rand McNally and Hammond to sell atlases and globes, and the *National Geographic* vied with myriad publications for readers and advertisers, the commercial firms paid taxes and the Society didn't. This gave the Society a subsidy with which to undercut its competitors, and the Society put this edge to good use.

A major publishing-industry trade magazine reported in 1973 that "there has long been a feeling in the publishing world that tax-sheltered publishing falls into the same general category as government publishing and that there is an element of unfair competition in both. . . . As a nonprofit institution, the *Geographic* can also sell advertising at less cost than commercial publishers. The publishers of the late *Look* and *Life* [recently revived as a monthly] must frequently have looked with anger as Cadillac or other juicy ads passed them by and ended up in the Geographic."[3]

Caleb D. Hammond, when he was chairman of the board of Hammond, was asked about having to compete with a major nonprofit publisher. He said, "I don't feel it's fair. The *National Geographic* probably does some good, but it's a real money-maker." Another competitor, Paul Gottlieb, then president of American Heritage Publishing Company, said of the *National Geographic*, "There is a substantial inequity vis-à-vis other publications because of their preferred position as a nonprofit organization, but the *Geographic* has an untouchable quality."

Other of the *National Geographic*'s competitors had complained that the Society could offer advertisers lower rates since it didn't have to add in corporate income tax expenses as part of overhead.

Rand McNally and Hammond had considered a possible legal challenge, but eventually decided to follow other strategies. Their efforts, combined with those of other publishers, apparently inspired the IRS to take another look at nonprofit organizations that engage in commercial activities. In December 1967, in a landmark IRS ruling, the National Geographic and other similar publications were stripped of one of their tax exemptions. In that year alone, the Society had sold 351 pages of high-income advertising in the *National Geographic*. Up to this time, most courts had ruled that no matter how nonprofits raised their money, as long as the revenue ended up at an exempt institution, the revenue was not to be taxed. Now, however, acting "to eliminate a source of unfair competition," the IRS ruled that ad revenue from the *Geographic* would from then on be subject to federal income tax levies. The IRS's logic was that an otherwise tax-exempt organization had to pay levies on income at regular corporate rates on money derived from any business "the conduct of which is not substantially related (aside from the need of such organization for income or funds or the use it makes of the profits derived) to the exercise or performance by such organization of its charitable, educational, or other [tax-exempt] purpose."

The IRS regulations raised a storm of protest from the tax-exempt publishers, and especially from the National Geographic Society, but the rules weathered a determined lobbying campaign aimed at getting Congress to scrap them. The rules were confirmed by Congress as part of the Tax Reform Act of 1969, giving the IRS a much firmer legal standing in the face of any expected court challenges.

While the legislation seemed to tap justifiably into the excess profits of the few high-income tax-exempt magazines, unfortunately for lots of other less endowed nonprofits, the IRS ruling also left their seven hundred or so publications with a new tax headache. At the time of the ruling, Philip Abelson, editor of the prestigious if unwealthy *Science* magazine, a publication sponsored by the nonprofit American Association for the Advancement of Science, said, "We're not making any money from our advertising. But now we're going to have to go out and hire lawyers and bookkeepers to prove it. It's just a nuisance for us, and the U.S. won't get a dime out of it."[4]

But whether this IRS ruling and the resultant legislation has had any serious effect—or indeed any effect at all—on the National Geographic Society's coffers is unclear. After the IRS ruling was incorporated into the 1969 tax law, one magazine writer in 1970 said that the law "was drawn so leniently that the *Geographic's* lawyers and accountants believe that it still won't actually have to pay anything anyway."[5] While the writer failed to quote anyone at the Society, the context of the quote makes clear that the conclusion was presented to him by "informed sources" at the Society.

And whether the Society does pay such taxes or not is unknown, since neither the IRS nor the Society is willing to talk about it. What is known is that for the year 1984, the Society told the IRS that it raised $29,629,088 in advertising dollars.

By contrast, in an early 1986 interview with the author, a high--ranking IRS official revealed that the total receipts during fiscal year 1984 from the unrelated-business-tax program for tax-exempt institutions throughout the nation was $37.9 million. The official explained the IRS's difficulties in making decisions concerning un-related-business-income-tax determinations. Under existing reg-ulations, the IRS formula for determining the applicability of taxes begins with subtracting all the costs of obtaining advertising reve-nue from the advertising receipts. If that tabulation leaves a sur-plus, then the tax-exempt institution is allowed to balance all of its "readership income"—that is, the ad and subscription receipts—from all of its "readership costs," the cost of producing the publica-tion and, of course, the portion of the institution's overhead that it attributes to the production of the magazine. Only if the institu-tion still shows a profit does it face any taxes from the IRS under the unrelated-business-income regulations.

As ineffective a federal revenue-raiser as the rules on advertising income have proved to be, the attempt to overturn them is far from over. As recently as September 1984, the U.S. Circuit Court of Appeal for the Federal District ruled in favor of a challenge to the IRS's 1967 rules by the American College of Physicians. The organization publishes a successful monthly journal called *Annals of Internal Medicine,* which had a circulation of 73,000 when the court case began in 1975. In that year, the magazine had $1.37 million in advertising revenue, on which it paid unrelated-business taxes of $153,388, a mere shadow of what the *National Geographic* earned and, presumably, paid to the U.S. Treasury.

The American College of Physicians challenged the IRS's levy-ing of the tax; the trial court upheld the rule, but the appeals court reversed. In May of 1985, the Supreme Court granted a writ of certiorari, and agreed to hear the government's appeal of the ap-pellate court's verdict.

One year later, the Supreme Court upheld the IRS's interpreta-tion of the rule and reversed the decision. Said a high-ranking IRS official, "The court saved the entire unrelated-business tax" with its decision. [6]

*   *   *

The next test of the Society's tax-exempt status concerned not money that the Society would have to pay to a governmental agency, but rather the Society's refusal to collect state sales taxes imposed by most jurisdictions on the sales of goods and the paying of those revenues to the appropriate states. The case stemmed from a suit brought by the State of California in 1964, challenging the Society's contention that it was immune from sales taxes on the maps, atlases, globes, and books that it sold through the mail to people living in that state. The Society refused to collect the taxes, saying it didn't have to because it only sold a small number of maps, atlases, globes, and books in the state, and only maintained two small advertising sales offices there.

Not having to collect sales taxes on the sales of its goods had two benefits for the Society. First, it would prevent the Society from incurring the administrative hassles and expenses of collecting, recording, and forwarding the taxes; and secondly, it made the Society's goods cheaper to the buying public, again giving the Society an edge against its commercial competitors, who had to add the sales taxes to the cost of their goods.

Lower courts had agreed with the Society's arguments, citing the relatively low number of sales it made in California and agreeing that the two small advertising offices that it maintained there were not large enough to represent a sufficient link between the Society's mail-order business and the state's taxing authority.

However, the U.S. Supreme Court in April 1977 overturned the lower-court rulings and ordered the Society to collect the sales taxes because it had a "substantial presence" in California. In a 7-to-0 decision that was said to have wide implications in the mail-order business, the Court ruled that "the slightest presence" of a business within a state gives that state the right to force a seller to collect the use tax, and to demand the payment directly from the seller if it fails to do so. The Society's "maintenance of two offices in the state and solicitation by employees assigned to those offices of advertising copy in the range of $1 million annually," wrote

Justice William J. Brennan, Jr., "establish a much more substantial presence than the expressed 'slightest presence' connotes." The Court also went to great pains to say that the justices also didn't agree with the "substantial presence" test in any event.

One of the two justices who failed to participate in this case was Chief Justice Warren E. Burger, presumably because, as chief justice, he is automatically a member of the Society's board of directors.

* * *

And as if tax exemptions weren't enough of a subsidy for the National Geographic Society, the organization also took full advantage of another perquisite offered by the Congress: discounted postal rates. These discounts are offered to nonprofits on the assumption that their funds are very limited and they thus need help with the costs of billing their members or distributing their appeals for funds. To the National Geographic Society, this assistance took a little different turn. In 1976 alone, the Society spent $3 million on third-class mailings to sell memberships and products. Had it paid the regular rates, its bill for the year would have been $9 million. Also during that year it spent about $3 million on second-class mailings for its publications, about $2.5 million less than it would have cost its commercial competitors to mail the same amount of material.

No doubt at least partially because of this discount mailing privilege, the Society sends out an almost endless stream of full-color, high-quality mailings pitching its various goods and membership plans to members, prospective members, and former members, the envelopes for each of which are clearly marked "Non-Profit Org." By 1984, according to Society officials, the postage subsidy was saving the organization $10 million a year.

As a result, the Society has become the fifteenth largest mail-order house in America, according to Maxwell Sroge, a consultant who specializes in that industry. "[I think] they have really an unfair advantage" over their competition due to their tax-exempt status and their reduced postage charges. Sroge estimated that the

Society mails "several hundred million pieces" of promotional material every year. [7]

* * *

All of these tax subsidies are granted to the National Geographic Society because of its educational functions and its status as a non-profit, meaning that no stockholders withdraw profits as dividends. The nation's tax laws as written today seek specifically to exclude from tax-free status organizations "operated for the primary purpose of carrying on a trade or business for profit" solely on the ground that their profits go to a charitable organization, themselves.

But looking at the Society's tax returns raises puzzling, and primary, questions. Why is the National Geographic Society considered a nonprofit organization? For what educational purpose does it exist? Other than for dispersal of income, how does it differ from the nation's for-profit publishing conglomerates?

Gardiner Greene Hubbard's goal was to create an organization of inquisitive, high-minded men both to help chart the globe and to inform other intelligent, curious people about their discoveries—in short, to promote "the increase and diffusion of geographic knowledge." Alexander Graham Bell's idea was to fund this research, exploration, and publication chain by selling memberships to the masses, but still keeping the Society focused as an educational organization. The Chief's goal was to funnel 15 percent of gross revenues into exploration and research.

And the Society's formula for commercial success was certainly succeeding. From the $60 million in gross income in 1968, the Society's gross revenue had reached $130 million in 1976. By 1984, the National Geographic Society was grossing $326,826,071 a year, had a net worth of at least $198 million, and recorded "profits" of more than $17 million, even under the peculiar rules that apply to it. In that same year, its interest and dividend income alone amounted to more than $18.7 million. And 1984 was far from a banner year—the year before, the Society had "profits" of $30 million on similar gross revenue.

Yet, astonishingly, in 1983, the National Geographic Society awarded research and exploration grants totaling only $3.18 million, less than 1 percent of its gross revenue. And even that figure is misleading, since many of those "grants" led to articles for the *National Geographic,* and would perhaps have been more accurately classified as publishing expenses. The next year, the Society reported that its research grants jumped to $4.3 million. But most of that increase involved projects destined for publication in a new research journal of very limited circulation that the Society was preparing.

The Society also spent about $3.4 million during 1983 on its little museum on the ground floor of one of its headquarters buildings, on running its news service and library, and in charitable contributions and memberships. In that year, the Society earned some $170 million from membership dues, almost $98 million in publication sales, $13 million from a new children's magazine, *National Geographic World,* and $2.5 million from television films and documentaries. It reported a "surplus" of $30,076,831.

The surplus included $162,781 in bequests from members concerned about the Society's financial future. However ironic a turn this was when balanced against the Society's enormous gross revenue, the Society made a subtle pitch for more such bequests when it dedicated the entire "president's column" in the September 1985 issue to a woman whom no one at the Society headquarters had met, but who had left money in her will to the organization.

What must be taken into account when assessing the Society's financial numbers is that federal policies actually encourage the Society to spend money. While not part of IRS and Postal Service regulations, agent field practices have evolved into a perceived rule that in order to retain its tax-free and reduced-postage status, 80 percent of the membership dues of an organization must go into the production of that publication. In other words, if a publication is a big money-earner, it had better cost the sponsoring organization a lot to produce. The Society reported that it spent $172.4 million preparing the twelve issues of the *National Geographic* in 1983, about $14.67 million an issue.

As a result of these rules, the Society has developed a well-justified reputation as a big spender. Its facilities are unsurpassed in the world of publishing, its technical facilities are state-of-the-art, and while its salaries aren't extraordinary, its lavish expense accounts are legendary. Writers and photographers are encouraged to spare no expense in pursuit of their quarry, and are often advised to "go first class."

As explained by a writer for *The Washington Monthly*, the IRS and Postal Service regulations don't "confront the possibility that there might be some nonprofit organizations that take in far more money than they spend, like the National Geographic. These organizations work hard to eat up their net income by artificially raising their overhead—hence the high salaries, the dining rooms, the free parking, the gleaming buildings, the generous investment portfolio. In a corporation that isn't protected by nonprofit laws, these perquisites might be protested by stockholders as unnecessary, but because the *Geographic* is nonprofit, it doesn't have to report any financial information to the members of the National Geographic Society, who fund it. The *Geographic*'s members know far less about where their money goes than do the stockholders of most corporations."[8]

One IRS official told the author, "It is very difficult for us to judge what is 'educational' and what isn't. . . . Where do you draw the line? I don't know. . . . What has evolved in practice is a general test of an organization's primary purpose. . . . If the primary purpose of an institution is an allowable charitable purpose, then the organization will be tax-exempt. . . ." He said there is no "percentage test" of an organization's unrelated business income or of how it puts its revenue to work. "It boils down to a question of reasonableness," said the official.[9] And reasonableness, it seems, is in the eyes of the beholder.

To Gilbert H. Grosvenor in 1922, being nonprofit was something he was proud of. "There is another point I want to make about these members of the Society. They do not merely get—they also give. The magazine, for instance, is not run for profit. No money dividends are paid to anyone. The treasury balance now is on the credit side of the ledger; but it is spent in increasing the scientific knowledge of the world in which we live. . . ."[10] But by the time of Gilbert M. Grosvenor's reign, *The Washington Monthly* had a very different view of the operation. "Mainly, what the government is subsidizing [through tax exemptions] is an expensively operated magazine, put out for the entertainment of an affluent readership and filled with innocuous articles on faraway places—something that, it seems, the readers ought to pay for themselves without the help of the nonreading public."[11]

19. GROSVENOR III

Aside from not paying taxes, one of the major reasons for the enormous success of the Society and the magazine is that they are operated according to sound aristocratic principles. Since the Society's founding . . . [except for brief periods] it and the magazine have always been run by members of the same family, and as far as anyone can tell, they always will be.

New York Times Magazine, 1970

After three years with no Grosvenor in either of the Society's two top operating positions, and with Grosvenor III approaching a respectable age—thirty-nine—for wielding power, the post–Melville Bell Grosvenor regency ended in October 1970, when *National Geographic* associate editor Gilbert Melville Grosvenor took over as editor.

While Melville M. Payne remained as the Society's president, "young Gil's" ascension clearly underlined that the Society was indeed a family dynasty to all but the powers that be at the organization's headquarters. "Members of the family do not, like Napoleon, crown themselves," said one magazine in writing about the Grosvenors, "and since they are not, technically speaking, the owners of the Society, which as a nonprofit organization has none but its members, they do not succeed to office by right of property. The choice, as the Society's executives never tire of saying, is made by [the organization's board of directors]."

In fact, however, most board members get to few meetings, and the Society is actually governed by its executive committee, which is dominated and controlled by members of the Grosvenor family and Society executives, chosen by the Grosvenors. One magazine found, "Aside from not paying taxes, one of the major reasons for the enormous success of the Society and magazine is that they are operated according to sound aristocratic principles. Since the Society's founding . . . [except for brief periods] it and the magazine have always been run by members of the same family, and as far as anyone can tell, they always will be."[1]

The company line—that the Society is an independent, non-profit corporation ruled by a self-perpetuating twenty-four-man board of directors full of high-powered business and governmental executives, and not by a family—was perhaps best illustrated by William McChesney Martin, a Society director who had been chairman of the board of governors of the Federal Reserve Board: "I hate nepotism," he told the New York Times in 1970, soon after Gilbert M. Grosvenor's appointment, "but I've interviewed forty-three members of the staff to find out who would be best choice. I give up. It was unanimous in favor of young Gil."[2]

When Grosvenor became editor, one writer described him as "a pleasant-faced, middle-sized man," with thinning black hair and horn-rimmed glasses, fond of wearing ostentatiously inexpensive suits. Soon after his selection, Grosvenor explained that he had been a premed student at Yale when the first thoughts of a career at the Society even entered his mind. He said he had never even entertained thoughts of a career at the Society until his junior year, when he traveled to the Netherlands to assist an international work force that was restoring that nation's dikes after disastrous floods that spring. While he had never expressed any interest in writing before, he took a camera along and wrote a story on the relief effort for the National Geographic. And he was hooked. After the article was published, he said, his plans for a career as a surgeon were soon discarded.

* * *

"I like to think that I can handle the job as well as anybody here," Grosvenor said soon after his selection. "I guess this probably is a break because of the family, but, hell, I've been in every damned division of this organization, including a few years in the business department. There's a view, which I don't necessarily agree with, that grandfather stayed around too long. Dad was fifty-seven when he took over. He had to wait a long time. He did tremendously well in ten years, but he decided he wouldn't do the same thing. So he stepped out, and I'm grateful to have the opportunity to come in at the age of thirty-nine."[3]

Young Gil brought youthful enthusiasm to the job, and set about to correct what he saw as some of the Society's, and the *National Geographic's* flaws. Being of the newer age of American publishing, one filled with more advocacy journalism, more probing investigating, he seemed particularly sensitive about the magazine's Pollyanna reputation.

Indeed, the continuation of the Chief's "Seven Principles," coupled with the Society's continuing anticommunist, pro-establishment point of view, had led to peculiarities in the *National Geographic's* presentation. For instance, it wasn't until 1970 that an article in the *National Geographic* about the American South had mentioned the Ku Klux Klan, lynchings, segregation, malnutrition, or, in later times, freedom rides or sit-ins.

In 1962, in "North Carolina—Dixie Dynamo," the magazine carried two pictures of blacks among the many illustrations that accompanied the feature. One of the blacks pictured was a maid in a starched uniform handing a camelia to a white woman who was wearing a long dress and white gloves; the other was a ragged tobacco farmer. That same year, "Southern Africa Close-Up" noted the existence of apartheid and presented a detailed explanation from a high government official elaborating on the reasons it was a desirable practice for all in the nation. The article, illustrated with many pictures of happy blacks doing their tribal dances while wearing gaudy paints, or cheerfully laboring in efficient, sterile mines, carried no opposing points of view.

As noted earlier, some allies of the Society have maintained that one of the reasons the *National Geographic* doesn't carry stories about the negative aspects of life is that its reproduction is so good; the bright cheery colors glamorize even the festering sores of the starving. But that explanation weakens on consideration of the Vietnam War era, when the vivid color of news photographs and videotape brought the horrors of death and destruction to the world in an all-too-real manner.

As his control over the magazine grew firmer, Grosvenor began gradually to exert influence over the magazine. Since so much of the *National Geographic* is prepared well in advance, and since its practices were so entrenched, Grosvenor's impact came very slowly. The first major public controversy that the Society faced under Grosvenor came as a result of the organization's good-news policy, coupled with its British-style pro-Arab slant in the Middle East.

In the April 1974 issue of the *National Geographic*, the Society reported in an article on the Middle East that Syria's Jews were satisfied with their situation in an Arab land. The article quoted leaders of the Jewish community in Syria as saying that Jews have "freedom of worship and . . . opportunity." American Jews were outraged. About twenty representatives from the American Jewish Congress and the Jewish War Veterans went so far as to picket the Society's headquarters, protesting what they termed a "whitewash of Syria's treatment of its Jewish citizens." The executive director of the American Jewish Congress charged that life for Syria's forty-five hundred remaining Jews is "so fraught with harassment, restrictions, terror, torture and even rape and murder, that the *Geographic* article was shocking in the magnitude of its distortions."

At the time, the Society's only reply was from Windsor Booth, then chief of its news service: "The only thing we have to say is that the issue has been banned in Syria as being too pro-Israel." But the protests obviously led to further investigation. In the November 1974 issue, in his new "editor's column," Grosvenor conceded that life for Syria's Jews was "worse than we led our readers to believe" in the article, but probably not as bad as the American Jewish Congress was claiming. "I am still not absolutely sure what the truth is," Grosvenor wrote, again reminding the readers that Syria had also denounced the article. His clear implication was that if both sides were unhappy with the story, then it must have been the truth.

236

The American Jewish Congress was delighted to have wrung out of Grosvenor what the organization termed the *National Geographic*'s first correction in history. Grosvenor seemed more concerned about setting the record straight on that than about resolving the Syrian questions. "This is nothing new," he told the *Washington Post.* "We've had many other corrections—from misidentifying Mount Everest to misplacing a comma." Grosvenor was playing with the facts a bit. In truth, the *National Geographic* probably expends more money and effort trying not to make mistakes than any other publication in the world. Its errors are so few as to be memorable, and its acknowledgment of errors is even rarer.

The Society regularly sends drafts of its articles to everyone quoted in them, and to government agencies of the nations that it writes about. People are given a chance to "correct" their quotes or to present opposing opinions on statements made in the magazine. While this minimizes confrontations and charges of inaccuracy, it also jeopardizes the integrity of the editorial product. Most periodicals that allow subjects to review articles send only those quotes directly attributed to the subject; at some publications, if a quoted source then claims his actual statements were different, the author is sent a copy of the claim and the discrepancies are worked out between the author and the editors.

In 1976, Melville Bell Grosvenor was shedding more of his responsibilities at the Society. On June 1, he resigned as chairman of the board and became chairman emeritus; he retained his basically honorary title of editor-in-chief of the *National Geographic*, while Melvin M. Payne succeeded him as chairman. Robert E. Doyle became the new president, replacing Payne, while Gilbert M. Grosvenor remained as magazine editor.

Up until now, Gilbert Grosvenor's changes had gone mostly unnoticed. But in 1977, as Gilbert was expanding his control over the operation, it seemed overnight that decades of tranquillity at the National Geographic Society were shattered by a string of unrelated controversies.

First, in the January issue, the magazine that had ignored communism and communists so successfully for so long painted a rosy view of Castro-controlled Cuba. The magazine that hadn't printed an article about the Soviet Union from World War II until 1959 had suddenly found in Cuba a communist jewel in the Caribbean. In a style vaguely reminiscent of John Patric's adoring piece on Mussolini forty years earlier, "Inside Cuba Today" began:

"May Day throngs filled Havana's Paseo. From the reviewing stand in the Plaza de la Revolución I could see the Cuban hierarchy approaching and beyond them a sea of waiting celebrators. . . . Prime Minister Fidel Castro and the Central Committee of the Communist Party advanced in a phalynx. . . . Precisely as [Cuba trade-union head Roberto] Viega pronounced the last syllable of his address, 130,000 parading participants burst into view, with uniforms, signs, posters, and banners all pounding out revolutionary themes. Educational goals were heralded, the United States denounced, Angola praised, Castro applauded. Thousands of workers passed before their 'Maximum Leader,' who is almost universally addressed by his first name. The crowd chanted the oft-heard slogan . . . [in Spanish] 'Fidel for sure, hit the Yankees hard!' . . ."4

The article accepted without question government officials' claims for Cuba's brightening economy, for its industrial and agricultural growth. Accuracy in Media, a right-leaning organization that monitors the American press in search of what it believes to be inaccurate reportage, pounced on the article as a classic biased distortion of the truth. And AIM was not the only quarter from which criticism was directed toward the *National Geographic's* seemingly sudden acceptance of communism. Conservative columnist Kevin P. Phillips opined that the magazine had inexplicably acquired a rather mild case of "radical chic."5

William Buckley's right-wing *National Review* jumped to the Society's aid. "*National Geographic* is not usually thought of as a fellow-traveling publication. Indeed, there are few more refreshing magazines, few so beautifully designed to take the reader out of himself and give him an instant vacation from politics and other humdrum distractions. So it comes as a shock to find Accuracy in Media accusing *National Geographic* of painting a flattering portrait of Cuba." *National Review* had already found the answer. "In a sense, of course, the magazine flatters everyone: . . . That is the virtue of the magazine, that it suspends judgment in introducing you to alien things."

Further, *National Review* reported, it must be remembered that "our free press is free only on our side of the Iron Curtain. To the extent it wants to stay in business abroad it must trade under conditions of what K. R. Minogue calls 'intellectual protectionism.' It shouldn't surprise or outrage us when it happens, but we should be alert to it: our journalists and scholars make frequent little pay-offs to foreign governments in the form of fudged phrases and the kind of terminological submission one finds in [*National Geographic* author Fred] Ward's piece. If they don't talk the totalitarian lingo, they at least find a neutral dialect. . . . When the market for truth is controlled, we pay a heavy tariff on every fact we import. . . ."[6]

In the very next issue, the *National Geographic* featured an article on New York City's Harlem neighborhood. While the article itself was on the whole the usual rosy Society special, the fact that the magazine was writing about the predominantly black and poor neighborhood at all was news. But the biggest furor was raised by the Society's advertising sales office, which sponsored a big party in the black community and took out an ad in the *New York Times* proclaiming: "The geography of Harlem: Poverty, dope, crime and people who wouldn't leave for a million dollars." The ad ended with a call to advertisers: "It's time you took another look" at the *National Geographic*.

Bob Kelly, then the sales-promotion director for advertising at the Society in New York, explained, "We have a tough sell and we wish Washington would realize it. Our theme was simply, 'We're certainly not old fuddy-duddy.'"[7] An unnamed Society official in Washington responded that the New York ad office didn't "know . . . beans about the magazine."[8]

Young Gil tried to calm the waters. "You can't fool very many of the people by not showing the world as it is. A magazine must evolve with its time. I'm hopeful the readers will never notice the subtle changes."[9] But the entire affair did not sit well in higher circles in Washington. Melvin M. Payne, who succeeded Melville Bell Grosvenor as board chairman, was outraged. "The ad guys organized this party and touted the article as a breakthrough. But the advertising tail is not going to wag the *Geographic* by a long shot. . . . Our feeling is that controversy is adequately covered in the daily press. Our responsibility is to hold up the torch, not apply it."[10]

No sooner had the Harlem controversy begun to die down than the *National Geographic* ran an article on South Africa, which seemed to try to make up for all the omissions in earlier articles on the nation. Blacks and apartheid occupied a goodly portion of the article. While the same article might well have escaped much notice in any other publication, in the *National Geographic* it set off a major furor. The government of South Africa went so far as to place large advertisements in major American daily newspapers to accuse the *National Geographic* of "anti-white racism," and of having made serious errors of omission and of attempting to "enter the realm of advocacy reporting."

It was all too much for the Society's directors and its readers to bear. Letters of complaint were arriving with unparalleled frequency at headquarters; some members were actually resigning, the Society's equivalent of canceling their subscriptions; the furor had attracted media attention, suddenly throwing the Society into an unprecedented role of political newsmaker. "Traumatic"[11] was Payne's term for the chain of events. Matters have "hit the fan,"[12] said Robert Doyle, the Society's president. "The *Geographic* Faces Life," headlined *Newsweek* magazine. "Change at the *Geographic*, Magazine's New Look Stirs Dispute," said the July 17 front-page headline in the *Washington Post*—perhaps the first time the city's largest newspaper had placed "Geographic" and "dispute" in the same headline since the organization's brush with having to pay taxes thirty years earlier.

Grosvenor tried to minimize the importance of the continuing furor, especially over the Cuba and South Africa stories. Showing a penchant for statistical comparisons that would have made his grandfather proud, he told a reporter that the "forty or fifty letters we get on a sensitive story," when compared with the Society's membership, was like walking once around the Society's headquarters complex "and then walking to the moon." The Society's research department later corrected that to "twice around the headquarters." [13]

But Payne knew how to handle it. At the trustees' meeting in June, he quietly created an ad hoc committee to look into the matter. The panel was created "not for censorship," he declared when asked about it by a reporter, "but to make sure we stay on the right track." He later said some three hundred letters of protest had been received concerning the article on Africa, an unprecedented flood of complaint mail for the Society. "South Africa is an emotional issue, and I considered the criticism serious enough to appoint the committee." [14] Payne said the Society had asked experts to check the South Africa story before it went to press, and as is its usual practice, had let the South African government see it in advance. "We accepted a number of changes urged by the South African government in an effort to be fair," he said. But, as is often the case in controversial matters, Payne said, "one man's objectivity is another man's bias."

Grosvenor, who was named to the committee by Payne, said he was unconcerned by the trustees' review. He pointed to a March 1977 vote of confidence in the magazine's general editorial policies from the board, and to a June study that he said showed that 97 percent of the Society's members "think the magazine is perfect." He assured a reporter in July that he wasn't about to change his editorial policies, and that he was not unhappy about the formation of the review board, "unless they suddenly decide that those stories were, in fact, biased. I don't think that will be the case," he confidently predicted. [15] And, Grosvenor told another reporter, he didn't expect the problems to continue. But, he added, "I didn't expect any problems with the others either." [16]

While that marked the end of the public discussion, the handwriting was already on the wall. The Society soon canceled its aggressive advertising campaign. The next victim was an article that had been planned on Beirut, which was once again being ravaged by one of its periodic civil wars, dominated by fighting between Moslems and Christians. W. E. Garrett, then the *National Geographic's* assistant editor for graphics, explained: "I saw it as 'Beirut Rises from the Ashes,' though I don't see that as a particularly controversial idea. I think in terms of pictures, and I saw a burned-out Holiday Inn with a tank sitting in the lobby," he told a reporter. The feature was canceled, Grosvenor explained, "because we don't know where Beirut is going." Sounding very much back in the fold, he continued, "We are not going to cover the destruction and demise of Beirut. This magazine has never dwelt on that kind of story."[17]

Quickly, the *National Geographic* returned to pre– Grosvenor III fare. "Salt—The Essence of Life" was featured. Next, "The Incredible Rat" adorned the pages of the magazine. And while rats plunder one-fifth of the world's crops every year and carry myriad diseases, the Society informed its readers, lest they become too critical of the rodents, they also have contributed to the cure of more human illnesses than any other animal.

* * *

On the business side, Gilbert M. Grosvenor has continued the enviable record of his father. While his earlier career at the Society centered on the editorial side, as he took over the operation he has become much more the businessman and much less the journalist.

His first major business change involved converting the Society's school newsletters, which raised little revenue for the organization, into a full-blown magazine. *National Geographic World* began in September 1975, and was aimed at eight-to-twelve-year-olds. When it was introduced, a year's issues cost $4.85. The Society had done much research before committing to the new project, and Grosvenor and his aides were so certain they would be successful that they ordered an initial press run of 750,000 copies.

To direct this effort, Grosvenor turned to Robert L. Breeden, the staff member his father had chosen to direct one of the Society's most important early moves in book publishing, the creation of the White House guide book with First Lady Jacqueline Kennedy. Breeden, as head of the book division, had launched a series of "Books for Young Explorers," aimed at four-to-eight-year-olds, which had been very successful, and had initiated a program of film strips for sale to schools. By 1983, *National Geographic World* was bringing in more than $13 million a year in subscription fees from its circulation of almost 1.5 million. The Society accepts no outside advertising in the publication; by 1985, subscriptions were up to $9.95 for a year's twelve issues.

Having quickly proved the profitability of appealing to the youth market, the Society turned its book division loose in that area, initiating "Books for World Explorers," a series geared at the same eight-to-twelve-year-olds as *National Geographic World,* also under Breeden's direction. To retain contact with teachers and school administrators after the end of the school bulletin, the Society created a multimedia learning kit for distribution in schools.

In February 1980, Grosvenor became president of the National Geographic Society, replacing Robert E. Doyle, who retired. In turn, Grosvenor relinquished the editorship of the *National Geographic,* which passed on to one of his assistants, Wilbur E. Garrett. Both men were forty-nine at the time.

By now, Grosvenor seemed convinced that the Society's future rested in areas other than the *National Geographic Magazine.* Increasing emphasis was placed on the diversification of product away from the magazine, with a special eye toward the coming advances in video technology and the resultant impact on reading and book-and-magazine-buying habits. In one of his rare interviews since the *National Geographic* controversies in 1977, Grosvenor in 1981 gave a reporter some insight into how he viewed the future. Pointing to a bookcase full of bound magazines, he said, "Here's the *Geographic* from 1890 to 1981." But, he told the writer, the entire collection could be reproduced on just a few videodisks and projected through disk players over color television sets. The disks wouldn't cost much more than a regular phonograph record, he continued, and the player would only cost about $600, he estimated.

"Look at that atlas," Grosvenor continued, as he lifted a copy of the Society's latest volume. "It sells for forty-four dollars. It costs me seven dollars just to bind it. Look what I could do with a videodisk of the atlas. I've got fifty-four thousand frames on each side of the disk. I could have infinitely more information for significantly less money if the technology expands as fast as I think it's going to." And if the Society's atlas were put on videodisk, he said, its illustrations and other graphics could be animated. "Here's the solar system. You could have that in motion, showing the revolutions around the sun. We could show a storm center by a series of satellite photos, showing how it developed.

"Talk about plate tectonics [the shifting of the Earth's continents]. You could take the planet Earth when it was one solid landmass, break it apart, and stop at any millennium you want to. An animated atlas, on videodisk, shouldn't cost more than twenty dollars," he said. [18]

Not that the Society's atlas sales have suffered by being on paper. In late 1985, the Society unveiled a new *Atlas of North America,* retailing for $29.95 for the regular edition and $39.95 for a deluxe version, which comes with a magnifier. Before the first copy was ready to deliver, the Society had already sold 200,000 of them, almost $6 million worth, even if all of the purchases were the lower-priced edition.

Under Grosvenor, who was paid $196,211 by the Society in 1984, Breeden has become a Society vice-president, in charge of "Related Educational Services," including books, special publications, television and films, and publications art. By 1984, this division was accounting for some 40 percent of the Society's annual sales. For his efforts that year, the Society paid him $127,335, in addition to the Society's impressive list of perquisites. That same year, the *National Geographic*'s editor, Garrett, was paid $130,711, and the Society's executive vice-president, Owen R. Anderson, was paid $158,056.

In February 1984, the Society launched *National Geographic Traveler,* a quarterly travel magazine more akin to the American Express Company's *Travel & Leisure* than to the *National Geographic.* Before the first issue was even off the presses, circulation exceeded 750,000. A year's issues cost $12.50, but subscribers must first be members of the Society. By applying the *National Geographic*'s formula to easily accessible destinations, the Society had another instant success. The first issue had 56½ pages of ads among its 208 total pages, so many, in fact, that its editor, Joan Tapper, suggested to Grosvenor that ad sales might have to be limited in the future.

Under Gilbert Grosvenor, the Society has emphasized its video operations. Its series on public and commercial television has attracted great critical acclaim. Many of the expenses for its television "specials" have been borne by the Gulf Oil Corporation; Gulf has been acquired by Chevron, which will apparently continue the association. But the Society is branching out in any event. Early in 1986, Grosvenor announced that the Society signed an agreement with Ted Turner, president of Turner Broadcasting, to bring the *National Geographic Explorer* cable television series to Turner's Atlanta-based superstation, WTBS. Turner signed a three-year pact to bring the weekly program to his station. While the contract price wasn't revealed, Gilbert Grosvenor said, "Turner Broadcasting has committed millions to produce a top-quality program every week of the year. It's a bold move on their part and we accept the challenge."[19] Of the weekly *Explorer* programs, about one-third are original Society projects, and the rest are documentaries from producers around the world.

Also in 1986, Grosvenor revealed that he is prepared to enter joint ventures with outside firms for the production of films or television shows. "If we are to be successful in impacting the geography curriculum nationally, we will need outside funding," he told the Society's employees in its full-color monthly newsletter, *National Geographic Society News & Views.*[20] One of Grosvenor's few public-service interests centers on what he has termed the poor state of the teaching of geography in the American school systems. His interest has inspired the Society to seek more ways to help classroom teachers present geography.

Grosvenor seems convinced that the Society's future is not in the magazine-publishing industry. When he speaks of tomorrow, it is almost always in terms of video products: films and disks. He speaks of increasing postage costs and all the things that are competing for the attention of his audience. The *National Geographic's* renewal rate has fallen somewhat, to 84 percent in 1981—a little lower than normal, but still unmatched in the industry—and the realities of its size mean that it has to sign up more than 1.75 million new members every year just to remain at 11 million. But Grosvenor's views seem strongly affected by his own habits, and, according to several employees, he isn't much of a reader. "One learns very quickly at the Society," explained one employee, "that Gil isn't a reader and that he has a short attention span. One doesn't send Gil a two-page memo if one wants to have it read."[21]

20. PERSPECTIVE

> *The National Geographic Society is an empire. . . . And it's something . . . we've never had in American geography: It's been a financial success. . . .*
> Geography historian Geoffrey J. Martin

To be sure, there is only one National Geographic Society. When speaking of it, superlatives—best and worst—come easily to mind. Almost thirty years ago, *Time* aptly summed the Society up in one sentence, calling it "the least exclusive, farthest flung and most improbable nonprofit publishing corporation in the world."[1] In mention after mention, it is the biggest, the best, the richest, the oldest, the smartest, and the prettiest. The *New York Times* quoted a Society executive as claiming that memberships in the National Geographic Society are the most popular Christmas presents in the world. It is also the richest and perhaps the stingiest nonprofit "educational" and "research" institution.

Geoffrey J. Martin, one of the few geographers in the world who specializes in the history of American geography, said, "The National Geographic Society is an empire. . . . It's the only geographical organization in the world that's been in one family" for almost one hundred years. "And it's something else that we've never had in American geography: It's been a financial success. . . . You see, this is a profession where everyone in it is always short of money, and no one's very good at getting it, except the National Geographic Society."[2]

Martin, a professor at Southern Connecticut State University in New Haven, said that at the turn of this century, all geography in America was concerned with the exploration of foreign and exotic lands. But in the second decade of the 1900s, most geographical professionals turned their efforts in the direction of pure science, while adherents of a popular school of geography, including most amateurs, branched off to form what Martin has called a "folk-model" geography. Thus the science of geography was going through the same sort of struggle that was being waged by Alexander Graham Bell and Gilbert H. Grosvenor against the traditionalists on the National Geographic Society's board of directors, and at approximately the same time in history. Bell, of course, prevailed, and the Society followed this "folk model" of geography, later becoming the leader of that school.

After the traditionalists lost the battle at the National Geographic Society, they went their own way, and have pretty much retreated from public view. In Martin's view, under the lead of the folk-model geographers, the science moved from a natural science to a social science, and the National Geographic Society's success was indicative of the change. "Riding the magic carpet of color photographs and bare breasts,"[3] to use Martin's words, the Society began slowly to emerge as the dominant American geographical organization, while the traditionalists, mostly members of the New York City–based American Geographical Society, faded into the science's background.[4] There were hurt feelings in both camps. Gilbert H. Grosvenor's bids to legitimize his standing as a professional by becoming a member of the American Geographical Society were rejected several times, according to Martin; disaffected traditionalist National Geographic Society directors resigned in protest of Bell's policies and formed the Association of American Geographers in Washington. Both of these competing professional organizations have continued to struggle in relative obscurity and to suffer from a chronic shortage of funds, all while the National Geographic Society has prospered.

Martin, who has received funding from the National Geographic Society for some of his work, seems ambivalent about the organization's impact on the entire field of geography. Martin has much praise for the Society's funding of geographic research and its sponsorship of several international conferences on geography in the United States, and its role in keeping geography alive as a field of study (since World War II, several universities, including Harvard and Yale, have closed their geography departments and merged them into other departments). But, he added, the Society has never had much real standing among professionals. Indeed, one geographer, who asked that he not be identified, said, "Today, the National Geographic Society is seen as the focus of American geography, and this has perhaps contributed to geography's demise as a subject of study at American universities."

This is surely a sore point at the Society. Interviews with employees and former employees indicate that this lack of scientific standing is the most troublesome thing faced by the Society; and under Gilbert M. Grosvenor, the Society is trying to do something about it. Since 1980, the Society has begun to fund what Martin called "intellectual geography," geography that is not aimed at its audience of nonprofessionals. While the amount of funding the Society is providing for such research is low, it does represent a new departure for the organization.

The Society has also very quietly begun a new publication, *National Geographic Research: A Scientific Journal,* in an obvious attempt to boost its professional standing. Begun in 1985 with a circulation of approximately five thousand, the journal seems to be having trouble; its circulation is rumored to have fallen off substantially. "It's not about geography," said one professional, "it's just a revved-up version of *National Geographic Magazine.*"[5] But to Martin, the Society's creation of the new magazine is, if nothing else, further evidence that the organization under Grosvenor "is now attempting to reconnect the two wings of geography," the scientific and the folk-model.[6]

Whatever tentative attempts the Society is making to increase its professional stature, Gilbert M. Grosvenor has no intention of losing his large, nonprofessional audience or abandoning general adherence to his grandfather's "Seven Principles" of reporting good news. In a rare public discussion of his feelings, Grosvenor told a reporter for the *Washington Post* in late 1984, "I would rather have a taxi driver than a Ph.D." as a reader. "A Ph.D. knows how to get information he wants from a library, but a cab driver doesn't necessarily know. . . . My feeling is that American journalists favor the rainy side of the street. We favor the sunny side of the street. It's a hell of a lot harder to do that, and stay interesting." [7]

Grosvenor told the reporter that the average National Geographic Society member in 1984 was forty-three years old, earned $25,000 a year, had 2.2 children, attended college for one year, was employed in a professional or managerial capacity, and liked to spend time outdoors. The Society's membership is about evenly divided between the sexes.

*   *   *

Grosvenor's push into high-technology products for the Society has led to another publishing-industry first, the use of a hologram on the *National Geographic*'s cover. The first attempt, on the March 1984 cover, was a three-dimensional image of an eagle with wings outstretched, and was used in conjunction with an article on the growing use of lasers. "We wanted to be the first to do it," said Wilbur E. Garrett, the *National Geographic*'s editor. He said he got the idea when a writer came to him "waving the American Bank Note Company annual report," which contained an eagle hologram on flat foil. Garrett decided that the *National Geographic* should be the first major magazine to use such a hologram, and struck a deal with the bank-note firm. The Society's order swamped the firm, however, and it eventually took ten presses around the country working three shifts a day to produce the holograms required for the almost eleven million copies of the magazine. "We did our R&D as we went," said Garrett, "and we went through an awful lot of foil" as the experiments continued. The holograms were eventually produced at a price rumored to be 10 cents a copy, more than twice the cost of a normal *National Geographic* cover. "We won't rush to do it again soon," Garrett promised. [8] However, in November 1985, a large and eerie hologram of the fossilized skull of a five-year-old child, buried for at least a million years in a cave in South Africa, dominated the cover of the *National Geographic,* promoting an article titled "The Search for Our Ancestors."

Grosvenor seems convinced that the *National Geographic Magazine*'s circulation is near its maximum possible audience, which is no doubt fueling his desire to diversify the Society's product lines further. "I'm absolutely committed to the theory that electronic communications of some sort is here to stay, that we should be a part of it," Grosvenor told a writer in 1985. "The magazine has been the flagship of the organization and probably will be during my lifetime. . . . But today's people are more accustomed to moving images, and we must establish ourselves as the premier moving-image organization in our field."9

But one has to wonder how the IRS will respond as video products and television shows consume increasing portions of the Society's enormous operating budget and generate more of its income. Grosvenor is obviously aware of the danger, telling a writer in late 1984 that the IRS had last audited the Society in 1982 and had left its tax exemption intact. "If we lost our tax-exempt status, we would lose our image as an educational institution, and that's what we're all about," said Grosvenor. "We don't have to make money on investors' money. If we want to spend one million dollars on a project, we'll spend one million dollars."10 If stripped of its exemption, the Society would also lose its $10 million annual postage subsidy and would have to pay income taxes on its enormous earnings and property tax on its vast holdings.

Grosvenor is as worried about the Society's financial performance as the chief operating officer of any profit-making corporation in America. When the Society's newest headquarters addition opened in downtown Washington in mid-1984 (variously estimated to cost between $35 million and $45 million), three of the building's seven floors were occupied by commercial tenants, most notably International Telephone & Telegraph and a large law firm. While the building was still under construction, Grosvenor explained that the rental income from the top three floors would pay for the building's entire cost in twelve to fifteen years. "That's how

I intended to get my capital back," he said. [11] But as a result of renting out the space, on the very day it opened the new building, the Society was still renting space from other landlords around the city to house its various offices that couldn't fit into the large headquarters complex.

The Society has also been revoking some of the traditional perquisites for its writers and photographers, such as always traveling first-class—although expense accounts still get far less scrutiny than they do at most other corporations. In addition, the Society is using increasing numbers of free lances and contract writers to lessen the salary load.

In all, Grosvenor behaves like a corporate executive who is expecting hard times at any moment. He makes vague illusions to falling revenue for *National Geographic Magazine* and of poor revenue performance for the Society's video projects, complains about rising postage rates, and moves to squirrel away every dollar he can find. This again raises the question of what the Society's function truly is. Grosvenor behaves as if the Society must first and foremost perpetuate itself; this is one general goal of most profit-making enterprises. But one has to wonder what has become of the "increase and diffusion of geographic knowledge." The longer the Society goes on, the higher its gross income rises and the lower its contributions to research and explorations become, at least as a percentage of income.

And this doesn't bode well for the future, since even the Society's management seems to think that the organization is presently living through its most profitable times. If net income starts to shrink, it seems reasonable to assume that the Society's grants for research and exploration will get even smaller, if the organization can manage it without alarming the IRS.

Despite Grosvenor's apparent fear of the future, that the *National Geographic Magazine* is dominant in its area was reemphasized in the past few years. The West German publishing firm Gruner & Jahr had created a magazine called *Geo*; successful versions of the publication were distributed in Germany and France. *Geo* was designed to be some of what the *National Geographic Magazine* is— that is, handsome, full of pictures, and expensively produced. But

Geo was also to be much of what the National Geographic isn't—
much of its excellent photography was innovative and interpretive, and many of its articles were timely and contained a point
of view. One editor described the magazine as "somewhere between National Geographic and Life, with Mondo Cane thrown
in."[12]

Geo's publisher brought the magazine to the United States, with
an obvious eye cast on making it a worldwide magazine capable of
competing with the National Geographic for the upside of its readership. But Geo's publisher was a profit-making company, subject
to the taxes from which the National Geographic was exempt, and
Geo had to pay the full rate for its postage. As a result, the new
magazine was much more expensive than the National Geographic.
The German publisher had obviously underestimated the loyalty of
the National Geographic's readers. After losing an estimated $50
million in the two years after its founding, the American version of
the magazine was sold to the Knapp Communications Corporation
of Los Angeles, the firm that publishes several up-scale magazines,
including Architectural Digest and Bon Appetit.

While Geo's audience remained small, it was composed of the
kind of readers that advertisers held in high regard. But advertisers
generally stayed away from Geo as it continued to grope for a distinctive style that would bring it success. By early 1984, Knapp's
losses on Geo were put at between $500,000 and $1 million a
month. "Articles illustrated with lavish, colorful photos from remote parts of the world and fine quality printing and paper made
the magazine particularly expensive to produce," explained the
New York Times in early 1985. At the time, Geo was selling for
$3.95 an issue; the National Geographic, based on the Society's $15
annual membership fee for twelve issues (which has been raised to
$18), was $1.25 an issue.

Finally, Knapp had had enough. In mid-January 1985, the firm
announced that the February issue would be Geo's last in America.
Geo's guaranteed readership base at the time was 255,000, about
half of what Knapp officials believed necessary to make the magazine profitable, and a mere shadow of the National Geographic
Society's membership. Once again, the National Geographic was

without a direct competitor. About the only magazine advertisers view as competition for the *National Geographic* is *Smithsonian Magazine,* another publication owned by a tax-exempt educational institution, although the Smithsonian is a peculiar quasi-public institution, with some of its budget coming directly from the U.S. Treasury.

*   *   *

In all, the National Geographic Society seems a good idea run amuck. It generates enormous amounts of money from projects all somehow at least vaguely related to the study of geography and natural science. But it has forgotten its reason for existence. Instead of taking the profits from its hard work and funding the exploration of the universe in order to unlock the secrets of existence, it plows the money back into its money machine, hiring more people and buying better machines with which to raise ever more money. That money, of course, goes to constructing buildings to house the new machines and new employees to run them, all as part of the Society's efforts to raise even more money tomorrow. And so on.

Even Gilbert M. Grosvenor is aware of some of the problem. While discussing the National Geographic Society's history with a reporter in 1984 during a visit to the magnificent estate in Nova Scotia that Alexander Graham Bell left for his descendants, Grosvenor III said, "The [organization's] founding fathers had no idea that we would evolve into the world's largest educational society. . . . They would probably be appalled."[13]

Perhaps the ultimate test for an organization founded for "the increase and diffusion of geographic knowledge" is the impact it has had on its chosen field of endeavor. But if that is the case, officials of the National Geographic Society may need to ask themselves some questions. Indeed, perhaps the time has come for the National Geographic Society's officials and directors, and its almost eleven million members, to ask the basic question that underlies all others: "Why?"

Asked during an interview in New Haven how American geography would be different today if there had never been a National Geographic Society, historian Martin thought for a moment and rubbed his chin before replying. "I don't suppose it would have been a hell of a lot different," he said.

And that, in a nutshell, is the problem. A group of well- intentioned people in 1888 founded an organization to expand man's knowledge of himself and his world. Other well-intentioned people made a success of the organization, eventually putting it in a position financially where it could afford to realize its founders' dreams and more. And in the end, it has not only failed to have a major impact on geography and exploration, but is as money-hungry as any publishing and mail-order conglomerate could be. Rather than a group organized "for the increase and diffusion of geographic knowledge," the National Geographic Society is today an organization dedicated only to its own survival.

ACKNOWLEDGMENTS

My goals for this book were relatively simple: to present an independent and balanced look at a major American institution that has helped shape our entire nation's perceptions about the world. I came to the task with few preconceived notions, other than a vague awareness of the types of articles that the *National Geographic Magazine* carries, boyhood memories of having rummaged through a bookstore's basement in New Haven madly searching for material to fill out a high school report, and, alas, taking time out to check each browsed issue for bare-breasted offerings.

I undertook this project neither to praise nor to bury the National Geographic Society. Lest the reader wonder why the Society doesn't speak directly for itself, let me say that the Society and its president were given ample opportunity to do so. The Society chose to utilize a feint that had been employed by one of its most important standard-bearers, Robert E. Peary. When Peary was asked to speak on the record concerning his claim to having discovered the North Pole first, he told a waiting world that he had signed a book contract, which prevented him from presenting his records to the Congress until the book was out. The congressional investigators were forced to cool their heels for months. This time, the Society informed me that it had just signed a book contract to celebrate its 1988 centennial, the terms of which prevented it from discussing itself with any other writer.

As a result, coupled with the fact that most of the principals involved in the evolution of the National Geographic Society are dead, I have relied on books and articles written by and about these principals. I thought that allowing these people to speak for themselves was the fairest thing to do, wherever it was possible.

In all, I would like to thank the people who gave of their time and energy through the course of this project, in many different ways. Special thanks to Elizabeth Knappman, my agent; to my editor David Groff and to Betty Prashker at Crown; and to the *Washington Post* for the many courtesies shown me. And in these budget-cutting times, I would like to acknowledge a special debt of gratitude to the Library of Congress, the repository of our past, without which this book could not have been written.

And I must pay special tribute to the members of my family for their patience and for their encouragement, and especially to Martha Robertson Gould, my wife and first reader, and to my son Nelson.

Howard S. Abramson
Washington, D.C.

NOTES

1

1. Susan Wagner, "The Phenomenal Success of the *National Geographic*'s Book Operation," *Publishers Weekly*, January 8, 1973, p. 40.

2. Anne Chamberlin, "Two Cheers for the *National Geographic*," *Esquire*, December 1963, p. 206.

2

1. Helen Elmira Waite, *Make a Joyful Sound: The Romance of Mabel Hubbard and Alexander Graham Bell* (Philadelphia: Macrae Smith, 1961), p. 20.

2. Ibid., p. 19.

3. Ibid., p. 52.

4. Ibid., p. 53.

5. Ibid., p. 59.

6. Harold S. Osborne, *Biographical Memoir of Alexander Graham Bell* (Washington: National Academy of Sciences, 1943), p. 2.

7. *The Career of Alexander Graham Bell* (New York: American Telephone & Telegraph Co., 1946), p. 7.

8. Osborne, pp. 16–17.

9. Catherine MacKenzie, *Alexander Graham Bell: The Man Who Contracted Space* (Boston and New York: Houghton Mifflin, 1928), p. 79.

10. Waite, p. 86.

11. *The Career of Alexander Graham Bell*, p. 31.

12. MacKenzie, pp. 79–80.

13. Waite, pp. 88–89.

14. Ibid., pp. 105–106.

15. Ibid., p. 106.

16. Ibid., p. 115.

17. *Events in Telecommunications History* (New York: American Telephone & Telegraph Co., 1979), p. 3.

18. Quoted in Osborne, p. 8.

19. Ibid., pp. 9–10.

20. Waite, p. 169.

21. Osborne, p. 10.

22. *National Geographic Magazine*, July 1965, p. 116.

3

1. Constance McLaughlin Green, *Washington: A History of the Capital* (Princeton, N.J.: Princeton University Press, 1976), Vol. II, p. 6.

2. Ibid., p. 6.

3. Ibid., p. 11.

4. Quoted in ibid., p. 77.

5. Quoted in ibid., p. 7.

6. Ibid., p. 92.

7. Ibid., p. 99.

8. Ibid., p. 99.

9. Gilbert H. Grosvenor, *The National Geographic Society and Its Magazine* (Washington: National Geographic Society, 1936), p. 9.

10. Ibid.

11. *Washington Post*, January 25, 1952.

12. Chamberlin, *Esquire*, p. 207.

13. *National Geographic Magazine*, Vol. I, No. 1, 1888.

4

1. Chamberlin, *Esquire*, p. 208.

2. *The Career of Alexander Graham Bell*, p. 25.

3. MacKenzie, p. 284.

4. Ibid., pp. 284–285.

5. Gilbert H. Grosvenor, *The National Geographic Society and Its Magazine* (Washington: National Geographic Society, 1957), p. 18.

6. Quoted in Hellman, *The New Yorker*, October 2, 1943, p. 30.

7. Grosvenor, 1957, p. 22.

8. Ibid.

9. Ibid., p. 23.

10. *National Geographic Magazine*, October 1963, p. 531.

11. Ibid.

5

1. *National Geographic Magazine*, October 1963, p. 532.

2. Grosvenor, 1936, p. 23.

3. Grosvenor, 1957, pp. 23–24.

4. *National Geographic Magazine*, October 1963, pp. 549–551.

5. Grosvenor, 1957, p. 24.

6. Grosvenor, 1936, p. 24.

7. *National Geographic Magazine,* October 1963, p. 532.

8. Ibid., p. 549.

9. Ibid., p. 525.

10. Ibid., p. 533.

11. Ibid., p. 536.

12. Grosvenor, 1957, p. 32.

13. *National Geographic Magazine,* October 1963, pp. 552–553.

14. Ibid., p. 553.

15. *National Geographic Magazine,* July 1965, p. 113.

16. Ibid.

17. Grosvenor, 1957, p. 34.

18. *National Geographic Magazine,* July 1965, pp. 105–106.

6

1. Geoffrey T. Hellman, "Geography Unshackled II," *The New Yorker,* October 2, 1943, p. 35.

2. Grosvenor, 1957, pp. 37–39.

3. Chamberlin, *Esquire,* p. 299.

4. Ibid.

5. Ibid.

6. Grosvenor, 1957, p. 43.

7. *National Geographic Magazine,* October 1963, p. 581.

8. Chamberlin, *Esquire,* p. 300.

9. *National Geographic Magazine,* July 1965, pp. 116–118.

10. Geoffrey T. Hellman, "Geography Unshackled III," *The New Yorker,* October 9, 1943, p. 32.

11. MacKenzie, p. 332.

12. Ibid., p. 333.

13. *The Career of Alexander Graham Bell,* p. 26.

14. Hellman, *The New Yorker,* October 2, 1943, p. 30.

7

1. Quoted in Andrew A. Freeman, *The Case for Doctor Cook* (New York: Coward Mc-Cann, 1961), p. 95.

2. *The National Cyclopedia of American Biography* (New York and Clifton, N.J.: James T. White), Vol. 22, p. 51.

3. Edwin C. Buxbaum, *Collecting National Geographic Magazines* (Milwaukee: Box Tree Press, 1935), pp. 21–22.

4. Freeman, p. 94.

8

1. Frederick J. Pohl, introduction to Frederick A. Cook, *Return from the Pole* (New York: Pellegrini & Cudahy, 1951), p. 21.

2. *New York Herald,* September 6, 1909.

3. Freeman, p. 160.

4. *New York Times,* October 16, 1909.

5. Freeman, p. 194.

6. Ibid., p. 196.

7. Quoted in ibid., p.196.

8. Russell W. Gibbons, *An Historical Evaluation of the Cook-Peary Controversy* (Ada, Ohio: Ohio Northern University, 1954), p. 27.

9. Freeman, p. 177.

10. Gibbons, p. 27.

11. Theon Wright, *The Big Nail: The Story of the Cook-Peary Feud* (New York: John Day, 1970), p. 234.

12. Freeman, p. 210.

13. Quoted in ibid., p. 211.

14. William Herbert Hobbs, *Peary* (New York: Macmillan, 1936), p. 392.

15. Freeman, p. 208.

16. Freeman, p. 208.

17. Cook, p. 553.

18. Frederick A. Cook, "Dr. Cook's Own Story," *Hampton's Magazine,* January 1911, cover.

19. Ibid, p. 51.

20. Ibid., pp. 51–52.

21. Wright, pp. 249–250.

22. Charles B. Driscoll, *The Life of O. O. McIntyre* (New York: Greystone Press, 1938), pp. 222–223.

23. Cook, *My Attainment of the North Pole,* p. 555.

9

1. Quoted in Freeman, p. 210.

2. U.S. House of Representatives, 61st Congress, 3rd Session, Private Calendar 733, Report 1961, p. 18.

3. Wright, p. 211.

4. Freeman, p. 234.

5. Quoted in W. Henry Lewin, *The Great North Pole Fraud* (London: C. W. Daniel), p. 90.

6. Ibid., p. 88.

7. Wright, p. 265.

8. Ibid.

9. Quoted in Lewin, pp. 88–89.

10. Ibid., pp. 91–92.

11. Gibbons, p. 30.

12. Wright, p. 315.

13. Quoted in Wright, p. 315.

14. Quoted in Wright, pp. 314–315.

15. Ibid., pp. 267–268.

16. Ibid., p. 330.

17. *National Geographic Magazine,* October 1953, p. 469.

18. *National Geographic Magazine,* March 1984, unnumbered page.

NOTES

19. Cook, pp. 541–543.

20. Ibid., pp. 555–556.

21. Gibbons, p. 37.

22. Ibid., p. 38.

23. Statement of Russell W. Gibbons at Duquesne University history forum, October 23, 1985.

24. *New York Times,* January 24, 1926.

25. *New York Times,* March 5, 1926.

26. Freeman, p. 236.

10

1. Daniel Cohen, *Hiram Bingham and the Dream of Gold* (New York: M. Evans, 1984), p. 11.

2. *National Geographic Magazine,* April 1913, p. 404.

3. Ibid., p. 14.

4. Ibid., p. 15.

5. *National Geographic Magazine,* April 1913, p. 404.

6. Cohen, p. 142.

7. *National Geographic Magazine,* September 1917.

11

1. Allison Gray, "We All Have a Secret Love of Adventure and Romance," *American Magazine,* May 1922, p. 26.

2. *National Geographic Magazine,* January 1917, p. 3.

3. *National Geographic Magazine,* June 1920, p. 529.

4. *National Geographic Magazine,* September 1925, pp. 301–302.

5. *National Geographic Magazine,* September 1926, p. 373.

6. *National Geographic Magazine,* August 1930.

7. Chamberlin, *Esquire*, p. 206.

12

1. Grosvenor, 1957, p. 37.

2. Ibid.

3. *National Geographic Magazine*, July 1906, p. 381.

4. *National Geographic Magazine*, January 1927, p. xii.

5. *National Geographic Magazine*, September 1930, p. 353.

6. Gray, *American Magazine*, p. 27.

7. *National Cyclopedia of American Biography*, Vol. 21, pp. 69–70.

8. Grosvenor, 1936, p. 38.

9. Grosvenor, 1957, p. 40.

10. Ibid.

11. Tom Buckley, "With the *National Geographic* on Its Endless, Cloudless Voyage," *New York Times Magazine*, September 6, 1970, p. 19.

12. Chamberlin, *Esquire*, p. 208.

13. Hellman, *The New Yorker*, October 9, 1943, p. 29.

14. Buckley, *New York Times Magazine*, p. 20.

15. Ibid., p. 209.

13

1. Grosvenor, 1957, pp. 44–45.

2. Ibid., p. 45.

3. Hellman, *The New Yorker*, October 9, 1943, p. 30.

4. Hellman, *The New Yorker*, October 2, 1943, p. 28.

5. Geoffrey T. Hellman, "Geography Unshackled I," *The New Yorker*, September 25, 1943, p. 29.

6. Buxbaum, p. 29.

NOTES

7. Grosvenor, 1936, p. 39.

8. Grosvenor, 1957, p. 5.

9. Ibid.

10. *National Geographic Magazine,* October 1966, p. 469.

11. Hellman, *The New Yorker,* September 25, 1943, p. 27.

12. Chamberlin, *Esquire,* p. 208.

13. Ishbel Ross, "Geography, Inc.," *Scribner's Magazine,* June 1938, p. 24.

14. Hellman, *The New Yorker,* October 2, 1943, p. 27.

15. Buckley, *New York Times Magazine,* p. 20.

16. Hellman, *The New Yorker,* September 25, 1943, p. 29.

17. Wagner, *Publishers Weekly,* p. 40.

18. Geoffrey T. Hellman, "How to Get a Rather Bad Case of Paranoia," *The New Yorker,* September 27, 1952, pp. 93–94.

14

1. *National Geographic Magazine,* February 1937, p. 170.

2. William L. Shirer, *The Rise and Fall of the Third Reich,* (New York: Simon & Schuster, 1960) p. 207.

3. U.S. Department of Justice press release, dated July 26, 1943.

4. Ibid.

5. Ibid.

6. Ibid.

7. "Former Newsmen Among 8 Indicted For Treason by U.S.," *Editor & Publisher,* July 31, 1943, p. 40.

8. George Seldes, "*Geographic* Published U.S. Traitor, Pro-Fascist Dope of *Reader's Digest* Man," *In Fact,* October 4, 1943, p. 1.

9. Interview with the author.

10. *National Geographic Magazine,* March 1937, p. 269.

11. Seldes, *In Fact,* p. 3.

12. Ibid.

15

1. *New York Times,* January 15, 1945.

2. *Washington Post,* December 8, 1950.

3. Hellman, *The New Yorker,* October 2, 1943, p. 27.

4. Grosvenor, 1936, p. 1.

5. Chamberlin, *Esquire,* p. 301.

16

1. Ross, *Scribner's Magazine,* p. 57.

2. Melville B. Grosvenor, quoted in his foreword to Grosvenor, 1957, p. x.

3. Chamberlin, *Esquire,* p. 299.

4. *National Geographic Magazine,* August 1982, p. 276.

5. *National Geographic Magazine,* September 1959, p. 351.

6. Buckley, *New York Times Magazine,* p. 18.

7. Ibid, p. 22.

8. Chamberlin, *Esquire,* p. 305.

9. Ibid., p. 300.

10. *Washington Post,* September 13, 1974.

11. Ibid.

12. *Washington Post,* July 17, 1977.

13. *Washington Post,* July 4, 1979.

14. Chamberlin, *Esquire,* p. 302.

17

1. Buckley, *New York Times Magazine,* p. 21.

2. Ibid.

3. Ibid.

4. Interview with the author.

5. *Washington Post*, December 18, 1984.

6. "The Wreck of the Bounty—And the Way of the *Geographic*," *Newsweek*, December 9, 1957, p. 62.

7. Ibid.

8. Ibid.

9. Wagner, *Publishers Weekly*, p. 41.

10. William Hoffer, "All the World's a Page," *Regardie's*, March 1985, p. 57.

11. Buckley, *New York Times Magazine*, p. 21.

12. Wagner, *Publishers Weekly*, p. 41.

13. *Washington Post*, July 7, 1974.

14. *Washington Post*, December 20, 1984.

15. Buckley, *New York Times Magazine*, pp. 20– 21.

16. Sonia M. Cole, *Leakey's Luck: The Life of Louis Seymour Bazett Leakey* (London: Collins, 1975), p. 15.

17. Ibid., p. 353.

18. *National Geographic Magazine*, July 1965, p. 120.

19. Chamberlin, *Esquire*, p. 305.

18

1. Alfred Balk, *The Free List* (New York: Russell Sage Foundation, 1971), p. 22.

2. *Washington Post*, April 20, 1941.

3. Wagner, *Publishers Weekly*, p. 41.

4. *Newsweek*, December 25, 1967, p. 74.

5. Buckley, *New York Times Magazine*, p. 10.

6. Interview with the author.

7. Ibid.

8. Lila Locksley, "The *National Geographic*: How to Be Non-Profit and Get Rich," *Washington Monthly*, September 1977, pp. 47–48.

9. Interview with the author.

10. Gray, *American Magazine*, p. 134.

11. Locksley, *Washington Monthly*, p. 48.

19

1. Buckley, *New York Times Magazine*, pp. 10–11.

2. Ibid., p. 13.

3. Ibid., p. 11.

4. *National Geographic Magazine*, January 1977, p. 32.

5. Tony Schwartz, "The *Geographic* Faces Life," *Newsweek*, September 12, 1977, p. 111.

6. M. J. Sobran Jr., "Tariff on Truth," *National Review*, May 13, 1977, p. 565.

7. Schwartz, *Newsweek*, p. 111.

8. *Washington Post*, July 17, 1977.

9. Schwartz, *Newsweek*, p. 111.

10. Ibid.

11. *Washington Post*, July 17, 1977.

12. Ibid.

13. Ibid.

14. Schwartz, *Newsweek*, p. 111.

15. *Washington Post*, July 17, 1977.

16. Schwartz, *Newsweek*, p. 111.

17. *Washington Post*, July 17, 1977.

18. *Washington Post*, December 7, 1981.

19. *National Geographic Society News & Views*, December 1985.

20. Ibid.

21. Interview with the author.

20

1. "Rose-Colored Geography," *Time*, June 15, 1959, pp. 47–48.

2. Interview with the author.

3. Ibid.

4. Ibid.

5. Ibid.

6. Ibid.

7. *Washington Post*, December 12, 1984.

8. *Washington Post*, March 6, 1984.

9. Hoffer, *Regardie's*, pp. 62–64.

10. *Washington Post*, December 19, 1984.

11. *Washington Post*, December 7, 1981.

12. *New York Times*, December 19, 1984.

13. *Washington Post*, December 19, 1984.

SELECT BIBLIOGRAPHY

Balk, Alfred. *The Free List: Property Without Taxes.* New York: Russell Sage Foundation, 1971.

Buxbaum, Edwin C. *Collecting National Geographic Magazines.* Milwaukee: Box Tree Press, 1935.

The Career of Alexander Graham Bell. New York: American Telephone & Telegraph Co., 1946.

Cohen, Daniel. *Hiram Bingham and the Dream of Gold.* New York: M. Evans, 1984.

Cole, Sonia Mary. *Leakey's Luck: The Life of Louis Seymour Bazett Leakey.* London: Collins, 1975.

Cook, Frederick A. *My Attainment of the North Pole.* New York and London: Mitchell Kennerley, 1913.

———*Return from the Pole.* New York: Pellegrini & Cudahy, 1951.

Driscoll, Charles B. *The Life of O. O. McIntyre.* New York: Greystone Press, 1938.

Everett, Marshall. *The True Story of the Cook and Peary Discovery of the North Pole.* Chicago: Educational Co.

Freeman, Andrew A. *The Case for Doctor Cook.* New York: Coward McCann, 1961.

Funk & Wagnalls New Standard Dictionary of the English Language. New York and London: Funk & Wagnalls, 1928.

Gibbons, Russell W. *An Historical Evaluation of the Cook-Peary Controversy.* Ada, Ohio: Ohio Northern University, 1954.

———*Frederick Albert Cook, Pioneer American Polar Explorer.* Hurleyville, N.Y.: Frederick A. Cook Society, 1979.

271

SELECT BIBLIOGRAPHY

Green, Constance McLaughlin. *Washington: A History of the Capital.* Princeton, N.J.: Princeton University Press, 1976.

Green, Fitzhugh. *Peary, the Man Who Refused to Fail.* New York: G.P. Putnam's Sons, 1926.

Grosvenor, Gilbert H. *The National Geographic Society and Its Magazine.* Washington: National Geographic Society, 1936. Revised edition, 1957.

Gurney, Gene. *The Smithsonian Institution.* New York: Crown, 1964.

Harley, Ralph Volney. *Story of America.* New York: Henry Holt, 1949.

Hobbs, William Herbert. *Peary.* New York: Macmillan, 1936.

Lewin, W. Henry. *The Great North Pole Fraud.* London: C. W. Daniel, Ltd.

MacKenzie, Catherine. *Alexander Graham Bell: The Man Who Contracted Space.* Boston and New York: Houghton Mifflin, 1928.

The National Cyclopedia of American Biography. New York and Clifton, N.J.: James T. White.

Osborne, Harold S. *Biographical Memoir of Alexander Graham Bell.* Washington: National Academy of Sciences, 1943.

Waite, Helen Elmira. *Make a Joyful Sound: The Romance of Mabel Hubbard and Alexander Graham Bell.* Philadelphia: Macrae Smith, 1961.

Weems, John Edward. *Race for the Pole.* New York: Henry Holt, 1960.

Wright, Theon. *The Big Nail: The Story of the Cook-Peary Feud.* New York: John Day, 1970.

Young, Brigadier Peter, ed. *The World Almanac Book of World War II.* New York: World Almanac Publications, 1981.

INDEX